Humanity  'King of Connemara' 1754-1834

SHEVAWN LYNAM was born in Dublin of Galway parents and educated in Ascot, Madrid, France and Germany. Linguist and journalist, she was Spanish specialist with the BBC and the Ministry of Information during the War as well as working for John Betjeman when he was Press Attaché in Dublin. After going to Paris in 1950 she worked for the Marshall Plan and UNESCO, and edited NATO's monthly review from 1958 to 1963, returning to Dublin to be Editorial Publicity Officer at the Irish Tourist Board until 1971. She now lives in County Wicklow and is well-known as a contributor to Radio Telefís Éireann's *Sunday Miscellany*.

Her novel on the Basque Resistance to Franco, *The Spirit and the Clay*, was published in 1954 and was recommended by the Book-of-the-Month Club in the USA and translated into French and German. Her biography *Humanity Dick* was first published in 1975.

Some reviews of the 1975 edition

'He waged a one-man battle to stop the ill-use of animals. For that alone he deserves to be remembered and to have won such a sympathetic and fair biographer as Miss Lynam' — T.G. Barker in *The Cork Examiner*

'The book is full of fascinating grace-notes about the history of both Ireland and England in a period of almost frenetic entanglement' — John Horgan in *The Listener*

'A courageous and attractive man who deserves to be remembered with affection' — Ruth Dudley Edwards in the *Irish Press*

'The most enthralling book I have read for a long time' — Hilary Boyle in *Hibernia*

'The most enjoyable book of 1975, I envy Shevawn Lynam her talents and her industry' — Maureen Potter

Presented with much respect to Miss Mary
Jane Martin: a Portrait of her illustrious Father
more illustrious than most "Princes and Lords"
"Humanity Martin"
                                    S. C. Hall

Humanity Dick Martin
'King of Connemara'
1754-1834

Shevawn Lynam

THE LILLIPUT PRESS
1989

First published by Hamish Hamilton Ltd, London, 1975.
First paperback edition published in 1989 by
THE LILLIPUT PRESS LTD
4 Rosemount Terrace, Arbour Hill, Dublin 7, Ireland.

A CIP catalogue record for this title is available from the British Library

ISBN 0 946640 36 X

Cover design by Jole Bortoli (The Graphiconies)
Printed by The Guernsey Press Co. Ltd, Guernsey,
Channel Islands

To the Memory of my
O'Flaherty Grandmother

Acknowledgements

My thanks are due to the directors and staffs of the various libraries and record offices in which I have worked in Ireland, England, France and the U.S.A. Mr. Kenneth Timings of the Public Record office, London, was an infallible guide, and I am also indebted to Miss Felicity Ranger of the Registry of Archives, London, for assistance in locating material. In a particular manner I wish to thank all those in the National Library of Ireland and the Irish Public Record office who have given me so efficient a service combined with such personal concern.

Without the generous cooperation of Humanity Dick's direct descendants in Canada the book would not have been possible. I have to thank them for supplying me with a valuable collection of letters, documents and photographs. I owe innumerable patiently typed copies of material to Mrs. Mary Collison (née Martin) of Vancouver, while her brother, Tim, of Toronto, has earned my gratitude by acting as a liaison officer between me and the Canadian Martins in general.

The RSPCA gave me most welcome encouragement when starting on a book about the man who played the leading part in founding their society, and kindly put their records at my disposal. Mr. Mullius of the History of Parliament Trust was good enough to allow me to make use of material collected by that body, and Mr. Malcolmson, Keeper of the Records for Northern Ireland, most generously supplied me with the notes for his history of the Galway constituency. I also have to thank him for providing material from the Mount Stewart archives and Lady Bury for permission to use it.

The Surrey Record Office authorized me to use material from the Goulburn papers, Lord Buchan has kindly given me permission to quote from Lord Erskine's papers, and I am grateful to Lord Kilmaine for allowing me to make use of the diary of the second Baron and the copies of the *Anti-Union* in his possession. Mrs. Teresa O'Neill kindly lent me the invaluable appendix to her thesis for an M.A., *The Sixth Parliament of George III*, for which I wish to thank her.

The Martin family have made a most valuable contribution to the illustrations. I am indebted to Miss Florence Martin of Grimsby, Ontario, the head of the Ballinahinch branch, for the picture on the dustcover which is a copy of one presented to Humanity Dick's daughter by S. C. Hall, the parliamentary reporter of *The Times*, and she also supplied me with a miniature of Humanity's son, Thomas. Richard Martin of Vancouver kindly sent me copies of pictures of Humanity Dick's father and two half brothers; Douglas Martin of Toronto provided me with a copy of the miniature of Humanity Dick's eldest child, Laetitia. Tim Martin filled what would have been an important gap by kindly sending me a copy of a portrait of Humanity Dick in old age.

Mr. Richard Martin of Ross, the senior branch of the Martin family, has my sincere thanks for allowing me to have the caricature of Humanity Dick leading a donkey into court photographed, and the same is true of Mr. Michael Gorman of the Irish Tourist Board in regard to the picture of Humanity Dick addressing his 'constituents'. I have to thank Colonel and Mrs. Lambert of Clareville for kindly allowing me to use a picture of their house, formerly Humanity Dick's, as an illustration, and Miss Norah McGuinness for doing the drawing of it. I am grateful to the National Library of Ireland for permission to reproduce the drawing of Ballinahinch castle and lake from the Edgeworth papers, together with several pictures from published works, and to the Governor and Company of the Bank of Ireland for that of the Irish Parliament. Mr. Patrick Tutty of Dublin is to be thanked for undertaking all the necessary photography.

Mr. Gerald Lee of Galway has been indefatigable in sharing his historical knowledge of the west of Ireland with me and in keeping me supplied with local anecdotes associated with Humanity Dick and the Martin family in general. Frank Comyn and Michael Vahy of Ballinahinch have added much from their store of information accumulated on the spot that Humanity Dick loved best.

I have to thank my mother for meticulously sorting my library slips, Ruth Lynam for helping to scan newspapers, and Valerie Randell for sorting press cuttings. And I must thank Aer Lingus for most valuable cooperation.

Above all others, I wish to thank Dr. Maurice Sheehy of University College, Dublin. He read the book chapter by chapter from the first draft to the final stage, giving me unfailingly wise advice and the benefit of his own very wide knowledge, and I am also grateful to Dr. Donal MacCartney of University College, Dublin, for checking the historical references.

Finally, I humbly express my thanks to Cecil Woodham-Smith for giving me that encouragement which only a great writer can give to a lesser, and which she has given me so unstintingly.

The great historian William Lecky, in volume 2 of *The History of European Morals in the Nineteenth Century* (London 1925), declared 'one of the peculiar merits of the last century' to be the introduction of the 'notion of duties towards the animal world,' singling out 'Mr Martin, an eccentric Irish member [of parliament]... to whose untiring exertions the legislative protection of animals in England is due.' Today societies world-wide continue the work Richard Martin began in 1794 to eliminate cruelty to animals on his own estates in the most westerly European province, and many more fight to safeguard the environment prompted by a respect for the balance of nature on which Martin based his crusade. All are represented in the World Society for the Protection of Animals, with the Eurogroup for Animal Welfare co-ordinating those of the European Community.

In 1970 the French authorities planned to build a road through Martin's burial-place in Boulogne, but England's Royal Society for the Prevention of Cruelty to Animals reinterred his remains beneath a marble slab bearing a bi-lingual tribute to him. Ireland pays daily homage to his warmth of heart through the 'Richard Martin Rest Fields' in which strayed, sick or abandoned animals are sheltered by the Irish Society for the Prevention of Cruelty to Animals. In 1989 Humanity Dick Martin was fittingly commemorated with a tablet of Connemara marble set in the wall of the place he loved best, his former residence, Ballinahinch Castle.

S.L.,
Ashford, April 1989

Illustrations

ix

before there was an act to prevent such abuses. *Printed for W. H. Bartlett and R. Wallis by Geo. Virtue of London*

8. A Galway election as seen by 'Phiz', illustrating Charles Lever's *Charles O'Malley* in which Uncle Godfrey, the Member for Galway, is supposed to be Humanity Dick.

Prologue

RICHARD MARTIN had earned the nickname of Nimble Dick. It contrasted with the more glorious name by which his great-grandson, another Richard Martin, was to be known, but it fitted equally well. An astute lawyer and County Galway gentleman, he was one of those people who manage to fall on their feet whatever the circumstances.

When James II of England was beaten by William of Orange at Aughrim in the west of Ireland on 12 July 1691, Nimble Dick was a captain in Luterell's cavalry, to whom the Jacobites attributed their defeat. Afraid for his life at their hands, he avoided retreating with them to Limerick. Instead he threw himself on the mercy of the High Sheriff of Galway who was acting a neutral part in preparation for the formal surrender of the city. Nimble Dick was a gentleman of standing, and for his protection the Sheriff took him to the Williamite commander, de Ginckle, then entrenched before the town.

The Dutchman was working out the terms of surrender, and Nimble Dick, an Irishman and a Catholic, remained with him throughout. As the articles began to emerge they proved to be exceptionally lenient. The city dignitaries and all within the town were to be pardoned; they could return to their estates, to which their titles were confirmed, or join the Jacobite forces at Limerick; and religious toleration was guaranteed.

These advantageous conditions were in part the result of Nimble Dick's exertions, but, due to a technicality, he himself was excluded from their benefits. The Mayor of Galway had added his name to the roll of freemen, which should have brought him within the scope of the Articles of Surrender, but with the brusque changes due to hostilities, he was never sworn and, thus, did not qualify for the general pardon.

The Irish Jacobites with whom Nimble Dick had fought represented Catholic Ireland. They considered that they were defending their legitimate King and regarded the English as traitors who had deposed three monarchs in forty years. Yet, the crown had been bestowed on William by the English parliament, and the Irish were rebels in the eyes of the law. Nimble Dick was, consequently, liable to all the penalties and, in particular, he faced the possible surrender of his vast estates.

But, as his nickname implied, he was resourceful. During the war he had saved the lives of some Protestant supporters of William's and, resolved to capitalize on this, he set off for England to make use of what a client was to call his capacity for 'plausible discourses'. Pleading his cause was a long and expensive business. It was said to have cost him his 'hat full of sovereigns' and took four years, but in the end he was successful. The King issued a warrant for his pardon, of 'all treasons, rebellions and crimes', making special reference to his having saved some Protestants 'from ruin', and confirmed his title to his estates. Only then was he able to feel they were safe for himself and his heirs.

By this time, more than five hundred years after the Anglo-Normans had invaded Ireland, the entire country was a patch-work of confiscated, divided and redistributed lands. The arrears of pay for successive English armies had been met by grants of Irish estates, but it was the Cromwellian conquest which brought to a climax the religious taboos introduced by the Reformation and the Elizabethan plantations, and put the westernmost province of Connaught in a special position. It was reserved, with County Clare, for the dispossessed native Catholics. They were transplanted to the west of the Shannon, the rest of the country became an English Protestant colony, and the population of Ireland sank to 850,000.

With boundless faith in the Stuarts, the displaced Catholics expected restitution at the restoration of Charles II. But he owed his crown to the Commonwealth army and his Act of Settlement confirmed the soldiers' titles to their Irish lands.

And when he attempted to compensate the disillusioned Catholics by an Act of Explanation, the compromise was so confused that the claims of thousands were never heard.

In the midst of these shifting sands, Connaught was full of contradictions. Some Catholics had been transplanted on to their Catholic neighbours' lands under Cromwell. Others had been granted the possessions of co-religionists whom Charles had failed to pardon, while the more prosperous had acquired new properties by the mortgages they had arranged with the older, impoverished classes falling in. Nimble Dick had come by his lands in all these ways, and, in particular, had been granted practically all the estates of the ancient clan of O'Flaherty. Consisting of almost a quarter of a million acres of mountain, lake and bog with eighty miles of indented coastline, they made him the largest proprietor in fee simple in the British Isles.

Having obtained the King's ear, he did not allow matters to rest. Scarcely had his pardon arrived than he addressed William. 'With great pain and industry,' he explained, he had acquired some thousands of acres in the remotest part of County Galway, but due to the rough nature of the country, he could not obtain tenants without great encouragement. He was 'so sensible of His Majesty's grace and favour' that he was determined to invest all he had, or could borrow, in order to improve the land, and he proposed to build a town at a place called Clare where a fair was held. He would produce every possible inducement to get tradesmen and handicraftsmen to settle there, but if his lands could be elevated to the status of a manor, which would entitle him to exact fees and services from the tenants, he felt that he could carry out his plan more rapidly.

William did not hurry to reply, but three years later, on 5 July 1698, he issued letters patent erecting all Nimble Dick's lands west of Galway into the manor of Clare, or Claremount, an event which his great-grandson was to turn to the advantage of the world at large. Nimble Dick and his heirs acquired for ever the right to hold a court-baron where their seneschals would have 'full power and authority and jurisdiction to hold pleas . . . in all actions of Debts Covenant Trespass Accompt Contract and Detenue and all other causes and matters whatsoever happening and arising within the said manor.' By special grace they could levy, collect and convert to their own use all fines, profits and emoluments arising out of the court, and they were to hold two weekly markets and two extra fairs at Claremount, as well as a court of Pye Powder during them.

With such a large estate the patent converted Nimble Dick virtually into a petty monarch, and there were rumblings of discontent. The House of Commons protested at such favour being shown a Catholic, while the Lords Justices pointed out to the Government that there was scarcely a Protestant in the area involved where, due to its remoteness, the inhabitants would be able to communicate easily with the King's enemies in the event of a foreign war. But William was not moved. He had given his word for himself and his heirs, and he stood by it.

The Martins were one of the fourteen great families of Galway whom the Cromwellian soldiers had christened the 'Tribes'. They were descended from Oliver Martin who was at the third crusade with Richard Coeur de Lion. Oliver was the only other survivor of the shipwreck on the King's return journey to Europe and shared his monarch's prison. It was Richard who gave Oliver the family arms: azure, a calvary cross, on five degrees argent, between the sun in splendour, on the dexter limb, and the moon in crescent, on the sinister, or. Their motto was: *Auxilium meum a Domino.*

The Martins came to Ireland following the Anglo-Norman conquest of 1169 in the retinue of the de Burgos and settled, like them, in Galway early in the thirteenth century. There the new arrivals took fright at the native Irish and walled themselves up in the town where they gradually built up a city state akin to those in northern Italy.

All rights and revenue to the mills of Galway were made over to one Thomas Martin, in 1365 at the period when the town began to come into prominence. With its fine port and vessels trading with Spain and Gascony, a thriving business in wine was built up over the centuries, and Galway became the *entrepôt* for the whole country. Hides and other commodities were exported, and the Irish beyond the walls supplied provisions.

By the beginning of the sixteenth century, the Martins were among the most affluent of a prosperous and proud community in whose civic life they played a leading part. Peter Martin was made a bailiff in 1498, and from then on the Martins produced

xiv

bailiffs and mayors in almost every generation, while Dominic Martin was the first recorder elected in 1595.

But the Martins had also been the first of the Tribes to venture out into the wild country of the native Irish. In 1590 Robert Martin had bought an estate from the O'Flahertys at Ross at the entry to the beautiful and rugged region of Connemara. Others had followed suit, and the Galway bye-laws about that time voiced a complaint against merchants taking to the country 'without answering tax and talladge, scott and lott' within the town.

The O'Flahertys of later generations, however, kept a jealous eye on the Martins with whom they had a standing feud, and when they saw Nimble Dick, the great-grandson of Robert Martin of Ross, growing fat on their lands, they could not be expected to suffer him gladly. The arrival of a riderless horse at Birchall, the house on the shores of Lough Corrib where Nimble Dick and his family lived, signified that the O'Flahertys had murdered his eldest son. The country people composed a dirge for him, 'Robin the beautiful, Robin the brave', but fortunately for the Martins they had another son, Anthony, and the succession was assured.

Anthony married his brother-in-law's niece, Bridget Kirwan, settled down at Dangan, a mansion Nimble Dick had built on the outskirts of Galway, and had two sons and a daughter. The Treaty of Limerick which had ended the Jacobite war had guaranteed religious tolerance, but the Irish parliament had refused to ratify it, and penal laws excluded Catholics from most of their rights, including education. Ignoring the law, Anthony sent his second son, Robert, to the University of Louvain where an uncle had been a priest. Yet, despite this act of defiance, Anthony was a quiet man, to judge by his epitaph:

> Esteemed in life, the Duitious Son, the
> Tender Husband, the truly Affectionate
> Father, Steady in Friendship, Frugal,
> Human, Temperate, Valient, Beneficient
> to the Distressed, only to punish
> Ingratitude and Impiety.

But his son, Robert, was turbulent. A crack swordsman and a handsome, swashbuckling dandy, he stabbed to death an unfortunate officer he thought had insulted him, but was lucky enough to get off with manslaughter. When a disagreement with the Governor of Galway led to a law case which Robert won, he was not satisfied until he had followed the Governor to London where he fought a duel with him in St. James's Street and gave him what he claimed was 'the most unmerciful dhrubbing that ever was heard of in the streets of London'.

An ardent Jacobite, like every student of Louvain, when the news of the Scottish rebellion of 1745 reached him, he set forth for Scotland disguised as a peasant in a heavy frieze coat. On the way he stopped overnight at an inn where he was thoughtless enough to order fricassee of chicken. Such refined tastes did not tally with his appearance, and the innkeeper, growing suspicious, had him arrested. The lace ruffs at his wrists, which were badly concealed, confirmed the suspicions and he was thrown into prison. Once he was released, he turned about and made for home where he gave some thought to his future.

According to one of the penal laws, gavelkind, only a Protestant could inherit an estate whole and entire. As a result, a great many converts to Protestantism were elder sons who changed faith in order to retain their property intact. A French traveller in later years who asked the owner of Oranmore Castle, near Galway, what had made him change his religion, got the simple answer, 'Oranmore.'

Robert's elder brother, Richard, was married to the 'sweet Mable Kelly' of the bard Carolan's song, but she had borne him no children, and no doubt in order to ensure Nimble Dick's heritage, Robert now took out a Protestant Certificate. But it was known that he continued to be the leader of the Galway Catholics. It was rumoured that at Dangan he was fitting out a ship for the Pretender, and the Governor informed the Government that he could 'bring to the town of Galway in twenty-four hours 800 villains as desperate and as absolutely at his devotion as Cameron of Lochiel'.

The Jacobite cause was, however, doomed and as the years passed and enthusiasm waned, Robert began to think of settling down. One of the great champions of the Catholic cause had been the eleventh Baron Trimlestown. The family, named Barnewall, were among the many Anglo-Normans who had gradually identified themselves with the native Irish, particularly after the Reformation when they were united by religious ties. The eleventh baron had left Ireland with the 'Wild Geese' —the cream of Irish society who departed after the final Williamite victory at Limerick. He had entered the Irish Brigade, but later returned to Ireland, and when he died in 1746, he was succeeded by his son Robert. It was this twelfth Lord Trimlestown's third sister, the Honourable Bridget Barnewall, whom Robert chose as his bride. Her two elder sisters, Thomasine and Margaret, were married respectively to Lords Gormanston and Mountgarret, both of whom were prominent in the Catholic struggle.

The wedding took place on 6 April 1753, when Robert was thirty-nine, and his brother, Richard, agreed to lease him the family seat at Dangan at a nominal rent of one peppercorn a year.

Chapter One

'NEAR TWO miles from Galway . . . beautifully situated on the banks of the fine river of Lough Corrib, is Dangan, the seat of Robin Martin, Esq. When the virtuoso contemplates this situation, its contiguity to the lake, and the various other beauties it unites, we doubt not but he will allow it to be one of the most delightful places for abode he may have viewed in the kingdom.' Thus wrote the editor of the *Post-Chaise Companion*.

The plantations which had been almost destroyed by a freak invasion of scarabaeus beetles blown in by the south-west wind a few years after Nimble Dick built the house, had by now grown again. They sloped down to the lake where pleasure boats were moored. The semi-fortified Elizabethan mansion of the Blakes stood only fifty yards across the narrow stretch of water at Menlo, and all around were green fields.

Galway, three miles away, was the remnant of an Anglo-Norman town in which for centuries the inhabitants had kept the natives at bay and enshrined their sentiments over the West Gate, 'From the ferocious O'Flaherties, good Lord deliver us.' There the Tribes had formed an oligarchy which throughout the medieval period had ruled with a rod of iron. Yet, they had taken largely to the Irish language, their French had grown rusty and their English, as exemplified by their bye-laws, was at best broken.

The city fathers kept a sharp eye on everything. Neither 'O' nor 'Mac' was allowed into the town. Prices were controlled, standards of workmanship guarded and rules for town planning

1

established. Widows were entitled to a third of their husband's goods, and the lot of the apprentice was regulated with as much justice as his master's.

With bourgeois solemnity, the Irish tendency to extravagance and lavish hospitality was discouraged, gate-crashing was penalized, young men were ordered not to wear 'gorgeous apparell', women were to confine themselves to black, and the aquavit sold in the town was pronounced to be more like *aqua mortis*.

Exhortations to morality were specific. A bye-law of 1519 declared that no man 'should be found by nighte time in any man's housse, to give coupillation, or to do with the good man's servant mayd or daughter, by ways of advoutrey, to less 20s., and also the good man, in whos housse the same person is found with the said facte or cryme, to lesse to that good man 20s. and he that begetteth a freeman or merchaund's daughter with child shall marry her, or give her a sufficient portion toward her preferment until another man.' By 1584, things had not improved all that much, and a fine of 20s. was imposed on 'any inhabitant comforting, lodging or mayntaining in his house or otherwise, any bawdry or harlotts'.

But the days of the little city state were numbered. It withstood a siege of nine months from Cromwell, and was defended by Mrs. Martin's great-grandfather, General Preston, the first Viscount Taragh. At the capitulation, the soldiers had taken over the sumptuously furnished tall, stone houses, with their high-pitched roofs and elaborately decorated arched doorways. They had torn down the wainscoting and pulled out the doors to burn them; and Galway, 'whose merchants were princes and great among the nations,' paid the price of not conforming to the new religion and regime. The Tribes were banished beyond the walls for a generation, and Galway never recovered her former prosperity and splendour.

By the time the young Martins settled down at Dangan, a great part of the town's walls were crumbling and many of the surviving old mansions were in a state of decay. The city which had been the second in Ireland had been surpassed by others, and was now just a struggling maritime town of 14,000 people. Neither the city fathers nor Cromwell had, however, managed to diminish the traditional hospitality. Galway women were still renowned for their beauty, vivacity and coquetry, and western conviviality made social life spontaneous and gay.

A year after their marriage the Martins had a son whom they christened Richard. It was a Martin family name. A Richard Martin had been Bailiff in 1519, another had been Mayor in 1535, and there had been Richards in every generation since; but it happened also to be the name of his great-grandfather, Nimble Dick, whose estates and privileges he would one day inherit.

The following year the Martins had a daughter, Mary; by then they lived partly at Dangan and partly in Dublin where Robert had taken a house. The journey between Galway and Dublin took several days, and they travelled in the style to which Mrs. Martin was accustomed, in a carriage and four accompanied by liveried outriders. Mrs. Martin shared the Barnewall family's passion for animals, so that, apart from all the paraphernalia essential in those days to the journey of a whole household, some animals would have had to be accommodated.

At Dangan the children grew up in the atmosphere typical of the Connaught countryside. There, history had had a levelling effect, and the peasantry of today all too often turned out to be the forfeiting gentry of yesterday. The landlords in the west, being predominantly Catholic, had suffered like their tenants, so that the cleavage between the two classes which was to be found in the rest of Ireland did not exist. The gentry did not stand on social distinctions and the peasantry for the most part gave them a feudal loyalty.

The Martin tribe had been prolific and there was always a multitude of little cousins at a variety of removes for Dick and Mary to play with. Indeed, that Corporation which had granted the freedom of Galway to Lieutenant-Colonel O'Shaughnessy, despite the obnoxious prefix, 'in consideration of his allyance in bloode to the whole town', need not have confined their remarks to him. Apart from the relations, there were the tenants' children, the farm, and the animals which Mrs. Martin brought up the children to care for and love. Finally there were the guests. Irish children were not excluded from the life of their parents, as in England, but were accustomed to mingle with the grown-ups, listen to their conversation and sit at table with

3

them. This gave them poise early in life, and when the children's aunts, Lady Gormanston and Lady Mountgarret, called, they were charmed by little Dickie and impressed with his excellent table manners.

Even the periods spent in Dublin had special attractions for the children, apart from those usual in a city. Turvey House, the Barnewalls' original home, had secret hiding places and a subterranean passage, and there was more excitement at Trimlestown Castle. Mrs. Martin's brother, Robert, 12th Baron Trimlestown, lived there. After his father had died in France he had returned to Ireland and his surroundings were the kind to delight a pair of children. Dressed frequently in scarlet, with a full powdered wig, he had a beautiful wife who defied fashion by wearing her hair loose and flowing. Robert was a doctor of great ability as well as a botanist, and, of course, an animal lover. He had a conservatory full of exotic plants, an aviary of rare birds and, chained up at the front door, an enormous eagle to whom the servants threw pieces of meat from a distance. Marshal de Saxe had presented him with a superbly painted coach, and he had a vast collection of books and prints.

But Uncle Robert, who had a number of distinguished patients, was not all-powerful; he could not save the life of his own sister, Bridget. She died in Dublin when the children were aged eight and nine, and this threw them both, but particularly Dick, into closer association with their father.

Dick was a sturdy boy, with rather ungovernable light brown hair and lively bright blue eyes. He was exceptionally warmnatured and loved all around him, whether man or beast. His powers of observation were highly developed and he had an acute sense of humour; and, as his father's companion, he was growing up a good fisherman, an expert shot and a practised yachtsman.

Robert had plans for his son which arose to some extent from the history of his caste. The Anglo-Norman settlers had early shown a spirit of independence and resented being governed at a distance by England. By 1366 their tendency to identify themselves with the natives caused such concern that the Statutes of Kilkenny were passed to make fraternization illegal and to exclude the native Irish from English law. But although the statutes remained nominally in force for two hundred years,

4

they could not prevent the Anglo-Normans from becoming 'more Irish than the Irish'. When a bill was brought into the Irish parliament to change Henry VIII's title from Lord of Ireland to King, it was found that, although all the members but one were Anglo-Normans, only one of them understood English, the rest knowing nothing but Irish.

These 'English irlandized', as they were called in England, gradually came to form a Middle Nation between the old natives and the new settlers who arrived with the different plantations. A high proportion of them were not converted at the Reformation. From then on they were united to the old race, and by the time the Battle of Aughrim had sealed the fate of the Gael, these people were among the acknowledged leaders of the Irish people.

Lord Macartney, a Lord Lieutenant of Ireland, described the penal laws under which they lived as 'the most complete code of persecution that ingenious bigotry ever compiled'. A Catholic might not go to school or university, study abroad or exercise a profession, possess land, own a horse worth more than £5, marry a Protestant, bear arms or sit in parliament. In practice these laws operated arbitrarily. If an invasion was suspected, they were applied; if peace prevailed, or England needed the good opinion of Catholic allies on the Continent, they were relaxed. These laws had decided how Robert Martin would be educated, and now they were to decide how he would educate his son.

One day when Robert and Dick were sailing on Lough Corrib, they were caught in one of the sudden squalls for which the lake is renowned. Dick was at the tiller, and Robert told him to keep the boat headed in to the western shore and his eye on the hill behind Dangan. This was the moment, as they made for safety, that he chose to announce to the boy what his plans for him were. He was to be sent to an English public school and university, and to be the first Martin to be brought up as a Protestant. This would entitle him to sit in parliament, and there he was to fight for Catholic emancipation.

In the beginning of 1761, the year that Dick was to be sent away to school, his father decided to remarry. His new wife was of a well-known Galway family, Lynch, and she was the childless widow of the Reverend John Vesey, grandson of an

Archbishop of Tuam. News of the event reached Dick's Aunt Thomasine Gormanston, who was now living with a part of her family in Belgium whence the first Lord Taragh had emigrated after the fall of Galway. The moment she heard of what had happened, Thomasine wrote home to her son, Lord Gormanston, 'I am in pain about poor Mary Martin. For God's sake give me a particular account of her in every respect and her brother.' Whatever account Gormanston gave of them did not satisfy their Aunt Thomasine. Ten months later, Gormanston's brother wrote to say that their mother was giving the greyhound Gormanston had sent her to the Belgian Princess Charlotte, because she had taken a resolution 'to have no dog of her own any more, on account of her growing *too* fond of them'. He then added: 'My mother is in great pain about R. Martin's children. When you write next lett us know how they are and what is become of them.'

Nothing dramatic had become of them, and the relationship with their stepmother worked out satisfactorily. But Dick had by now gone to public school. He was fortunate in his father's choice of Harrow; it was going through one of the most remarkable phases in its history. Under the headmastership of Doctor Sumner, assisted by Samuel Parr, one of the best classical educations was available, and the school was turning out men who made their mark in the field of learning.

Sumner, who was thirty-nine at the time, was a cheerful, good-tempered man with a brilliant classical reputation and a gift for eloquence. Parr, aged twenty-two, was small and benign, except when roused. He spoke with a slight lisp and vibrated with indignation at the slightest show of cruelty, servility or injustice. Both men were adored by their pupils.

There were over two hundred boys in the school when Dick arrived, and lessons only occupied about four and a half hours a day. During these, Mr. Parr dinned Caesar's Commentaries, Ovid and the Greek Testament, and the whole range of classical writers into Dick and his companions. When they had gone to bed, he and Sumner talked what amounted almost to sedition—civil rights for the American colonists who were clamouring for their freedom.

Both men were Whigs, and the boys were accustomed to hearing the name of Wilkes and popular politics, while Parr was never tired of repeating what years later he was to sum up, on cruelty to animals, in a famous sermon on education: 'He that can look with rapture upon the unoffending and unresisting animal, will soon learn to view the sufferings of a fellow-creature with indifference; and in time he will acquire the power of viewing them with triumph, if that fellow-creature should become the victim of his resentment, be it just or unjust.' He believed that children should be taught at an early age to be kind to animals, but that this would be impossible 'if the heart has been once familiarized to spectacles of distress, and has been permitted either to behold the pangs of any living creature with cold insensibility, or to inflict them with wanton barbarity.' Dick heard the words 'wanton barbarity' reiterated constantly throughout his school-days, and he never forgot them.

Twice a year he went home to the west of Ireland. During his first year at Harrow, his father's cousin Jasper of Birchall had died and had left Robert all his property in West Connaught which included Birchall where Nimble Dick had lived. If the family were there rather than at Dangan, young Dick had a sixteen-mile drive along a bumpy track. As he approached, bonfires would be lit along the way to welcome him, bare-footed children would run alongside the carriage cheering, and their elders would try to approach within earshot of 'the young masther' to voice some grievance he could see redressed. It was a foretaste of his adult life. Then when he arrived there would be the view across the lake, the blue humps of the Maamturk Mountains, the water lapping at the garden walls, and fishing and shooting to his heart's content.

When he left Harrow in 1771, he was sent to 'cram' for his entrance to Trinity College, Cambridge. He was under the Reverend Joseph Gunning, a young man in his thirties who was a Fellow of Corpus Christi and had been vicar of Sutton in Suffolk for the previous three years. There, in an Elizabethan vicarage beside a pebble-built twelfth-century church, Dick studied well and was admitted a gentleman-commoner at Trinity on 4 March 1773; he matriculated that Easter.

The university at the time was more preoccupied with politics than learning, and gentlemen-commoners enjoyed special privileges which made it unnecessary to take their studies too seriously. Dinner in Commons was generally the only firm engagement of the day and was treated with some ceremony. It was usual to attend the barber and have one's hair curled, then to change into knee breeches, a white waistcoat and white silk stockings. In the evening people mostly ate in their rooms where the bedmaker brought the bill of fare. No wine was drunk; instead, an enormous teapot of hot punch was kept on the hob. Drinking was not a Cambridge failing at the time, and Dick Martin was notoriously abstemious all his life. But Dr. Ewin complained of the 'lavish way of spending both money and their time' of the Irish and the sons of the big West Indian planters.

The counter-attraction to the tavern was the coffee house where the students perused the London newspapers with avidity. A boy of fourteen called William Pitt had just come up to college, and the rumour may already have circulated that his father intended him to be Prime Minister one day. At Trinity, Dick was sharing rooms with George Ponsonby, the son of the Speaker of the Irish House of Commons, and among his companions was the Marquis of Granby, soon to be the Duke of Rutland, who had won the university seat the year after Dick's going up to college, and who spoke out in favour of the American colonists.

In the vacation Dick continued to pay his cherished visits to the west of Ireland where he now had two half-brothers, Robert and Anthony, but he also spent much time in London where he was a gay, sophisticated young man about town. His cousin, Lord Gormanston, had a house in Burlington Street, and was on close terms with the Royal Family, and through their mothers the two men shared an interest in animals. However far from one another the members of the Gormanston family might be, dogs, cats and canaries were passed around between them like so many picture postcards.

Dick shared a love of travel with his cousin, James Jordan of Rosleven Castle in County Mayo. Together they visited Europe where Dick, an excellent horseman, rode in all the leading riding establishments, and then they sailed for Jamaica, which was full of Irish planters, and remained there some time. When the American War of Independence at last broke out, they were in New England.

Dick came down from Cambridge without taking his degree,

but, on his return from America, he intended to continue reading for the bar. He was admitted to Lincoln's Inn on 1 February 1776, a couple of weeks before George Ponsonby, but probably under Rutland's influence he decided to go straight into Irish politics.

The Americans were busy making comparisons between their situation and that of Ireland, and Franklin had been to Ireland to convince people that America's cause was Ireland's cause. This theme was to make the reputation of the parliament to which Richard Martin was now to offer himself as a candidate for Galway.

The cut and thrust of a Galway election became in later years proverbial. An old refrain, 'He's not the man for Galway!', referred to somebody who could not fight a duel before breakfast; ride all day to hounds, jumping six-foot walls in the process; entertain on so lavish a scale that he was in permanent danger from the bailiff, whom, however, he could always foil by swamping him in yet more hospitality; drink bumpers of claret or rum-shrub into the small hours of the morning; then adjourn in order to fight another duel, jump more walls and evade more bailiffs. 'The man for Galway' had to live up to a tradition not demanded of candidates east of the Shannon.

Parliamentary representation at the time was based on property, not popularity. The entire country was composed of big estates and the tenants formed the greater part of the electorate. Every member of the established Protestant church who leased freehold land worth forty shillings a year or over was entitled to vote. He was called a forty-shilling freeholder, and he automatically voted according to the landlord's wishes. The majority of the Martins' tenants were Catholics, therefore not entitled to vote, and at the end of a long and momentous parliamentary career, Richard Martin must have looked back with a faint smile to his first election contest. It was a tame affair in which only 360 votes were cast and he footed the poll with fifty-three; but this did not keep him out of parliament. In common with a large section of the House of Commons, he purchased a seat for the freeman borough of Jamestown in County Leitrim at a cost of approximately £2,000.

On Tuesday, 18 June 1776, Richard Martin, in full court dress with a powdered wig, took his seat with the three hundred members of the Irish parliament. Situated at right angles to Trinity College, the parliament house was the most impressive public building in Dublin. Begun in 1728 and designed by Sir Edward Lovet Pearce who had travelled in Italy, it was built in the Italian style, with Ionic columns, a forecourt and arched entrances. The House of Commons was circular, with the members' seats ranged around the middle in concentric circles, each rising above the other. Sixteen Corinthian columns supported a dome and behind a balustrade between the pillars there was a public gallery. One rule of political significance was that this was not cleared for a division, so that members' votes were public. The whole combined magnificence with intimacy.

But the Irish parliament had little control over the Irish Government. This was composed of a Lord Lieutenant, or Viceroy, representing the Crown, a Chief Secretary with the powers of a Prime Minister, and Secretaries for the other Departments of State; and it was appointed by the English parliament at Westminster. The Irish parliament might irritate the Irish Government, but it could not change it. The Government, on the other hand, due to the borough system which gave the owners the control of several seats in parliament, was generally in a position to achieve the majorities it wanted by bribing a few individuals. The Administration was generally referred to euphemistically as 'the Castle' because Dublin Castle was its headquarters.

When the members took their seats in 1776 in this rather anomalous assembly, a large number had been bribed by the Government with places or pensions, one third of the members were new, and eighteen election results were disputed. The House included some of the most remarkable men Ireland has ever known, the standard of oratory was high, and leading the Opposition was Henry Grattan after whom the next parliament was to be named. Four years Martin's senior, he was the son of the Recorder of Dublin and a lawyer who had found his way into politics through his friendship with Lord Charlemont and his political associate, Henry Flood. Grattan had entered the House earlier in the year, and he had now assumed the leadership of the anti-governmental forces Flood had been obliged to relinquish upon accepting office as Vice Treasurer. Small and misshapen, with a head which seemed to be stuck on to the back of his neck and a protruding chin, Grattan was characterized by the enthusiasm and impetuosity which he combined with a shining integrity and disinterestedness. He had a habit of weaving to and fro as he spoke in a shrill and inharmonious voice; but due to its glowing eloquence it was to become the voice of Ireland.

The Viceroy, Lord Harcourt, had procured an address from the previous parliament authorizing the despatch to America of 4,000 men from the Irish military establishment of 12,000. There had been time since then for the unpopularity of this measure to increase and for such a formidable opponent as Grattan to prepare to attack him on the grounds of corruption. Harcourt took the precaution of proroguing parliament the very day it assembled, and he continued to do so until his recall to England the following November.

Richard Martin scarcely had the feeling of having sat in parliament at all. Yet, before he was to sit there again, Harcourt, for whose policies he had no admiration, had died in a manner which could not fail to make Martin warm to him as a man. His favourite dog had fallen into a well, and when he went to the rescue, the ground had given way and flung him foremost into the mud where he had been suffocated. Such a generous effort would probably have counterbalanced a score of pensions in Richard Martin's mind.

Chapter Two

FEW CONNAUGHT gentlemen in those days looked east of the Shannon for a bride, and there was a considerable likelihood of the ladies of their choice being connections. Richard Martin was no exception. His stepmother by her first marriage had a niece, Elizabeth Vesey, whose family was from County Mayo, just across Lough Corrib from the Martins' estates, and at the age of twenty-three he fell deeply in love with her.

Elizabeth's father, George Vesey, who was married to his own first cousin, was heir to Lucan House, one of the most impressive mansions in the neighbourhood of Dublin. But his elder brother, who was childless, was still resident there, and when a marriage had been arranged the wedding was planned to take place at the ancestral home of the Veseys at Holymount in County Mayo.

It was a large, square, stone house set in a splendid park traversed by the river Robe. Rolling along through the flat, fertile country, criss-crossed by loose stone walls, to be married there on 1 February 1777, Richard Martin had every reason to feel pleased with himself. He had won a beautiful, exceptionally gifted bride with whom, unlike many bridegrooms in similar circumstances, he was in love. And, related as he was by blood to all Connaught, he was now about to become related by alliance to some of the leading families in the kingdom.

Elizabeth was descended from a famous and prolific Archbishop of Tuam whose palace had been burned by Catholic extremists during James II's reign. He fled to London, and on his return after the Williamite victory, settled down on the family estate at Holymount to rear fourteen children. Between them they produced fifty-eight grandchildren and nearly all of his great-grandchildren had made excellent matches.

As a result, Richard Martin was in due course to become linked with the great banking families of La Touche and Dawson. In the Irish parliament he was to be allied to Brownlow and Sir Vesey Colclough; and in the nobility to Baron Knapton, Viscount Northland, Viscount de Vesci, Lord Adare and Lord Lucan. More important still, he was to be connected with the Earl of Buckinghamshire who had just replaced Harcourt as Viceroy and who had married, when she was only fifteen, a sister of the Right Honourable Thomas Connolly, the descendant of a former Speaker of the Irish House of Commons. One of Connolly's sisters was married to Elizabeth's first cousin, Staples.

However rich she was in relations, Elizabeth was not so in fortune; it only amounted to £5,000. To Richard Martin this was immaterial. Throughout his life he considered money a disagreeable subject and, as time went on and he grew increasingly short of it, he was able to ignore it. His father, Robert, had recently suffered some financial reverses, but he had been impressed by Elizabeth's charms and accomplishments —she could both paint and write—and readily gave in to the idea of a marriage.

He made a settlement on the couple to which Sir Michael Cromie, who had also just entered parliament, was a witness. Out of an annual income of some £6,000, he settled £1,500 on Dick, £900 of which was secured for any children in the event of their parents' death, and £600 on Elizabeth in the case of Dick's death.

While awaiting the recall of parliament, the young couple settled into Dangan with Robert and his family. There Elizabeth got her first taste of Galway politics. The family of Denis Daly, who was both a member of parliament and Lord Mayor, had acquired a virtual monopoly of the Corporation which they had 'packed' with their friends, and the Martins were among those foremost in trying to re-establish independence.

The summer assizes at Clonmel also gave them plenty to discuss at Dangan. Duelling was widespread, but it had been

13

especially so in Ireland since the disbanding of the Irish army after Aughrim. It replaced the opportunities for displaying valour previously offered by the military life. A gentleman was scarcely a gentleman unless he had 'smelt powder', and to have 'shot up at the bar' more often than not meant to have fought well in a profession where duelling was particularly current.

Galway was considered one of the two greatest 'fire-eating' counties. The old saying, 'as proud as a Galway merchant', was said to point to characteristics acquired through long contact with Spain, and gentlemen were inclined to send a challenge on the slightest provocation. It was now felt that the whole science was in danger of falling into disrepute through being indulged in too lightly, and it was decided to establish regulations. Delegates from Tipperary and the different counties of Connaught met at Clonmel summer assizes and laid down the rules for the future conduct of affairs of honour.

Richard Martin would not have been his father's son had he not been a duellist, and Elizabeth would probably not have accepted him had it not been known that he had 'blazed'. Like Robert, he was expert with the small-sword. This was Galway's speciality, calling for great agility in a very exacting form of fencing; and he was considered to be equally good with pistols.

The rules and regulations were now sent to all duelling clubs with the recommendation that copies should be made and kept by gentlemen in their pistol cases. In Galway they came to be known as the 'thirty-seven commandments' and a committee was established to meet alternately at Galway and Clonmel during the quarter sessions to examine complaints and give judgements in cases of doubt. Young Mrs. Martin, like most ladies in high society, was to have good reason to remember the commandments.

In preparation for the opening of parliament, the young couple moved up to Dublin and took a house in Kildare Street. The Duke of Leinster had built a house there in 1745, designed by the German architect, Cassels. A stately mansion in the Palladian style, it had set the stage for Dublin's future development; people of fashion began to migrate from the north bank of the Liffey to the south, and around it there grew up terraces of houses with classical façades punctuated by decorated fanlights over the doorways, and elaborately stuccoed interiors.

Dublin was the second city in the empire, and, with a population of 160,000, it was a quarter of the size of London. Its social life was so strenuous that an appointment there was regarded more as a marathon than a performance of public service. Buckingham had chosen as his Chief Secretary Richard Heron, but, under pressure from his wife, he turned down the offer. 'I have not, she thinks,' he wrote to his brother, 'constitution enough for the social meetings of that country.' Buckingham interceded with a faint reproach to the lady, and her husband took her to the Bishop of London who had witnessed her vows of obedience on marriage.

After much delay, she gave in, and even did so with such a good grace that she was not deterred by a letter from Mrs. Waite at Dublin Castle which could only strike terror into her.

'Mr. Heron and you will be visited by the whole town,' it ran, 'immediately after your arrival, and the whole town will expect you to return their visits as soon as possible. *To omit one*, either on your part or on his, will be a deadly sin, and therefore you should be fortified directly with a good porter, who is to be *very exact* in booking the names and places of abode of your visitants.' Even the parting shot did not deflect the martyred Mrs. Heron from the path of duty. 'Give me leave to tell you,' the letter concluded, 'that at this moment, Mr. Heron, and you, are as well known in Dublin, as if you had lived here for twenty years.' The Bishop of Gloucester delivered the final blow. 'Mrs. Heron,' he wrote to the couple after their arrival, 'will want all her health and spirits among her new acquaintance, the Irish.'

Fortunately for the Martins, they had good constitutions, and threw themselves into social life with enthusiasm. He already had a wide circle of friends in Dublin and through her connections they were at once associated with the Viceroy and his entourage. She was beautiful and graceful and he, though only of medium height, had a manly, athletic figure and a wit which was becoming proverbial. They were equipped to succeed in society.

Gentlemen at the time wore knee breeches, buckled shoes, coats down to the knee and lace at the neck and wrists. The ladies had full skirts, often with panniers, stiff bodices with a corset laced openly down the front, low, square-cut necks, and

15

sleeves reaching to just below the elbows. They wore their hair raised up on towering structures of wire and padding, and the men wore wigs.

It was now a decade since it had become obligatory for the Viceroy to reside in Ireland, and this had given a great impetus to society which revolved to a considerable extent around the Viceregal court and the parliament. People vied with each other in the splendour of the houses they built and the lavishness of the hospitality they dispensed. It was the custom to serve seven-course meals accompanied by endless quantities of claret, many people kept open house, and overcrowding was general.

The Viceroy gave levees and balls with buffet suppers at Dublin Castle, the gentry attended charity balls and concerts all the year around, and the Martins, like the Buckinghams, were ardent theatre-goers; they both shone in the amateur theatricals which were the rage. Masquerades were popular, and it was not unusual after one of these for a few fashionable ladies to throw open their houses where food and drink would be served until dawn.

There were a number of fine mansions in the surroundings of Dublin for a young couple such as the Martins to visit. Elizabeth's uncle, Agmondisham Vesey, the Accountant-General, had built an elegant classical house at Lucan to replace the old Sarsfield Castle his father had inherited through marriage to Charlotte Sarsfield. His wife, who was a friend of Dr. Johnson, Burke and Reynolds, had been the centre of a literary coterie in London; and the Swiss artist, Angelica Kauffman, who had made her name in the British capital, painted medallions to decorate the interior of the house ornamented by a leading Irish stuccoer, Michael Stapleton.

Only a few miles away there was Castletown, the home of Thomas Connolly, where the Buckinghams were constant guests. Built in 1722, it was the largest and one of the most splendid Irish mansions, and the Connollys, like the Duke of Leinster not far away, created a hub for society. The Duke's country house, Carton, had been remodelled by Cassels and had a saloon with a superb coved ceiling decorated by two Italian stuccoers, the Francini brothers.

Further afield there lay County Wicklow, the beautiful and mountainous region south of the city. One of the fashionable

16

pastimes was to drive out to visit some of the large houses built there by members of parliament and other prominent persons. The expedition took several days, and people travelled accompanied by their retinue of servants bringing sumptuous picnics. The La Touches had built a moss house in their grounds at Bellevue where visitors could eat and shelter, and they had even erected a lodge on the shore of Lake Luggala, high up in the mountains, especially for the use of such guests.

By the time parliament was due to open Buckingham had been almost a year in Ireland and knew what he had to face. His dilemma was that of every other Viceroy: how to govern in the best interests of Britain and Ireland through the influence of parliamentary supporters whose interest was chiefly their own. He was pressed on the one side by those seeking posts, pensions and perquisites, whilst on the other he had to handle people like Mr. Tighe, a member of parliament, who protested when offered a post that he was, always had been and felt 'exclusively English'. When Buckingham wrote to Lord George Germain, Secretary of State for the Colonies, 'Nothing . . . remains to me but a choice of difficulties,' he summed up the lot of the Viceroys in general.

Now, however, a new dimension had been added to the difficulties. For eighteen months the American colonists had been at war with the mother country and this had set in motion a chain of events which was to have a profound effect on Ireland. Many of the disabilities under which Ireland was suffering were similar to those which in America had produced exasperation, then war. The analogies created widespread sympathy with the colonies and provided politicians with an ideal ground on which to argue Ireland's case.

Ireland had a parliament of her own, but it was completely subservient to the English parliament. Under Poynings' Law, dating from 1495, no bill could be introduced in the Irish parliament until it had first been approved by the Irish Privy Council, appointed by the British Government's representative the Lord Lieutenant; then by the English Privy Council. A Declaratory Act dating from 1719, similar to that relating to America which was passed following the repeal of the Stamp Act, asserted the right of the English parliament to legislate for Ireland.

Under the cover of these laws, England had gradually managed to regulate the whole of Irish commerce. The Navigation Acts of Charles II's reign forbade her to trade directly with the British colonies. At the Revolution her staple industry was restricted when she was forbidden to export woollen goods in order to protect the English manufacturers. Her glass manufacture was nipped in the bud by similar prohibitions, and she could not export corn or cattle to England. Irish exports to England bore heavy duties, but parliament was forbidden to impose similar taxes on English imports, so the market was flooded with English goods. Ireland's export trade had gradually been reduced to that in linen and in provisions; but the loss of the American market for linen due to the war, and the placing of an embargo by England on the export of provisions, had now had a disastrous effect. The result was summed up by Yelverton in the Irish House of Commons when he asked: 'Is it generous of England that those winds which bring home wealth to her from every point of the compass, should here produce no other effect than to touch with aching cold a naked, half fed, half famished peasantry.'

With such grievances, the example of America fighting to liberate herself from the thraldom of the British legislature was an obvious stimulus to Ireland. When Buckingham drove in state to open parliament on 14 October 1777, these were not his only preoccupations. He had to obtain approval for the 4,000 men who had been removed from the Irish military establishment to remain abroad while there were not enough troops in Ireland to defend her. Furthermore, these men were fighting the Americans for whom there was growing sympathy. This was particularly true of the north of Ireland where the Presbyterians had been concentrated during the plantations. Due to religious persecution they had now been emigrating in great numbers to America, where they in turn had planted whole areas. Six Ulster Presbyterians had signed the Declaration of Independence, and the unrest in the northern province was liable to flare up at any moment. The Catholic leaders were loyal, but there was no knowing the sentiments of the silent masses. Meanwhile, all over the country among the toasts being drunk were 'Mr. Hancock and success to him!', 'May every Mercenary be obliged to pile his arms and march to the

18

tune of Yankee Doodle!' and 'To the memory of the saints and martyrs that fell at Lexington!'.*

With such an explosive atmosphere around him, Buckingham did the statesmanlike thing; in the Speech from the Throne opening the session he did not even mention America. Grattan declared, 'I approve of the silence from the throne from a delicacy to the feelings and circumstances of individuals,' but the Government in London thought otherwise. So many eyebrows were raised at the omission that for several weeks Buckingham had to justify his conduct by explaining what should have been obvious, that in Ireland the question of America was a vexed one. The measures being taken to subdue the colonists were so universally disliked, that any reference to the matter could only have produced an outburst of pro-American feeling.

There were no political parties in the modern sense, but Grattan headed a group calling themselves the Patriots and having Whig tendencies, and from the first Richard Martin supported them. Corruption, pensions and the extravagance of the Administration were among their principal hobby-horses, and Martin, who viewed with such distaste his personal accounts, became an able speaker on those of the public. He was not an orator, but an alert and astute debater. His interventions were generally brief, but very much to the point. The pith was often contained in the line he threw away, and he had an almost Socratic gift for exposing to people the weaknesses in their own arguments. He had the kind of originality which could lead to his being misunderstood, but the opponent who described him as 'an odd, absurd character with something like abilities, but of no consideration or consequence', did not foresee how far his abilities might ultimately carry him.

He had the necessary finesse to be politely rude when the occasion demanded. In a discussion on extraordinary payments to various public servants, it turned out that Sir Roger Palmer, Paymaster of Corn Premiums, had incurred expense in obtaining a new house, but when offered £40 towards the cost, had

* *John Hancock*: first President of the American Continental Congress and first signatory of the Declaration of Independence. *Lexington*: Engagement of 19 April 1775 between colonists and British forces which touched off the American Revolution.

19

refused it saying he would rather pay it all himself than accept such a paltry sum. 'When a gentleman condescends to ask anything,' observed Martin, 'who has an independent fortune, he suffers much more by receiving it from the House than we by granting it to him.'

His refusal to mince words was well demonstrated when it was suggested that the Collector of Customs in Cork was indulging in corrupt practices. Martin admonished those who adhered 'steady to the banners of corruption', and then continued:

> The King, unfortunately for this country, is not very much interested in the embezzlement of the public revenue. His situation resembles that of a man, whose goods and chattels are insured for more than they are worth. If the servants commit depredation, or his house is set on fire, he recovers more than he could have lost, a system which for some time past has rendered it unnecessary that he should be provident of the Public Revenue. The supply has always been made up two-fold to him. If he has been so corrupt as to bribe the majority in Parliament. . . .

At this point he was called to order.

Before Buckingham had time fully to convert the Government to his Speech from the Throne, a thunderbolt fell. At the beginning of December 1777 General Burgoyne and his entire army were forced to surrender to the Americans at Saratoga. In England the news caused dismay, in Ireland it was the signal for rejoicing among America's sympathizers, and there were illuminations in Belfast.

France, always smarting under the English policy which for decades had concentrated on capturing French markets, now saw a chance to bring England to her knees. The Count de Broglie brought up to date a plan he had made in 1763 for an invasion of Britain. 'This expedition,' he declared, 'can strike a blow from which she will never recover. We can dictate the peace to her in London, and put her back again to the place she should occupy in Europe, which is to say, that of a second, or even a third class power.' Spain was to assist by causing a diversion with an invasion of Ireland. The scheme was presented to Louis XVI on 17 December 1777. On that day the King informed the American emissaries that France recognized the independence of America.

Meanwhile, England was faced with the problem of inadequate manpower to replace her lost army. All eyes were turned to Ireland, but there England found herself caught in the cleft stick of her own past policies. Catholics were forbidden to carry arms. Consequently, any move to raise regiments under Catholic officers would involve repealing the law and brought forth from Lord George Germain the inevitable question: 'Would our friends support?'

The impropriety of employing Catholics at home was granted, but the intention was to send them to America. When, however, Buckingham started to put out feelers, the result was discouraging. He had to write to Lord George that, when the question arose at a dinner party, he could see that 'the idea alarmed the company in general', and when George Ogle, the popular and witty member for Wexford who had written the ballad, 'Molly Asthore', but who was one of the staunchest opponents of concessions to the Catholics, asked in the House if a step was contemplated in which 'our civil and religious rights are so essentially concerned', Richard Heron stalled.

Gradually it became clear that the Protestant ascendancy would not support the idea. They feared that the forces would either desert to the Americans or return home well trained and prepared to attack them. The idea was dropped and Buckingham himself came to the conclusion that even the 2nd Antrim Regiment which was being raised in the North should be sent anywhere but to America 'as they would make admirable recruits for Washington'.

Meanwhile, things were moving fast. At the beginning of 1778, France had signed a treaty of alliance with America, and in March the British Ambassador in Paris was recalled. War was imminent, while in Ireland the economic situation continued to deteriorate and the Government was heading for bankruptcy. Buckingham's repeated requests to London for money remained unanswered, and gradually the point was reached where there was not enough in the public purse to cover salaries and the other day-to-day expenses of administration.

France and Spain were well armed and had large navies ready to put to sea. At this crucial moment in Britain's history, Ireland, at her back door, was in such desperate straits that two-thirds of the country was uninhabited due to the lack of employment. The majority of those who remained were linked by spiritual ties with Britain's enemies and lived discontented under a cruel oppression. In Britain's own interests, the moment had arrived for conciliation.

Chapter Three

GEORGE III himself raised the question of the Catholics. When Pery, the Speaker of the Irish House of Commons, saw him in the spring of 1778, he expressed a wish that in the next session of the Irish parliament the laws against the Catholics should be relaxed 'as far as might be admitted with propriety'. Buckingham wrote to Weymouth: 'It is a matter not only of the highest importance, but of very great difficulty to determine where the line shall be drawn.' This was the quandary which was to dominate Irish politics for half a century.

Richard Martin did not want any line to be drawn. He stood for the total emancipation which would give the majority equal civil rights with the privileged minority; but those in parliament who thought like him were few. Little over a dozen of the three hundred came from families who had been more than a century in Ireland, a country whose people were, of all those north and west of the Alps, the longest settled on their own soil. Even the most tolerant of the members were the prisoners of their own origins; most of them owed their wealth and rank exclusively to legalized theft. As Lord Clare was to declare later: 'From their first confiscation they have been hemmed in, on every side, by the old inhabitants of the island, brooding over their discontent in sullen indignation.'

The laws against the Catholics were no longer based on creed, but on land. Religious practice had been tolerated for some considerable time, and the Protestants had never shown any marked inclination to proselytize. Religion had been associated with land for the purpose of the confiscations, but had there been a massive conversion of the Irish people to the Protestant Church, it would have sufficed to revive and revise the Statutes of Kilkenny, or draft some new ones, to exclude the majority from the possession of their estates. Religion had by now become largely an excuse for the penal laws.

Concessions were being granted to the Catholics in England, and while the British Government hoped that the Irish parliament might follow the English lead, they did not wish to appear over-solicitous. Germain merely wrote to Buckingham that he hoped the Irish Catholics would meet with 'that favor and protection which may induce them to be loyal subjects and which may prevent their quitting Ireland in pursuit of civil and religious liberty'.

Buckingham saw this very aspect of the case from another point of view. The members of the House of Commons lived by the landlord system, and the majority of their tenants were Catholics. If the tenantry left, the landlord system would collapse, and he hoped that those who might otherwise be against any concessions, would recognize this fact and unbend.

One of the most independent and long established members in the House, Luke Gardiner, the future Lord Mountjoy, brought up the question. Belonging to a family closely associated with the development of Dublin city for which he sat, he was a man who went deeply into any subject with which he had to deal. When, therefore, he moved on 25 May 1778 for leave to bring in the heads of a bill to alter the popery laws, nobody could doubt that his proposals for the amelioration of the Catholics' lot were the result of the most thorough research.

The discussion was lively, but at length it was proposed to commit the bill. Then Ogle declared: 'By this the great bulwarks of the Constitution will be overturned; the flood gates of popery will be laid open.' He was not just harking back to the reign of James II when the Protestants had had justifiable fears of Catholic intolerance, but to the Protestant apprehensions of Catholicism as an international conspiracy illustrated by the claim the Pope had formerly made to the right of deposing monarchs. But inadvertently he was also providing a warning of what was obvious to a man like Richard Martin. Short of keeping the majority under lock and key, there could be no halt between giving a little and giving all. The flood gates were about to be slowly prised apart.

An earlier concession had been derisive in essence and in name. The Bogland Act of 1771 allowed Catholics to take leases for sixty-one years of fifty acres of unprofitable land with half an acre of profitable land adjoining, provided it was not within one mile of a town. The whole was to be free of taxes for seven years, and half must be reclaimed within twenty-one. Gardiner's bill proposed to grant them the right to unrestricted purchase.

Nothing can show more clearly the heart-searchings to which such a proposition subjected members of the House of Commons than the attitude of Henry Grattan. His fragile frame was illuminated by a burning sincerity. Whenever Catholic hopes sank low, it was this descendant of Protestant planters who was to revive them. He was to go down in history as their advocate. Yet, even he at the outset faltered.

When Ogle introduced an amendment to substitute the right to lease for the right to purchase, Grattan voted for the amendment, and declared:

> I have attended the debate with the most unbiased veneration for every argument that fell from either side of the House. I was undecided for a long time. I formed an opinion and I altered that opinion. I listened to every gentleman, and I find that the objections to the bill as it now stands are unanswerable. . . . Whenever you pass a law to enable Roman Catholics to purchase, what will be the consequence? That the Protestants, who maintain only an artificial superiority by virtue of the law will be subjected to the natural superiority of the Roman Catholics. . . . In the course of a year, by the natural circulation of property, the lands of this country must be in the possession of the Roman Catholics. . . . The present bill is not merely to repeal an Act of Parliament; it is to subvert a system of policy. . . . Under the operation of the penal law, the landholder is a Protestant. Under the operation of the law whatever influence exists is Protestant. Under the operation of that law whatever power exists is Protestant. I will not say I would maintain them as a code of behaviour, but I would maintain them as a code tending to preserve the Protestant authority.

He paid a tribute to the loyalty of the Catholics, but urged the

House not to let out of its hands 'the golden reins of Protestant government'.

Martin was not on the Committee, which continued its discussions throughout June, often sitting until two or three in the morning. The majority wanted to give something, and agreed with Flood on the 'inexpediency, apart from the inhumanity' of the laws, but when it came to deciding what precisely they should give, they were faced with the bogey of popish power; and, ultimately, it was Ogle's and Grattan's views that prevailed.

Catholics were not to be allowed to purchase land, but they were to be entitled to take leases of 999 years on condition of taking an oath of allegiance. More important still, the offending gavelkind clause was to be repealed and Catholics were to be allowed to inherit in the same way as Protestants. Martin, of course, voted for the bill, and it was greeted by the Catholics with addresses expressing loyalty and gratitude. It got through in the nick of time, for while the Committee was sitting, war had at last broken out between England and France.

As steps were being taken to conciliate the Catholics, Buckingham was pressing the British Government to end the commercial restrictions and tranquillize the country at large. Distress was widespread. Without markets for their products, people were left with them on their hands, and the prices of everything dropped. The value of estates had fallen by a quarter, and in Dublin alone twenty thousand manufacturers had been thrown out of employment in two years. People exhausted with hunger were seen fainting in the streets, and several had died of hunger in the north.

The Prime Minister, Lord North, was prepared to be generous, and Ireland had a brilliant advocate in Edmund Burke, one of the leading exponents of free trade in the English parliament. North's proposals meant relaxing almost all the restrictions. Those on wool were to remain, but Ireland was to have direct trade with the English settlements and plantations in everything except tobacco.

But no sooner were the proposals known than an outcry was raised. The large English manufacturing towns, particularly those in the north, saw in them a challenge to their supremacy, and Bristol was so incensed that Burke ultimately lost his seat because of his stand. There were even rumours that the loyalty of the big industrial centres to the King was at stake, and, intimidated by what began to look like a rebellion, North gave in and watered down the plan.

Ireland was now to be entitled to export a certain number of restricted goods to the colonies, but no wool, woollen and cotton manufactures, hats, glass, hops, gunpowder and coals. She was to charge duty and taxes on all exported manufactures equivalent to those imposed on similar items in Britain; and iron and ironwares were only to be exported if the Irish parliament placed a duty on them. But one of the most crippling restrictions was to remain: Ireland was still forbidden to import directly from the colonies whose payment for Irish goods was more likely to be in goods than in money. These concessions did so little to alleviate Ireland's desperate situation that, as Buckingham put it, they 'were scarcely received with gratitude'.

Meanwhile, the war was giving rise to more frequent rumours of invasion and threw into relief the undefended state of the country. The Irish parliament had never accepted Britain's offer to replace 4,000 men who had been despatched to America by an equal number of Protestant troops, principally from Hanover. It was estimated that only about one third of the establishment necessary to the defence of the country was on foot, and the Irish Government's finances were at such a low ebb that it was incapable of raising and equipping a militia.

The Irish gentry now produced their own solution. They proposed to assemble as many as possible of their Protestant tenants, to arm and equip them out of their own pockets, and to form them into Volunteer Corps. However apprehensive the Lord Lieutenant might be of such a move and whatever the long-term consequences he foresaw, he was in no position to refuse the offer.

Soon the entire country was caught up in a volunteering fever. A great many Irishmen had participated in the Seven Years' War, and these old soldiers were canvassed to instruct and train the emerging army. The corps evolved their own uniforms and tailors were kept constantly busy. Most coats were scarlet, but some were green, blue or orange, faced with varying colours. Epaulettes, buttons and lace were silver or gold, and the emblem on the belt plate was a crowned harp symbolizing what came to be the dual objectives of the Volunteers—loyalty and independence.

Each corps elected its own officers, and although Martin had never been a soldier, and was at the time still reading for the bar, his prowess with sword and pistol was renowned. He had the kind of open character and genial nature which make for popularity, and when the Galway Independent Volunteers were embodied on 31 May 1779, they chose him as their colonel. Gradually the Volunteers became the focus for the whole social life of the country, and through their resolutions, they frequently stole a march on parliament.

The Galway Volunteers' first resolution was to establish a precedent and called, among other things, for the liberation of parliament through the abolition of Poynings' Law. It was equally emphatic about the commercial restrictions. The members and their families undertook not to buy wool, cotton or silken goods, or refined sugar or porter which were not of Irish origin, and threatened to make an example of anybody who did by publishing their names. Soon Volunteer Corps all over the country were following their example, and it became a patriotic duty to wear nothing but clothes of Irish manufacture.

The Volunteers were now practically all that stood between Ireland and the invasion which the French continued to plan. In the summer of 1779 they sent Edward Bancroft, an American merchant and friend of Franklin's, on a scouting mission, but his report to the French War Minister expressed disappointment. He had found the Irish Catholics pacified by the recent legislation, the Volunteers ready to take up arms with the English, and nobody even thinking about independence.

Several plans were made during the summer, one of which emphasized the importance of holding Galway and Limerick in order to cover a possible retreat, and in September the Count de Vaux, an infantry commander, produced a plan for twenty-five to thirty thousand men to land in Kinsale, Cork and Waterford.

He assumed success sufficiently to go into Ireland's constitutional future. Republicanism, he claimed, could have no hold on a country traditionally monarchist, and he recommended that a younger son of the Bourbons, elected by the members of the Irish Brigade in France, should land in Ireland as the liberator. 'The little kingdom,' he concluded, 'wisely governed and allied to France and Spain through the blood ties of their respective sovereigns as well as by treaties, will become in a few years a flourishing and respectable state among the European powers.'

Neither the Volunteers nor the members of the Irish parliament had their minds on this future king. They were concentrating on the stranglehold Britain had on Ireland's trade, and in October the Speaker proceeded from the parliament house to the Castle, between rows of Volunteers presenting arms, to deliver to the Lord Lieutenant a resolution: 'That it is not by temporary expedients but by free trade alone that this Nation is now to be saved from impending ruin.'

On King William's birthday, 4 November, it was customary to gather around his statue in front of the parliament house and Trinity College. This year the Volunteers assembled there, placed their cannon in prominent positions and on them put a notice reading, 'Free trade or. . . . '

Three weeks later it was the turn of parliament to rebel. They had jealously guarded their control over the revenue, but had always made over supplies so promptly that Britain took them for granted. Now, by way of protest, they decided to make over supplies for six months only. The Prime Serjeant, Hussey Burgh, one of the most brilliant and incorruptible of men who had been called 'the Cicero of the Senate', though a servant of the Crown, gave expression to the general indignation when he said:

> The words penalty, punishment and Ireland are synonymous. They are marked in blood on the margin of their statutes; and though time may have softened the calamities of the nation, the baneful and destructive influence of those laws have borne her down to a state of Egyptian bondage. The English have sowed their laws like serpents' teeth, and they have sprung up armed men.

He struck his breast as he spoke and was greeted with enthusiastic applause from the gallery, but the outburst cost him his office.

Measures which common sense and equity should have dictated to Britain were now achieved through parliamentary pressure backed by arms. They were rushed through the British parliament and brought to an end the throttling embargoes. Ireland was to be allowed to export wool, woollen cloth and manufactured glass, and to have free trade with the colonies except with the West Indies in sugar.

This was not, however, the end of a battle, but the beginning. Lord North himself described the commercial concessions as 'resumable at pleasure', and a reminder of what lay ahead was sent out in Dublin on 20 December in the form of a printed handbill which was distributed throughout the city and read: 'No illuminations, no rejoicings, until the English parliament shall do away all its acts that in any manner affect this country, and our constitution is made free.'

On 19 April, Henry Grattan introduced a Declaration of Independence in the House of Commons. This asserted that the Crown of Ireland was inseparably annexed to that of Britain, and that the two nations were united under one Sovereign and indissolubly connected by ties of interest, loyalty and freedom, but that no law on earth except the King, Lords and Commons of Ireland was competent to make laws for Ireland. The question was indefinitely postponed, but soon Grattan's words were being reiterated throughout the kingdom.

The day to day political life of the country was shackled by Poynings' Law more than by any other thing and on 26 April a proposal was made for its modification. The mover, Yelverton, was one of Grattan's closest associates. A man of exceptional charm and eccentric habits with a liking for unorthodox companions, he was one of the best advocates of his age. Speaking to his motion, Martin declared that he rose to assert the need for the freedom of the legislature from any intervention, 'a truth so self-evident as to need no demonstration. Indeed, self-evident truths may serve to demonstrate, while they are themselves hardly demonstrable.' To the argument that Britain intended to repeal the Act anyway, he replied: 'Can the requisition of the Commons be an injury and prevent the sisterly affection of Britain in our behalf?' To the argument that she would not grant the repeal he countered: 'Will it not . . . be prudent to go into the framing of this Act, certain as we are of a refusal on the other side of the water. Let our legislature comply with the wishes of their constituents; let the English

Humanity Dick. Colonel Richard Martin, M.P.

A Street in Old Galway, 1840

Clareville, the house Robert Martin built where Nimble Dick had
established his Manor of Clare, and which later came to be known as
'Dick Martin's Gate Lodge'

The Irish House of Commons, with Richard Martin third from the
left in the back left-hand row

Theobald Wolfe Tone.
From a drawing done by his wife

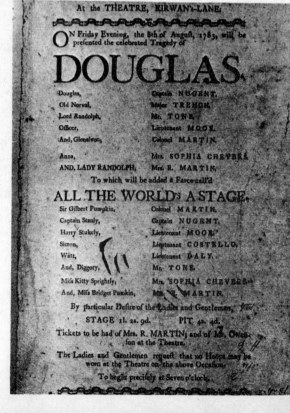

Playbill from Martin's
theatre in Kirwan's
Lane, Galway,
announcing the opening
performances in which
the Martins and Wolfe
Tone played

At the THEATRE, KIRWAN-LANE,

ON Friday Evening, the 8th of August, 1783, will be
presented the celebrated Tragedy of

DOUGLAS.

Douglas,   Captain NUGENT.
Old Norval,   Major TRENCH.
Lord Randolph,   Mr. TONE.
Officer,   Lieutenant MOOR.
And, Glenalvon,   Colonel MARTIN.

Anna,   Mrs. SOPHIA CHEVERS.
AND, LADY RANDOLPH,   Mrs. R. MARTIN.

To which will be added a Farce call'd

ALL THE WORLD's A STAGE.

Sir Gilbert Pumpkin,   Colonel MARTIN.
Captain Stanly,   Captain NUGENT.
Harry Stukely,   Lieutenant MOOR.
Simon,   Lieutenant COSTELLO.
Watt,   Lieutenant DALY.
And, Diggory,   Mr. TONE.
Miss Kitty Sprightly,   Mrs. SOPHIA CHEVERS.
And, Miss Bridget Pumkin,   Mrs. R. MARTIN.

By particular Desire of the Ladies and Gentlemen,

STAGE 1s. 2s. 9d.   PIT 4s. 4d.

Tickets to be had of Mrs. R. MARTIN; and of Mr. Orierfon at the Theatre.

The Ladies and Gentlemen request that no Hoops may be
worn at the Theatre on the above Occasion.

To begin precisely at Seven o'clock.

administration have the censure of refusal.' Yelverton's motion was defeated by 130 votes to 105, but Martin's intervention brought him a unanimous address from the Clanricarde Cavalry Corps of Volunteers, thanking him for his 'just and genuine' approach and applauding his 'steady and uniform zeal for the liberties of this kingdom, both as a senator and a freeholder.'

Before the end of the year, Martin's Volunteer Corps was to sound a warning. There had been rumblings of dissatisfaction in certain official circles at the habit of armed men meddling in politics. Members frequently appeared in parliament in their Volunteer uniform, and there were no subjects of national discontent upon which the Volunteers did not feel qualified to pass comment.

The Galway Corps now concluded a series of resolutions with a stirring clause which smacked of Martin's pen and ran: that 'a whole people self-armed, self-paid, are not to lose the citizen in the subordinate character of the soldier. . . . It is the indefeasible right of a free people publicly to declare their sentiments on public measures by which they are affected. . . . We are resolved not to be deterred from exerting the last liberty of the injured—the liberty of complaining.'

Chapter Four

'URBANITY TOWARD women; benevolence toward men; and humanity toward the brute creation,' was how Martin's friend, Jonah Barrington summed up his character. An incident now occurred which was to test Martin's devotion to animals in a peculiar way.

At Turlough, in County Mayo, there lived George Robert FitzGerald, commonly called 'Fighting FitzGerald' because of the number of duels in which he had engaged. His family were distinguished Anglo-Normans transplanted west of the Shannon by Cromwell. His mother, who had been one of the ladies of the bedchamber to Princess Amelia, was the sister of the notorious and eccentric Frederick Harvey, Earl of Bristol and Bishop of Derry, and George Robert had spent much of his early childhood at the bishop's magnificent mansion of Ickworth in Norfolk. He himself had married one of Thomas Connolly's sisters who had just died, and was thus connected with Elizabeth Martin.

He was slender, elegant and almost effeminate, his manners were gentlemanly and often mild. He was accustomed to the best international society, and during a prolonged stay in Paris he had counted among his friends the King's brother, the Count d'Artois, and had moved in court circles. Yet his behaviour was more often than not that of a monster. He deliberately insulted people in order to provoke a duel, sometimes resorting to elaborate tactics. For instance, he would stand in the middle of a narrow part of a dirty street where all passers-by had to choose between walking in the mud or jostling him to avoid it. If they did the latter, he challenged them.

He had a pet bear whom he treated as a boon companion, travelling everywhere with him, even in stage coaches, to the terror of the other occupants. On one occasion his lawyer who was on a journey with him in his carriage, discovered with the first light of dawn that the gentleman beside him swathed in a blue travelling cloak and red cape, with his head wrapped in a white cloth, was covered with fur and had enormous teeth in a huge mouth. When, upon Fitzgerald's command, the brute kissed the attorney, the poor man leapt from the carriage and ran for safety.

While Martin was still a child and FitzGerald was a young man, he had been involved in a duel in Galway over the advances he had made to a shop girl. He was wounded in the head, and had to be trepanned, and his grotesque behaviour was attributed to this.

However much his treatment of his bear might have aroused Martin's sympathies, FitzGerald was now to lose them. He had a deep-rooted hatred of the Brownes, Lord Altamont's family, with whom the Martins were on intimate terms. One day, he rode over to Westport House, an impressive mansion built by Cassels for Altamont's father on an inlet of Clew Bay in County Mayo. He mounted the double flight of broad steps up to the front door, and when it was opened asked for the great wolf-hound, the Prime Serjeant. These dogs stand about three and a half feet high; they are brindle or grey and have beautiful, haunting eyes the colour of amber. In particular, they are exceptionally gentle and affectionate.

When the dog came out on to the steps, FitzGerald raised his gun and shot him dead. He then instructed the servants to tell their master that until he became charitable to the wandering poor whose broken meat was devoured by hungry wolf-dogs, he would not allow any of these to be kept, but he would allow Lord Altamont's three sisters each to keep one lap dog. He then went down into the little town and announced that he had shot the Prime Serjeant dead.

Altamont's brother had been appointed to Hussey Burgh's office and the wolf-hound had been called after him. Browne was considered an oracle by the country people throughout

Mayo, and in no time the entire place was in an uproar, everybody wondering if they should not get FitzGerald arrested for murder. But he quieted it all by declaring; 'I have shot a much worthier animal, the big watch-dog.'

Martin was outraged. He had known and loved the wolfhound, but even if he had not, the fact remained that, so far as he was concerned, FitzGerald was a murderer. His instinctive reaction was to send a challenge to a duel, but this would have made it appear as if Altamont had not the courage to stand up for his own honour. Therefore, he decided instead to bide his time until he should find some other plausible ground for a quarrel.

This was not long in presenting itself. It so happened that FitzGerald's father was himself a reprobate. He had abandoned his wife early in their married life and settled down to live openly with another woman. Upon George Robert's marriage, he had entered into a number of financial undertakings with his son in connection with the property, none of which he had observed, and the son had retaliated in a manner typical of himself. He had imprisoned his father, and kept him sometimes chained to a dray in a cave at Turlough, and sometimes bound to the muzzled bear. His brother, Charles Lionel, now lodged information against him.

By a fortunate coincidence, Martin, who was now twenty-seven, had been called to the Irish bar in the Trinity Term of the same year, 1781. Fighting FitzGerald's case was due to come up at the summer assizes at Castlebar in County Mayo and this presented Martin with his chance of at last getting FitzGerald within his grasp. He gladly accepted the brief without a fee. It was the only one he ever held and it was appropriate that it should be connected with a dog.

In Castlebar he usually stayed with Elizabeth's cousin, Lord Lucan, or nearby with his friend, Mr. Browne of Castlemacgarrett, a house where Fighting FitzGerald and he had often met. The case came on before Lord Justice Carleton on 7 September, and Martin opened by suggesting that the best way of proving Fighting FitzGerald's innocence would be for his father, one of the magistrates for the Commission of the County Mayo, to be in attendance. To this Counsellor Lennon, appearing for FitzGerald, remarked that the father was one of the worst men alive.

'The greatest crime against society and the greatest sin against Heaven that he ever perpetrated,' replied Martin, 'was that he had begotten such a son as George Robert FitzGerald.'

The trial, which excited great local interest, lasted fifteen hours, and during it Martin heckled FitzGerald so wittily that the prisoner remarked with a cool smile: 'Martin, you look very healthy. You take good care of your constitution. But I tell you that you have this day taken very bad care of your life.'

This provided Martin with the opportunity he had been seeking. He replied that he would resent the remark on a suitable occasion.

It was proved beyond doubt that FitzGerald had imprisoned his father and chained him up as described by his brother, and in the small hours of the morning, after only a couple of minutes' deliberation, the jury brought in a verdict of guilty. Fitzgerald was fined £500 and condemned to three years' imprisonment.

This meant that Martin would be obliged to postpone sending a challenge in order to avenge the great wolf-hound. But just as the judges were due to leave Castlebar, armed supporters of FitzGerald's began lining up in front of the court house where he was being held, and the Solicitor-General realized that an escape was planned. There was no armed force in Castlebar at the time, and, as Martin and the rest rode off at a brisk pace with their briefs in their saddle-bags and accompanied by dragoons, the Sub-Sheriff was left behind to assemble as many gentlemen as he could to enforce the law.

FitzGerald had remarried soon after his first wife's death, and a servant of his father-in-law's now brought him a livery coat to the gaol. Then, on 14 September, he received a visit from his lawyers, and, as they emerged from the gaol, he followed them. He scattered some silver among the guards, telling them to help themselves, and this caused a diversion during which he fired a few shots, leapt on his wife's mare which was waiting for him, and rode away. At Turlough he seized his father and hauled him off to the coast near Ballina where his supporters had ships waiting.

By the time parliament reopened on 9 October, everybody knew of the death of the great wolf-hound, Martin's part in the trial, and the escape, and with FitzGerald at large it was plain that the duel could take place at any moment. A proclamation was issued for FitzGerald's rearrest, and a week of suspense followed. Then on 17 October he was recaptured in College Green, literally a few yards from the parliament house where Martin was sitting. Thrown now into Newgate prison, he spent his time writing lengthy and well-composed letters to the papers justifying his treatment of his father. Martin saw his duel being indefinitely postponed.

Since the last session of parliament, Lord Carlisle had replaced Buckingham as Lord Lieutenant, and Heron, whose wife had survived the rigours of Irish social life, had been replaced by Eden. With a little imagination the English Government could have foreseen the effect of sending this team to a country where comparisons were always being drawn with America. In 1778 it was Carlisle who had been sent at the head of the peace commission, which included Eden, to offer terms to the Americans in an attempt to prevent their ratifying the alliance with France.

Grattan was quick to seize upon this as a fresh ground for arguing Ireland's case. He contrasted the behaviour of the Americans, who had been offered everything, with that of the Irish, who had been offered nothing. The colonists had opposed England in arms, yet they had been offered 'a perfect freedom of legislation, no army, freedom of trade'. The people of Ireland had agreed 'to turn out a greater army at their own expense in support of the King of England than the Americans had given to the King of France', they had voted supplies and incurred a heavy debt. Were they now to accept as an answer, 'You ask for more, you shall get less.' He put the question bluntly to the Viceroy: 'I ask whether he has offered to the ally of France what he will refuse to the sister of England?'

And now Ireland was about to prove her loyalty once more. Cornwallis's surrender to the Americans at Yorktown in December was a major catastrophe for Britain, and Yelverton, who was poised to move again for the repeal of Poynings' Law, moved instead an address of loyalty to the King's person. But this did not prevent several members arguing against a continuation of the American war.

In January 1782, the Lord Lieutenant appointed Martin High

Sheriff of County Galway, a much-coveted honour, but the appointment did not interfere with his attendance at parliament where once again the Catholic question was to be discussed. Luke Gardiner's second Relief Bill renewed the proposal that Catholics should be allowed to purchase land.

It was four years since the first bill. Grattan had found plenty of time to ponder on the entire question, and he now came forward with a changed attitude which heralded that he was to adopt for the rest of his days. Two major objections were raised to the bill. It was felt that if Catholics owned property they would be able to influence tenants at elections and that would give them in due course political power. Another and more genuine fear arose in connection with the Acts of Settlement under which many of the members held their lands, confiscated from Catholics. According to John Fitzgibbon, a very able lawyer, these acts would be endangered if the Catholics could acquire property, and the threat appeared so serious that at one juncture the Committe was nearly adjourned in order to examine the full legal implications. But first Grattan had summed up Ireland's dilemma. 'A Protestant colony or an Irish Nation? That is the question,' he said. ' . . . If you exclude four fifths of the inhabitants you will not be a nation.' It was one of his most prophetic sayings.

But before the Committee had concluded its work, an event occurred which was to have profound influence. On 15 February, the delegates of one hundred and forty-three corps of the Ulster Volunteers, fully armed, marched two abreast to a convention in the Presbyterian church at Dungannon in County Tyrone. There they passed a series of resolutions similar to those passed by the Galway Volunteers the preceding autumn, but drafted by Grattan, and they added: 'That a claim of any body of men, other than the Kings, Lords and Commons of Ireland, to make laws to bind that kingdom is unconstitutional, illegal and a grievance.' Then, in the name of the northern Protestants who had elected them, they passed, with only two dissenting voices, a resolution drafted by Grattan approving a relaxation in the laws against their Catholic brethren.

These were not just Volunteers passing resolutions; they were the representatives of 25,000 men, and the effect was electrifying. When Grattan rose in the House on 22 February he was in a state of great animation and spoke very rapidly. He took his lead from America and Dungannon. America, he declared, was about to be freed at any minute. She would become a great nation while Ireland was kept as 'a secondary state, engaged in a lingering contest for freedom, with some inferior Minister calling her factious, making her corrupt and spending the last farthing of the Treasury to stifle the voice of the nation'. He went on to move an address to the King which re-echoed the Dungannon demand for legislative independence. But the House voted for the question to be postponed and, when Flood moved for a declaration in a different form a few days later, he was defeated.

Grattan had said that he thought the assizes would produce something like a declaration of rights and had urged members to consult their constituents. Martin now took up this claim:

> An honourable gentleman has told you he thinks the Assizes may produce unanimity upon the question. I think nothing can be more effectually binding upon the representatives of this country than the instructions of constituents. Nothing could coerce me so strongly as those instructions. As he thinks it will be the sense of every county it will be better to postpone it. I do not favour this claim by giving a negative to the motion, nor do I pledge myself after the assizes to supporting it.

This kind of statement was typical of his legalistic approach, but it was open to misinterpretation. It could mean precisely what he said, namely, that he wished to have the instructions of his constituents before deciding how to act. It could mean that he held himself free to oppose the declaration regardless of what happened at the assizes, but it could also mean that Flood already felt that Grattan was not going far enough, and that Martin supported this view. His Volunteer Corps interpreted his attitude as support for Lord Carlisle and his Administration, which they considered inimical to Irish claims. In fact, the Viceroy was at variance with the instructions he had been given to prevent the question of independence being brought to the fore. He had consistently tried to get the English Government to understand the Irish point of view, and shortly after he wrote to London suggesting that a repeal of the Declaratory Act might be 'becoming and wise'.

38

Putting their own interpretation on Martin's behaviour, the Galway Volunteers met at the Tholsel on St. Patrick's Day and resolved unanimously that the command should be 'entrusted to none but men invariably attached to the rights of Ireland', and that Colonel Martin, by supporting the Administration, 'had deviated from that line of conduct which induced us to give him the command of this corps'. They agreed to meet again on the 31st to elect a colonel in his place.

Such a misunderstanding of his motives was particularly galling to so disinterested a man. However robust physically and serene spiritually he appeared, the man who would have fought a duel to avenge the death of a dumb creature was obviously one who felt things deeply. As High Sheriff, he convened a meeting of the Grand Jury, gentlemen, clergy and freeholders of County Galway for the very day on which his successor in the Volunteers was to be elected. The meeting gave its full support to the Dungannon resolutions; but he himself was too ill to attend. Possibly on this account the Volunteers put off their meeting for a few days, for, on hearing of his dismissal from the corps, he had made up his mind to do himself the justice others had failed to do him, and to offer an explanation for his behaviour.

When the two hundred men met at the Tholsel many must have been surprised to see their discarded leader in their midst, but his action was typical. He was not a man to run away. Now he brought all his powers of argument to bear upon the subject. He could point to a long record of supporting Ireland's claims, and only the previous year, following Grattan's first declaration of rights, he had remarked in the House that on that famous occasion 'not one of the servants of the Crown could be found profligate enough to vindicate English legislation in Ireland, so that it was asserted without any reservation whatsoever, that no law of any kind made in England, could be in force in this kingdom'. Candour was one of his qualities, and by the time he had finished he had totally vindicated his vote and his utterances. There was only one dissenting voice when a resolution was passed reinstating him.

Grattan had given notice that he would renew his declaration on the first day after the Easter recess, and there was a call of the House for 16 April which announced to members that on that day they would 'tender the rights of the Irish Parliament' but Martin was detained in Galway by the assizes.

Grattan, in an emaciated condition following a serious operation, walked through streets lined with Volunteers into a House whose gallery was crowded with the cream of society. England had by now recognized American independence, North's Government had fallen, and the Whigs were in power. Carlisle had been abruptly recalled and replaced by the Duke of Portland who presented the House with an address from the King in which he desired them to take into account the 'discontents and jealousies' prevailing in Ireland 'in order to effect such a final adjustment as might give mutual satisfaction'.

This meeting of Ireland half-way could have cut the ground from under Grattan's feet, but he was determined not to yield. He moved an amendment to the motion on the address and used it to make a full and unequivocal declaration of rights:

> I have had to admire by what inexplicable means and steady virtue the people of Ireland have proceeded, till the whole faculty of the nation is now braced to the great act of her own redemption. I am not very old, yet I think I remember Ireland when she was a child. I have watched her growth with anxious wishes. I have beheld with astonishment the rapidity of her progress from industry to arms, from arms to liberty.

His voice was heard in England. It was backed by 80,000 armed men who had never fired a shot and it could no longer be resisted. The Declaratory Act was repealed and it was agreed that Poynings' Law should be modified. All that had been asked was conceded magnanimously and unconditionally, and in moving an address to Portland, Grattan included the words, 'We do assure his Majesty that no constitutional questions between the two nations will any longer exist which can interrupt their harmony.'

The Catholics' situation was again taken up and now Gardiner's Bill was passed. By allowing Catholics to purchase land it started a new era in Irish history. They were also to be permitted to teach, and some minor laws which were social irritants were repealed as well. A Protestant could no longer take over a Catholic's horse on payment of £5, Catholics' horses could no longer be commandeered upon an alarm of invasion, and they were no longer required to pay for the damage done by enemy privateers; but the law forbidding them to marry Protestants was retained.

Martin continued to act as a kind of watch-dog for all signs of extravagance or corruption. He graciously allowed Grattan to move for the committee he himself had suggested on the collection of the revenue, and had a typical exchange of words with John Fitzgibbon, the future Lord Clare. A small, vehement lawyer, the son of a Catholic who had relinquished his religion in order to practise at the bar, he was arrogant, vindictive and obdurate in his opposition to all concessions to the Catholics. He was to play a leading part in the junta which came to dominate Irish politics and his ambitions were crowned when he became Lord Chancellor. Martin was sufficiently perceptive to recognize Fitzgibbon's aims at this early stage of his climb to fame, and when, commenting on the creation of two new posts, Attorney and Solicitor General to the Queen, Fitzgibbon remarked: 'Whether this is determined to lessen influence I do not know.' . . . 'I do beseech the Honourable Gentleman,' Martin interjected, 'to suspend his judgement 'till he is appointed to one of them.'

'I would not condescend to accept either the one office or the other,' Fitzgibbon retorted. 'The honourable gentleman gave himself a good deal of unnecessary trouble in exercising his wit upon me. I was not at the trouble of making him a serious answer.'

'I suppose the honourable gentleman is serious in his compliment,' replied Martin graciously, 'and thank him for it.'

But another aspect of corruption was occupying Martin at the time. To him, people were always more important than politics, and he had heard that Coppinger, who was Counsellor to the Commissioners and advanced in years, was to be deprived of the office and to be replaced by Martin's old college friend, George Ponsonby. Martin knew Coppinger's office was almost his only source of income, and that he had a family and was crushed by debts. He had been seen driving past with the blinds of his carriage drawn down, so ashamed was he of his poverty.

Martin's heart was wrung by the whole situation. He drove down to the law courts with Ponsonby in his carriage and tried to persuade him to relinquish the post. He stirred up the feelings of the members of the House and canvassed Coppinger's case so successfully that there was scarcely a soul who did not come around to his point of view.

Now, at the very end of the session, he took the matter up in the only long speech he ever made during the seven years he had spent in parliament. He proposed to bring in a motion for Coppinger's restitution or indemnification.

He was completely carried away by his sense of the disaster that had befallen the old man. He was always indignant at an injustice, but this filled him with deep personal anguish. He claimed that those who shared his views had also shared his expressions: 'Poor Coppinger! He is deprived of his place! He is ruined!'

'If gentlemen do not get up and support me,' he cried, 'I shall repeat them name by name.' When he was interrupted by Rowley, he snapped, 'I am astonished when I hear a gentleman of gravity and age interrupt a gentleman like a boy. If I hear that gentleman utter a single syllable, I shall move the censure of the House upon him.' But then he apologized: 'For my feelings upon this occasion, I hardly hold myself accountable for anything I say.'

He argued that Ponsonby should never have accepted the post, and that now he should resign it. If he did not, then the Government had an obligation to compensate Coppinger. If the House felt that Ponsonby, being a younger man, was more equal to the task, then they should pay for it with a pension to Coppinger. He was, he said, prepared to have his property taxed five shillings in the pound to provide for the old gentleman. The Chief Secretary, Fitzpatrick, assured him that it was the intention of the Government to do something for Coppinger, but Martin pointed out that it now seemed likely that Portland would leave the country earlier than anticipated, and, therefore, if he was to have anything done for Coppinger, it must be done now. He pilloried Ponsonby for accepting the office, but paid a sincere tribute to his abilities; perhaps because Martin's wife, Elizabeth, was on bad terms with Ponsonby's mother, he laid some blame at her door.

The Ponsonby family had long been accustomed to patronage, and George was no exception in his desire for a privileged position. But he had the kind of temperament best suited to withstanding Martin's harangue. Aristocratic and somewhat cold in bearing, he had a temper which could not be ruffled, a generous spirit and a capacity for discretion which stood him in good stead in later life when he was called upon to lead the Opposition at Westminster. Martin looked around the House for Ponsonby's father, the former Speaker. He did not see him, but he urged him or his son to go personally to the Lord Lieutenant and hand back the office to Coppinger while it could still be done with honour. Pouring himself forth in an uninterrupted agony of compassion and indignation, he called upon the Lord Lieutenant to settle the matter now. If he were to leave it to some future administration, he declared:

'I will tell you what I shall do, though I have not worn out the Castle pavement by my horses trampling upon it, though I have not unnapped the carpets of the Castle, though I have not been guilty of servile flattery. If he does not redress it here, I will follow the Noble Lord into Great Britain. If he does not redress it, I will tell my Royal Sovereign of the deed. . . . '

If Ponsonby were to relinquish the post, it would have to be filled by Coppinger because the administration would not find a man base enough to accept it. He went on:

'If they expect to find any man, they must go into some dark cells of some dark dungeon, they must go where the wicked only are to be found. They must seek for some wretch with a savage heart and savage principles to accept the donation. No man who regards his character would accept of it, it is grown so unpopular. I don't mean a satire on the Gentleman, for he will not keep it. He did not know the wrong he did; now, knowing it, he will do every means in his power to make restitution . . . It was not a man that solicited this place. No man of a manly disposition solicited this place, but some female. Somebody in the garb of a woman might have whispered to the Lord Lieutenant, some toothless Dame . . . ' When he had finished, the House remained silent except for Fitzpatrick. He had been convinced; provision ought to be made for Coppinger, he said, and gave an undertaking that it would be, whereupon Martin withdrew his motion

Chapter Five

THE GENERAL satisfaction that followed the repeal of the Declaratory Act was short lived. What seemed at first like a legal quibble ended by splitting the country into two camps. As a result of Flood's taking an unorthodox line in a parliamentary debate, Carlisle had brought about his resignation, and he now set himself up in opposition to Grattan, attempting to recapture his former leadership. With a dome-like forehead, lantern jaw and broad, flat nose, he was a man of brilliant and profound intellect who could probably claim a vaster knowledge of constitutional affairs than any other man in the House, but his popularity with his former followers had suffered severely due to his having accepted office.

Flood maintained that a repeal of the Declaratory Act did not amount to a renunciation by Britain of the principle on which it was based; in fact it did no more than rescind the actual act, while Britain could at any time renew her legislative control. Grattan, on the other hand, was satisfied that all that needed to be done on the matter had been done.

Martin supported Grattan in the House, and called his address 'a production of consummate wisdom and great deliberation'. He had even tried to silence Flood with, 'The Honourable Gentleman is not the Advocate of Ireland.' But he was very rapidly to eat his words. The Lawyers' Corps of Volunteers came out with a declaration supporting Flood, whereas the National Council of the Volunteers in Dublin, to which Martin was the Galway delegate, supported Grattan. But by the time

Martin returned home to the west of Ireland at the end of the session, he had been completely converted, and his admiration for Flood was never to diminish. Years later he was to refer to him as the greatest mind Ireland had ever known. His own Corps and the Central Division of the Connaught Volunteers, at both of whose meetings he took the chair, voiced strong support for Flood, Martin was instructed to invite him to attend Lord Altamont's review of the Connaught Corps and eventually he was made an honorary Colonel of the Galway Volunteers.

As Flood's views gained ground, Grattan's popularity declined, and the man who only recently had been hailed as Ireland's liberator now became known as the author of what was called 'the bubble security'. Events were ultimately to prove Flood correct. Various incidents, most notably the reversal by Lord Mansfield in an English court of a judgement given in an Irish court, reinforced the feeling that, in fact, Britain had not fully relinquished her old right. When Lord Temple took over from Portland as Viceroy, he was foremost in convincing the British Government that something more was needed to tranquillize Ireland. And once again Britain responded generously to Irish demands. In January 1783 a Renunciation Act, introduced by Lord Townshend and seconded by the Lord Lieutenant's brother William Grenville, was passed.

About the same time, a meeting of the independent freeholders of County Galway expressed their thanks to 'Colonel Martin, our late Sheriff, for his just, his upright and active conduct while invested with that important role.' Martin was already acquiring that reputation for probity which was to increase with the years. But he now heard of another step of Lord Temple's which was to affect him more intimately than the Renunciation Act.

Fighting FitzGerald, was still in prison where he had by now served over a year of the sentence imposed as a result of Martin's pleading. He had addressed a memorial to the Lord Lieutenant, and his brother-in-law, Connolly, now appealed to have him released. Temple acceded to the request, and from that moment the whole of the counties of Galway and Mayo lived in a constant state of suspense, awaiting the predicted duel between the two great 'fire-eaters'.

Parliament was now dissolved, and Martin, while awaiting

the elections in which he was to stand with his cousin, Martin Kirwan, for the town of Galway, settled into Dangan with his wife. They were childless, several children having died at birth, but they had a common passion in the theatre, and both of them were exceptionally good actors. Martin found that his friend, Joseph Blake of Ardfry, had an actor protégé, Robert Owenson, whom he had arranged to have trained in England and who knew David Garrick. After a successful tour in Irish provincial repertory, principally in the western counties, he had arrived the previous autumn in Galway. Performances there usually took place in an upper room at the Tholsel, but Owenson decided he would like to establish a proper theatre.

He could not have found a more ideal backer than Martin. A site was provided on a corner of the narrow, sloping street called Kirwan's Lane, where the mills in which Thomas Martin had held the rights in 1365 were situated, and Martin provided the money to erect a tiny building. It had an auditorium without either boxes or gallery, but the sloping pit, designed to hold one hundred, was so built that each person could see without being inconvenienced by those in front or blocking the view of those behind.

There was a young man staying at Dangan who was to play his part in the theatre and in the Martin family. He was called Wolfe Tone and was a student at Trinity College. He was acting as tutor to Martin's two half-brothers, Robert and Anthony, now aged thirteen and twelve. Tone was a thin, boney, handsome young man of twenty, rather refined and effeminate-looking, with a long pock-marked face and low forehead. He had the same high-bridged nose and curiously waving lips as Martin's, and he talked fast and enthusiastically and, to Mrs. Martin, passionately. He 'became in love to a degree almost inconceivable,' he afterwards wrote in his diary. 'I have never met in history, poetry or romance a description that comes near to what I actually suffered on her account.'*

* Tone states in his diary that he fell into disfavour at Trinity in 1782 through having acted as second in a duel in which a student named Anderson was killed. The *Freeman's Journal* of 24 November 1798 asserted, no doubt wrongly, that the duel had taken place while Tone was at school, but went on to declare that Tone was barred from college for some years while his father's patron, Lord Kilwarden, the future Attorney-General, was interceding for him. This time, the paper claimed, Tone spent at Dangan.

Martin was always busy. Apart from his political and volunteering activities, and the launching of the theatre, he had to attend to a constant stream of people of all descriptions who looked to him to solve their problems. He was frequently away from home, and when he returned, even if it was late at night and his wife was already in her nightdress, she would run downstairs and out on to the steps to embrace him. Among their circle of friends they were known to be a very happy couple.

Tone, however, felt that Martin neglected his beautiful wife, and, as he began to gain her confidence, he made comparisons for her between his own attentiveness and Martin's negligence. Gradually she began to respond to his advances until she, too, fell in love and returned his affection with what seemed to him an ardour equal to his own.

Due to Martin's frequent absences, the couple were thrown together a great deal, and rehearsing for their parts in the theatre they often found themselves in intimate situations. Tone had a rather colourless manner of speaking and difficulty in pronouncing his 'Rs' which he enunciated with a curious guttural accent—defects which coaching from Mrs. Martin, whom he considered the best actress he had ever seen, could help to efface. To him she was 'more divine than human' and he wrote in his diary that 'he adored her as a deity'.

The Kirwan's Lane theatre was due to open just before the elections began, but in the meantime the Martins were invited by Lord Altamont, the son of the owner of the great wolfhound, to a round of festivities at Westport House. The great English architect, Wyatt, had just completed some additions to Cassels' mansion, as well as laying out the town of Westport. The new rooms in the house were not in the extravagant style later adopted by Wyatt, but along the classical lines of the original structure, the most perfect being the dining-room overlooking the water-pieces which had been made by Cassels from an inlet of Clew Bay.

The extensions were inaugurated by banquets, balls, concerts and theatricals lasting over a period of several days. The theatre was set up in a large room with a raised stage, gallery, scenery and magnificent chandeliers, and across the proscenium was emblazoned the motto: 'Since life is no more than a passage, at best, let us strew the way over with flowers.' The Martins appeared in *Douglas*, a tragedy with a Scottish setting in the period of Danish raids, and the most performed play of the time. Mrs. Martin played the small part of maid to the heroine Lady Randolph, for which she was much admired, but Martin played the strong role with which he was to open at Kirwan's Lane, namely, Glenalvon, the villain of the piece who attempts to murder Douglas. His success was outstanding, and one critic wrote; 'We have seen this gentleman in so many walks, that he wanted but this to make the *omnistrous*, the *all accomplished*, as Pope calls Bolingbroke. His powers of voice, elocution and action were inimitable.'

Martin went on to Dublin after the festivities at Westport House, and found the whole city flocking to see Kemble and Mrs. Crawford at the Crow Street Theatre in the title roles of *Edward and Leonora*. As a devotee of the theatre who never missed what promised to be a good performance, he did not even rest after his journey, but made straight for the theatre.

He took his seat in the front row of the stage box, and almost immediately he heard a voice outside imperiously demanding that the door should be opened. Within seconds, Fighting FitzGerald was sitting near to him. Martin at last saw the opportunity he had been awaiting for over two years, and moved over to seat himself beside the recently released prisoner.

'Have you anything particular to say to *me*?' he asked.

'Only to tell you,' answered FitzGerald, 'that I followed you from Castlebar to proclaim you the *bully* of the Altamonts.'

'You have said enough, Mr. FitzGerald,' Martin replied. 'You no doubt expect to hear from me, and it shall be early in the morning.'

'*I* shall hear from *you* tomorrow!' exclaimed FitzGerald disdainfully. He then struck Martin, adding, 'This will refresh your memory.'

FitzGerald promptly left the box and made for the lobby. Martin leapt to his feet in order to follow, but in his hurry became entangled in a curtain and fell. Helped to his feet by Major Craddock, he rushed into the foyer. There he found FitzGerald and immediately accused him of being coward enough to have deliberately created the scene in order that they should both be bound over to keep the peace. FitzGerald retorted: 'You have got a blow. I desire to disgrace you, and when you are punished to my liking *that* way, and not before, you shall have the *satisfaction* of being shot, or run through the body.'

The next day Lord Donoughmore offered to take a challenge from Martin to FitzGerald, but Martin did not want to involve any friend of his with such a man. He preferred, instead, to wear his sword and to rely upon meeting his antagonist around the town. But although he watched FitzGerald's house at 23 Upper Merrion Street for several days, he could not, as he himself put it, 'unkennel the fox'.

It was a cousin of FitzGerald's who ultimately delivered the challenge. FitzGerald beat him up, made him hold out a finger on which he wore a handsome ring, promptly broke the finger with a cudgel, then picked up the ring which he wrapped in a piece of paper and returned to the owner. The young man was by now terrified out of his wits, and, running to the window, opened it and screamed to the passers-by for help. FitzGerald and his cousin were both bound over to keep the peace, but the magistrate so implicitly believed what FitzGerald told him, that he ended by congratulating him on having refused to fight a duel with Martin, and released him on condition that he undertook never to fight a duel again.

Martin, thinking his quarry had once more evaded him through being flung into prison, had meantime returned to Galway where rehearsals were in full swing for the opening of the theatre. Play-bills announced this for Friday, 8 August 1783, at 'precisely 7' in the evening, and tickets were to be obtained from Owenson at the theatre or from Mrs. Martin at Dangan. A stage seat cost as much as £1. 2s. 9d., one in the pit was 4s. 4d. and ladies were requested not to wear hoops in order to allow as much space as possible. The Volunteer printing office produced the play-bill, and the actors, who were mostly members of the Corps, included Trench, one of Martin's opponents in the forthcoming election for County Galway.

When the great night came, the curtain was rung up under the proscenium which was strung with roses and ribbons joining two medallions bearing the figures of the Tragic and the Comic Muse; below, there stood out the lively motto: 'Vive la Bagatelle'. Here Tone and the Martins made their début before the general public. In *Douglas* Mrs. Martin now played the heroine, Lady Randolph, opposite Tone, with Martin once again as Glenalvon. There was also a farce, *All the World's a Stage*, which was remarkable in the light of later events for the role taken by Tone. Destined to play the most serious part in Irish history, he here appeared as a comic—the stage-struck butler, Diggery. He was constantly discovered in incongruous situations, from kneeling in front of the sideboard instead of serving the wine to trying to kill himself with a large key while exclaiming; 'I have tried a thousand times and never could kill myself to my own satisfaction in all my life,' until the final curtain dropped almost prophetically upon him making his last attempt at suicide and declaiming:

> 'My tragic thirst of blood not yet allay'd
> I must again draw forth my shining blade;
> Nor shall I live in peace till all I kill,
> And at the last my own blood bravely spill.'

The performances were enthusiastically applauded.

The elections were now only three weeks away. The *Freeman's Journal* claimed, 'Patriotic and incorruptible Kirwan and Martin will need all their circumspection to overcome the base designs of their enemies.' One of these was Daly, an intimate friend of Grattan's, a fine speaker, the owner of a library of priceless first editions, but also the Mayor who had usurped for his family the corporation whose independence the Martins were striving to re-establish. Tenants' holdings, called freeholds, had to be registered in advance for them to be qualified to vote, but it was common before elections for landlords to create new freeholds in order to increase their potential electors. In this context, the *Freeman's Journal* accused the Rector of the Cathedral of St. Nicholas of having refused the sacrament to the 'undisputed registered freeholders of Mr. Martin while giving it to the perjured vassals of Daly'.

When polling started, each Protestant with a 40s. per annum interest in freehold land declared his vote verbally at a booth after swearing with respect to his land-holding. From the very first day, the difference between the first and the last of the candidates was never more than eight to ten votes, with Martin at the bottom. The *Freeman's Journal* kept up a continual tirade against the Sheriff and Sub-Sheriff whom they accused of debarring most of Martin's freeholders. In fact, Martin was at a grave disadvantage. There were no roads in Connemara, and he had to bring in his freeholders by barely passable tracks, or else around by sea from assembly points on the coast. The other candidates' freeholders had easy access to the town.

Polling continued throughout the latter part of August and the whole of September. It was not until 13 October that the booths were at last closed, and the results of the county election were announced: the sitting members, Daly and Trench, were re-elected. But the contest proved such an expensive affair that the fortunes of all those concerned were seriously impaired for many years.

While the elections were in progress, the peace treaty had been signed, formally recognizing American independence; and, at home, the Volunteers, who had come into existence due to the American struggle, had not been idle. The Ulster Volunteers had once again met at Dungannon and had called on the other Corps to co-operate in summoning a Grand National Convention in Dublin to discuss the question of parliamentary reform. The other Corps rapidly agreed, and at the end of September the Galway Independents elected Martin with Flood and four others to represent them at the Convention which was to take place on 10 November.

It had become obvious to many people that, despite the Renunciation Act and the repeal of Poynings' Law, the Irish parliament was not really free because of the influence of the big borough owners. Furthermore, the new Viceroy, Northington, who had replaced Temple, was not liked, and he was in a position to put pressure on parliament whenever he wanted. Flood was the great protagonist of reform, and Martin fully supported him, while in England a movement in the same direction, largely sponsored by the Whigs, was gathering momentum.

When news reached Martin of the Dungannon meeting and his own Corps had backed it, he wrote to Temple:

'The resolutions entered into at Dungannon have, I suppose, before this reached your Lordship and I think you cannot but see that they bode a certain removal of the present Irish Administration and perhaps may also bring about an alteration in the Administration in England. At all events, the exertions of the virtuous and independent in this kingdom may be directed so as to co-operate with your Lordship's friends on the other side of the water. That it may have this effect, no pains shall be wanting on my part.' As for the National Convention, he declared: 'I shall certainly propose a resolution tending to point out the unpopularity of the present government here. . . . I know the delicacy of your situation. I will not, therefore, expect to be informed relative to a subject upon which perhaps it may not be proper that you should be communicative. I shall, however, receive any hints from your Lordship with gratitude and execute them with fidelity. From the part your friends have taken on this question in England, I feel myself entitled to address you relative to a more equal representation of the people.'

In the event, however, the number of delegates from the different regions to the National Convention was reduced to five, and Martin was not one of them. But he was on the committee of thirteen formed to prepare a report on the mode of election in Galway giving, as near as possible, the numbers of Catholics and Protestants and their respective property.

On 11 November, the hundred and sixty delegates of the different Volunteer Corps assembled at the Royal Exchange in Dublin and elected Lord Charlemont, the Commander-in-Chief of the Volunteers, their Chairman. They then proceeded, two abreast, down Dame Street in front of the Parliament House, and crossed the Liffey to the Rotunda, the fashionable assembly room. The Dublin Volunteers, under the command of the Duke of Leinster and with their colours flying, lined the streets, and there were several thousand spectators. At the Rotunda the main room had been arranged as an amphitheatre, and in the orchestra sat some three hundred ladies of fashion.

Flood, who was to dominate the proceedings, had to be carried in a chaise due to gout, and was greeted with an ovation, but it was the arrival of the Earl-Bishop of Derry that was the highlight of the pageantry. He was dressed entirely in purple, with diamond buckles at his knees and on his shoes, and long gold tassels hanging from his white gloves. His landau was drawn by six magnificently caparisoned horses, and accompanied by dragoons in splendid uniforms commanded by none other than Fighting FitzGerald.

The object of the deliberations, which lasted until 29 November, was to purify the system of representation. Two hundred of the three hundred members of the House of Commons were returned by a few individuals; from forty to fifty were returned by ten people; and there were some boroughs which had only one resident elector, whilst several others had none at all. A third of the House and half its active members were pensioners, and, therefore, under the thumb of the Administration. But the main difficulty lay with the twenty or thirty great borough owners who could always command a majority in the House and who did so according to how the Government prevailed upon them to accept that some measure was or was not in their interest.

Martin was among those who obviously believed that any scheme for parliamentary reform in a country which was predominantly Catholic would take the majority into consideration; this despite the fact that two of the dominant figures of the Convention, Charlemont and Flood, were totally opposed to rights for the Catholics. Both generously agreed to relinquish their borough interests, but when it came to the Catholics, the extravagant Earl-Bishop stood almost alone. It was he who raised the question and who found himself foiled by a Government ruse aimed at excluding discussion of the subject by conveying a fictitious message from one of the great Catholic leaders, the Earl of Kenmare, to the effect that the Catholics were content for their situation not to be discussed. But even when this flagrant dishonesty had been exposed, the Catholics found themselves without support except from a section of the northern Presbyterians.

Throughout the three weeks of the Convention, the Earl-Bishop entertained in almost regal style in Fighting Fitz-Gerald's house, which came to be known as the headquarters of the extremists. This extraordinary vain and reckless man—who was known as the 'edifying bishop' because of his passion for building, rather than his manner of living; who had an annual income of £20,000 a year, yet was to be found in Italy without the price of a bottle of wine, so vast were the sums he had expended on art treasures; who was probably maligned by the suggestion that he wanted to be king of a Catholic Ireland—was able to see through the clouds of rhetoric and the more rarified air of self-righteousness to that conclusion which Grattan had already prophesied: there could be no nation without the people.

On 29 November, while the Convention remained in session awaiting the result, Flood, Brownlow and the others who were members of parliament went down to the House and moved 'that leave be given to bring in a bill for the more equal representation of the people in Parliament'. No sooner had Flood explained the plan of reform than Yelverton, who was now Attorney-General, attacked him on the grounds that he and Brownlow had disavowed their commissions in the Volunteers to bring in the motion which they presented as their own. The Attorney-General went on: 'Nor has the Honourable Member mentioned who those persons are from whom this motion originated; for if it originated with an armed body of men, it is an invasion of the dignity of Parliament; it is inconsistent with the dignity of the House and the freedom of debate to receive it. We sit not here to register the edicts of another assembly, or to receive propositions at the point of the bayonet.' He proceeded to accuse the National Convention of forming 'a Pantheon of Divinities' and assuming 'the fastidious state of a great legal body'.

This drew forth from Flood a eulogy of the Volunteers and their past services. 'Who got you free trade?' he asked. 'Who got you the Constitution? Who made you a nation? The Volunteers.' But it was of no avail. Leave was refused by 158 votes to 49 to introduce the bill, and even Grattan, whose principles should have set him in the fore as an advocate of the measure, although his differences with Flood had reached the point at which a duel had been barely avoided, gave nothing but half-hearted assent. The big borough owners immediately followed with a motion 'against all encroachments whatsoever', which was carried, but during the discussion most of the minority absented themselves in protest.

Thus ended dismally what might have been a glorious passage in Irish history. Charlemont, a man of popular but moderate principles, had advocated the delegates' returning home to communicate the plan to their corps and to organize public opinion to work on parliament through petitions and addresses. Doubtless this would have been the wisest manner of proceeding, but Flood was not only a brilliant, but a vain and ambitious man; he was going abroad and wanted, with justification, to have the honour of introducing the measure himself. His haste was to convert what would have been wise advice to parliament into what appeared like a menace.

Had parliament accepted the proposition of reform, the Government would have been deprived of those means of exercising pressure which in due course would bring that parliament to an end. Yet people such as Martin, who had expected the plan to include the emancipation of the Catholics, may have seen that, even in the short run, it was fraught with dangers. A more broadly-based parliament, still representing a minority, could have ended by merely increasing the number of people interested in perpetuating its exclusiveness. The more independent the parliament and the more prosperous the nation, the greater the taunt to those four-fifths of the population who were excluded from their civil rights.

The delegates to the National Convention had sat on resplendent in the Rotunda throughout the parliamentary deliberations, awaiting the return of Flood and Brownlow with the account of their victory. When they received the news of defeat, there was nothing left to them but to disperse. This they did on 2 December after agreeing upon an address of loyalty to the King in which they expressed their wish to have 'certain manifest perversions of the parliamentary representation of this kingdom remedied'.

Chapter Six

WILLIAM PITT was now Prime Minister of England, at the age of twenty-four. He was the advocate of parliamentary reform, and despatched to Ireland as Lord Lieutenant another man equally associated with the movement, the Granby of Martin's Cambridge days, now Duke of Rutland. Martin took the chair at a meeting in County Galway where it was agreed to send an address of welcome to the new Viceroy, and the *Freeman's Journal* commented that Martin had used his great influence in the county in Rutland's favour. 'His popularity could even recommend an *un*popular Viceroy,' the journal concluded, 'but in this case Rutland is the proven friend of the country.'

Flood had gone to England to look for a seat in the English parliament, and no doubt under Rutland's influence Martin decided to do the same. The former Viceroy, Lord Temple, wrote to Rutland: 'I have introduced Mr. Martin to Mr. Pitt, but have taken care to prepare him for a disappointment in his object of an English seat. He asked me for a letter to Orde on the subject of Scott's seat, but I only gave him a letter of a very general kind.'

Neither Martin nor Flood was successful in obtaining an English seat at the time, although Flood was to achieve this later. Nor was the new Chief Secretary, Orde, able to do anything about obtaining for Martin the seat vacated by Scott in the Irish parliament upon being raised to the peerage. After six months in England, Martin returned home.

He now heard that Fighting FitzGerald, who had spent a certain amount of time since his release from prison with the Earl-Bishop, was in Castlebar. It so happened that Martin was accompanying Flood to Galway for a triumphal entry as General of the Galway Volunteers, and he decided that they could travel via Castlebar and at last bring to a close the feud over the great wolf-hound.

He immediately sent a challenge to FitzGerald. At the same time he wrote to Lord Altamont to announce the forthcoming duel and to say that he would gladly accept a slight wound in settling this curious affair of honour, but that he would request His Lordship to send his carriage the few miles from Westport to Castlebar to collect him. Flood, himself a noted duellist, offered to be Martin's second; but the younger man was afraid of exposing a friend to possible insult, and, seeing that the seconds frequently suffered more than the principals, he was reluctant to endanger the life of so distinguished a statesman.

He gave his duelling pistols to a man whom he told to reach Castlebar before him, and set off with Flood in his carriage. But when they arrived at their destination, the man carrying the pistols was not there, and they had to wait for him at Lord Lucan's house. Several people gathered there, and in due course they heard that FitzGerald was parading around the town with his henchmen and had been heard to declare: 'Mr. Martin expects Altamont's carriage, but he may wait long enough; for though the horse is a brave animal, I fancy Altamont's are like the owner, and will not stand the smell of powder.'

When Martin heard this he decided to wait no longer—which was just as well, for it turned out that the man to whom he had entrusted his pistols had got drunk on the way and forgotten what he was supposed to be doing. Instead, Martin grabbed his servants' common holster pistols, but when he tried the triggers they were so stiff that he could hardly press them. So he fastened on his sword, took the arm of Dr. Merlin, who was to act as his second, and walked into the town.

He very soon caught up with FitzGerald and his supporters. FitzGerald was also wearing his sword and Martin at once called upon him to draw; but FitzGerald answered that he was lame and that the pavement was uneven. In other words, he refused to fight. Martin then said he would await him in the barrack yard. He ordered the soldiers to post sentries to keep out everybody except his antagonist and the seconds, and in due course FitzGerald arrived, calling on people to back the Mayo cock against the Galway cock.

FitzGerald, who had no real courage, but who was extremely agile, had discovered during his long duelling career that a pistol loaded to strike at nine yards will not cause nearly as much damage if fired at five. He also knew that, if a man could be distracted from his first aim before he could discharge his pistol, his subsequent aims would be far less accurate. As for the distance between adversaries, the second of two articles added to the Thirty-Seven Commandments by the Galway duelling delegates specified that if the ground between the opponents was measured, neither could advance or retreat, but if it was not measured, they could advance as close as they pleased and even touch muzzles.

Martin was notoriously cool and daring, and as the ground between them had not been measured he now took up his stand against a projecting piece of the barrack wall and asked Fitz-Gerald to come as close as he pleased. FitzGerald, no doubt aiming to get Martin to fire at a closer range than that for which he had loaded his pistol, replied that a cannon ball would not carry that far.

'I will soon cure that,' Martin retorted. 'I will now march up until I lay my pistol to your face.'

With that he advanced until their pistols touched. Both of them fired. FitzGerald missed Martin, but was himself hit. He fell back upon a projecting rock and called: 'Honour! Martin! Honour!'

'If you are not disabled,' Martin replied, 'I will wait as long as you choose.'

Among FitzGerald's many tricks was the ability to shorten his body by stooping very low. The moment his adversary fired, he would make as elongated an outstretch as he could, so that he not only presented as little of the surface of his body as possible, but actually lost sixteen inches of his height. In this position, and by keeping his eye level with the muzzle of his opponent's pistol, he could cover his head and heart. In order to reach his brain a bullet would have to pass through the palm of his hand, and to reach his heart it would have to travel through the whole length of his right arm.

This was the trick he now played. Crouching like a cat, he fired and hit Martin, who returned the fire and for the second time hit FitzGerald who once again recovered. Then he came up to Martin, begged his pardon and asked to shake hands. 'Altamont has caused all this,' he said, 'and now would not send you his carriage. Let us both kick him.'

Flood was waiting at the barrack gate and Martin leaned on him while being taken to Dr. Lendser's to have his wound dressed. FitzGerald had appeared to walk normally, but Martin did not know how badly he might be wounded after being hit twice, and with typical generosity of spirit decided to send his servant after FitzGerald to enquire how he felt. Flood implored him to do no such thing. If FitzGerald lived, he pointed out, there would be a second fight. But Martin's heart got the better of his head, and he insisted on sending his man with the message.

When they reached Dr. Lendser's house, Martin was immediately put to bed. He had hardly been there a few moments when, to his great surprise, FitzGerald appeared and asked the doctor what he thought of Martin's condition. Martin himself replied from the bed that he was very well, and, still astonished at seeing FitzGerald apparently in perfect health, said he hoped he was not badly hurt. But, despite Martin's having shown such good will by sending his servant to enquire after him, FitzGerald now did exactly as Flood had predicted: he produced fresh grounds for fighting. He claimed he had been insulted by Martin's second, Dr. Merlin, and said he would make Martin accountable. Martin replied: 'If I account with you, on a mutual understanding that Dr. Merlin is beneath your notice, I shall have to fight him also for such an imputation—so put your renewed quarrel on some other ground. If you say you did not ask my pardon, I will fight you again; or if you say you are fond of such an *amusement*, I will fight you until my eyelids can no longer wag.'

Flood was to review the Volunteers in Sligo following his reception in Galway, and FitzGerald now asked Martin if he would be present. Martin replied that he had not intended to be there, but if FitzGerald wished it, he was prepared to go there immediately. FitzGerald promptly named a day, to which Martin assented, and thus the settling of accounts over the Prime Serjeant was once more put in abeyance.

Martin's wound was slight and he and Flood proceeded to Galway according to plan. The *Freeman's Journal*, promoting Martin on the way, described their arrival: 'On Monday 5 General Flood arrived in Galway where he was received with all the honours due to his patriotism and abilities. Second only to him in honours was the manner in which they received Major General Martin, after an absence of six months; nor is their estimation of him decreased by his descent into private life.'

No doubt Martin was greeted with the customary enthusiasm when he arrived at Dangan, particularly when he was able to relate how he had escaped from Fighting FitzGerald with his life. He was of so unsuspecting a nature that it would not have occurred to him that his absence could have changed anything. Yet, Tone and Mrs. Martin had had the stage to themselves for almost half a year. Although Tone admitted that she was as much in love as he was, he did not absolve her from a certain coquetry. He wrote in his diary later: 'As I preserved, as well as felt, the profoundest respect for her, she supposed she might amuse herself innocently in observing the progress of this terrible passion in the mind of an interesting young man of twenty; but this is an experiment no woman ought to make.' The couple were now so close that on the rare occasions on which Tone had been obliged to absent himself, they had been able to find an accomplice to carry letters to and fro.

Martin was totally occupied with Flood's visit. It lasted three days and was the occasion of the greatest review of troops ever seen in the town. One thousand men in their brilliant uniforms, accompanied by bands and cavalry, filled the place with pageantry, and when Flood's duties were completed, Martin rode at the head of a troop of horse which escorted the great man out of Galway.

Flood proceeded to Sligo to review the Volunteers there, and Martin eventually followed in order to keep his appointment with Fighting FitzGerald. Scarcely had he arrived, however, than he received a message from FitzGerald to say he did not wish to renew the quarrel. Then, too, Martin discovered how it was that FitzGerald had survived two shots full-on from horse pistols. He had plated his body so as to make it completely bullet-proof and had only been knocked down by the force of the balls hitting him.

It was three years since FitzGerald had shot the wolf-hound. During that time such wanton cruelty had never ceased to rankle with Martin and he had continually looked forward to the day of reckoning. Now, with one duel fought and another cancelled, he was able to rest assured that he had acquitted himself honourably. It would be difficult to find any dog in history whose death has been so punctiliously avenged.

Mrs. Martin now announced that she was expecting a child. In view of past experience, the news was as much a cause for apprehension as for rejoicing, but in the meantime life at Dangan pursued its normal course. It was not only his passion for Mrs. Martin which put young Tone in a position that was novel; he had been living for two years in a society very different from that to which he was accustomed.

As a Protestant brought up among Protestants, he had come into contact with few Catholics apart from the labouring classes and the peasantry; but in the west conditions were very different from those in the rest of the country. Due to the Cromwellian transplantations, Catholics predominated in society, and Galway was the most Catholic county in Ireland. Dangan was a hospitable house, where many Catholics came and went constantly, and Tone was to write later that Galway and Mayo contained 'the cream and flower of the Catholic gentry'. At the same time, the conversation was very frequently about politics in which parliamentary reform and Catholic emancipation were the dominant themes. Tone claimed that he learned from Mrs. Martin how to make himself agreeable to women, and no doubt he, who started with rather orthodox ideas, also picked up something from her husband. He may have improved his mind as much as his manner.

But one evening the course of this pleasant life was rudely interrupted. When Tone was with Martin in his room, a strange thing occurred. A couple of ruffians broke in to arrest Martin. So extraordinary an occurrence could not be allowed to pass, and Martin set about getting the affair investigated. In the process he asked Tone to swear an affidavit, but the young man refused, claiming for some reason that it would be against his principles. A correspondence ensued in which Martin pressed the matter and, according to Tone, even threatened him; but Tone remained adamant.

He commented with a certain smugness in his diary: 'Though I adored his wife beyond all humans, and knew well that my refusal was in effect a sentence of banishment from her presence for ever, I had the courage to persist in my refusal.' As he rightly foresaw, the incident brought to a close the Dangan idyll, and so ended in his own words, 'a passion of the most extravagant violence', but it was one from which he was quick to recover. A few months later he eloped with a girl of fifteen whom he married.

That same year Martin fought another duel of a very different kind from the one with Fighting FitzGerald. His cousin and close friend, James Jordan, was with him on the Connaught circuit, and during a bar dinner Martin remonstrated with him for criticizing the way his mother was educating his sisters. Jordan took offence, and although Martin apologized, Jordan insisted on an apology before the people in front of whom Martin had made his remark; but this was impossible. Martin implored Jordan not to fight, and even turned up at the appointed place without pistols, hoping this would settle the matter once and for all, but Jordan merely handed him one of his own.

Martin hit Jordan in the groin, and the young man died after a few days of terrible agony which was fully matched by the spiritual anguish Martin suffered. He was seen some time afterwards at the Brownes' at Castlemacgarrett holding a carving knife in his hand as if it were a pistol and exclaiming absent-mindedly: 'No, I could not have missed him. Poor Jordan, I could not have missed you.'

Martin had only returned from his stay in England in July 1784, and already in February of the following year Mrs. Martin gave birth to a daughter. The fact that the child was a month premature could not fail to cause some alarm, but she survived and was christened Laetitia. After eight years of marriage, Mrs. Martin at last made her husband, who was now thirty-one, into a family man. Mrs. Martin was a devoted mother, and if she missed Wolfe Tone, her husband certainly did not suspect it.

Although he was no longer in parliament, Martin had his hands full with the family estates, the theatre and the Volunteers who, since the National Convention, had been passing through a new phase. The idea had been growing, especially among the Ulster Presbyterian dissenters, that there could be no genuine reform that did not include the granting of the franchise to the Catholics. At the same time the composition of the Corps began to alter. In the Liberties of Dublin the ranks were thrown open to working-class Catholics, while in the north special drilling sessions were organized for them. Grattan complained that what had been the 'armed property' of the country was turning into the 'armed beggary' and the Government viewed the new developments with alarm. Parliamentary reform in England meant one thing, but in Ireland it meant another—the weaning of parliament from that power of the executive which was essential to English rule. In particular Rutland looked with concern on the activities of the Earl-Bishop who was one of the leaders of a liberalizing movement in Ulster.

But once again an old spectre was effectively raised. The idea was put about that the Catholics, if they got the political power that would result from the vote, would start to claim back their lands. Renewed fears that the Acts of Settlement might be endangered were accompanied by an intensive campaign organized by Charlemont in the north. Gradually his exclusivism gained the ascendancy, until the point was reached where the Lord Lieutenant could report that the Earl-Bishop would not be able to go beyond 'talking treason over his claret'. Little did he know what a fertile seed the bizarre ecclesiastic had sown, and that others even less acceptable to the Administration would come to cultivate it.

The Bishop's nephew, Fighting FitzGerald, had not in the meantime been inactive. Jealous of a local solicitor, Randall McDonnell, who had been made Colonel of the Mayo Volunteers, FitzGerald organized a gang to assassinate him, and then disappeared. The army sought him in vain for some time, and then found him ignominiously hiding under some blankets in a chest in his own house. Once again he was imprisoned in Castlebar, and when his trial was due to start, Martin went there expecting that Altamont would attend. There was serious friction between the two men, possibly because Martin resented Altamont's not having sent his carriage to collect him after the duel over the Prime Serjeant. The Attorney-General, Fitzgibbon, who was to prosecute, wrote to the Lord Lieutenant: 'Martin came here yesterday in quest of Lord Altamont, whom he means to beat wherever he can find him. The noble peer, however, does not mean to give him the opportunity for the present, as he chooses rather to attend to his duty in Parliament than to visit his Connaught friends. . . . The gentlemen of the sword suspect that he has had intimation of brother Martin's business with him.'

Before FitzGerald's trial began, a mob broke into the gaol and injured him. He claimed that he was so badly hurt that he could not stand his trial, and finally it was postponed for a couple of months. Then, Castlebar was packed with fashionable people for the occasion, and the trial lasted for fifteen hours during which FitzGerald never spoke. After a quarter of an hour's absence, the jury brought in a verdict of guilty, and he was condemned to death; but wagers were laid that his powerful connections would once again intervene to have him pardoned.

But this time his fate was sealed. After he had been attacked in prison he had claimed that he had no clothes, and when his final hour came, the man who had worn diamond buckles on his shoes and a string of pearls as a hatband, stepped jauntily out to his execution dressed like a beggar in an old coat of the Connollys' hunt at Castletown, a flannel waistcoat and drawers, coarse shoes and an old battered hat. His death was destined to be as extraordinary as his life: the rope broke and he had several extra hours in which to await the fatal moment, by which time his spirit was broken and he died pathetically, overcome with contrition.

His notorious uncle was abroad. He had been reported as setting out the previous year from Oxford dressed in a light lilac coat, with 'his volunteer's hat, fiercely cocked, laced, and with a cockade'. He was now in Rome, where the news of his nephew's execution took three weeks to reach him, and there he managed to keep it out of the newspapers.

The Martins' little daughter, Laetitia, had thrived, and Mrs. Martin was now expecting again, but that did not prevent her taking part in the performance at Kirwan's Lane theatre during the summer assizes of *The Fair Penitent* by Rowe, a tragedy set in Genoa.

Mrs. Siddons had created the part of the inconstant fair penitent, Calista, which Mrs. Martin played opposite Martin in the Lear-like part of Sciolto. Their performances drew forth the most extravagant praise from the critic of the *Freeman's Journal*. He wrote of Martin: 'He was venerable, eloquent, dignified and pathetic, as the character alternately rendered each necessary. I had known him to be the best mimic of public men, but it remained for me to know that he is also one of the best actors. The struggle between honour and nature in the scene with Calista . . . was so uncommonly affecting that not a dry eye was to be found among the audience.'

As for Mrs. Martin, the critic confessed that he had difficulty in finding words adequate to praise her. 'It would require her own pencil to depict the grace, the dignity, the elegance of her attitude—it would require her own pen to describe the *beauties* of her performance. . . .'

The audience whose hearts Martin had wrung was well accustomed to the recital of the pathetic; it was composed almost entirely of the gentlemen of the bar. After the play, the Martins entertained them to a sumptuous dinner at Dangan, and one of them, who was considered one of the foremost judges of taste, was heard to say that 'Mrs. Siddons excelled every other English actress, but that Mrs. Martin excelled Mrs. Siddons, and every other woman in the world.'

On 4 October 1786 Mrs. Martin gave birth to a son. After all the disappointments of their early married life, the survival of yet another child, and a son at that, gave the event more than ordinary significance in the eyes of the parents. The child was christened Thomas; there had been many Thomases in the Martin family since the Thomas who was granted the rights in the Galway mills in 1365, and for a second name the boy was given Barnewall, the family name of the devoted mother and lover of animals whom Martin had lost so early.

Although they lived principally at Dangan, the Martins had not abandoned society in Dublin where they still had a house. They were on close terms with the Lord Lieutenant, Rutland, although he had fallen away from the idea of parliamentary reform with which he had been associated in England, and, in particular, had a deep suspicion of the Volunteers. But he was a popular, if rather dissipated man, more distinguished for passing around the claret than for his politics.

When he decided in the autumn of 1787 to do a tour in the west of Ireland, it was natural that the Martins should be closely involved. They planned to put on *Douglas* for him at Kirwan's Lane, and this time the part of Douglas, Lady Randolph's long-lost son, was to be played by Martin's young half-brother, Anthony, now a tall, handsome, graceful lad of sixteen. The Martins had composed an address to Rutland in verse which Mrs. Martin was to read as a prologue.

Once the Lord Lieutenant was on the way, Martin went to Ballinrobe in County Mayo to welcome him to the west, and set him on his way to Westport House where he was to be the guest of the Altamonts for a couple of days. This time Martin spent with Lord Louth, at Bermingham House, a fine mansion he had not long before built on the outskirts of Tuam where Rutland was due to stay after Westport.

On the day that Rutland was expected, Martin went over to the Veseys at Hollymount to meet him. Rutland had ridden very hard the twenty odd miles from Westport and was complaining of a pain in his side and weakness in his back. Martin advised him to take Doctor James's Powder or a small quantity of tartar emetic, but, nonetheless, they rode on the remaining twenty miles to Bermingham House where they arrived at 8 o'clock in the evening. Dinner was served immediately, but Rutland was very dejected and could eat nothing. He withdrew upstairs to his room before the cloth was removed from the table for the customary toasts and after-dinner conversation.

Martin knew that there was a very good doctor in the town and wanted Rutland to send for him, but he refused. Instead, he followed Martin's original advice and sent out for Doctor James's Powders. He was a good deal better the following day, but stayed in bed and would not even take chicken broth. He was supposed to be receiving the freedom of Tuam, but had to excuse himself, though he did receive an address. After a couple of days at Bermingham House, he decided he was well enough to continue his tour and set off to ride the twenty-five miles to Denis Daly's at Dunsandle, one of the finest houses in the county, while Martin proceeded to Galway in order to have the town ready to receive him.

The following day Rutland went to the Kirwan's Lane theatre. Most of the nobility and gentry were in the audience, and while Mrs. Martin was reciting 'with that graceful animation' for which she was distinguished the poetic address to Rutland, he bowed continually in recognition. The performance caused something of a sensation, and the *Freeman's Journal* claimed that the audience did not know whether to admire most in Mrs. Martin 'the justness of her elocution, the marked propriety of her emphasis, or the uncommon grace of her attitudes'.

Young Anthony was praised for his performance of Douglas, the production and scenery were much admired, but the palms went to Martin for the variety he gave to the character of Glenalvon, one full of 'envious malice' and 'designing ambition' which he played with that 'discriminating judgement which he possesses in an eminent degree'. The critic referred to his 'sharp penetrating eye', his 'dispassionate irony and unruffled contempt', the 'blended expression of wonder and derision', and a sarcastic smile which no words could describe. His versatility was so remarkable that, news of it having reached the capital, the *Dublin Chronicle* published a report that he had 'performed several characters in such a style as scarcely to be equalled on any stage'.

After the play, the Viceroy and his suite adjourned to Dangan, and there they were entertained to a magnificent banquet and, in the words of the *Freeman's Journal*, 'that conviviality and elegance reigned for which Mr. Martin and his consort are so peculiarly distinguished'. The Duke did not leave Dangan until 4 a.m. when he rode back to Dunsandle where Martin was invited to dine with him that night.

When Rutland returned to Dublin, he did not shake off his indisposition. He took to his bed and the reports showed his condition to be fluctuating. On 20 October he was declared to be much better, but by the 25th the papers announced there was very little hope for him. In fact he had already died the previous day at the age of thirty-two. With him Martin lost a friend of fourteen years' standing and one who had probably played an important part by advising him to go into politics. Rutland's

67

death was ascribed to various causes, among them to a chill caught in riding from Dangan to Dunsandle in the middle of the night; but Martin, who knew so intimately the condition in which he had arrived at Bermingham House, attributed it to a cold caught while dredging for oysters at Westport with Altamont.

Rutland was replaced by the former Earl Temple, who now returned as Marquis of Buckingham. His previous reign had been particularly popular, and on his return there were illuminations calling him 'the Patriot Viceroy' no doubt for the part he and his brother had played in getting through the Renunciation Act. Early in the new year, which the Martins ushered in by playing Shylock and Portia with great success, Martin attended upon the new Lord Lieutenant with the two members for Galway, to present the county's address of welcome.

The Martins' estates were heavily encumbered, but about this time the prospect of a new and vast fortune had suddenly opened up before the family. A valuable copper mine was discovered on their Connemara lands. The vein was of great length and breadth, and when samples were sent to a manufacturing company in Liverpool, it was reported that the ore should sell at a net profit of about £9 per ton. There was the advantage that the copper was in the vicinity of the Corrib, which flows into the sea at Galway, thus rendering transport cheap.

This was only the beginning. Martin, with his usual energy, was soon on the spot. He stayed at Clareville, a charming little house of classical design which his father had erected on the site of Nimble Dick's manor of Clare, and followed all the drilling operations closely. By the summer he was able to write to the Lord Lieutenant: 'In one vein we have cut two veins or lodes, the one, 3 feet from wall to wall, is solid ore and so tender as to work without powder; the other course is above 4 feet broad and what perhaps is remarkable, the ore in each differs much from each other, the first being purple and the other yellow ore. Altho' we have not yet sunk 7 fathoms, we intend on Monday to start stopeing both these veins, and at the same time to bring up our lead which will be done in the stopeing as we have a hill 200 fathom above our present work. . . . I sent your lordship some time ago some specimens of the ore and I have now packed up a box containing samples of the different ore we are now raising and some other fossils which I dare say you will think curious.'

To Martin the parliamentarian and Martin the actor was now added Martin the mineralogist.

Chapter Seven

IN THE spring of 1789 Martin decided to take his family on a visit to France. He now had a second son, St. George, aged three months, and it was no easy matter to transport a group of people ranging from that age to thirty-five, with their servants and luggage, across two islands and on to the Continent. The journey by road from Galway to Dublin was familiar, but the sea voyage from the Pigeon House, outside Dublin, to Holyhead or Liverpool, was hazardous and of unpredictable duration, and the shorter English passage from Dover to Calais was not much better.

In view of all this, Martin set out ahead early in March to make what preparations he could and thereby to smooth the way, and a few weeks later the entire family reached Lille in the north of France. This was on the main road from the French coast to Paris, and Martin's two first cousins, Lord Gormanston's brothers, Jenico and Martin Preston, were already installed there.

It had been an exceptionally hard winter. Temperatures in Paris had dropped to seventeen degrees below zero, the water had frozen in the fountains and the water carriers had been extracting exorbitant sums. There had been a shortage of bread, which was generally supposed to be due to the export of wheat and speculation, since the preceding harvest had been average, and there was widespread discontent. The war which the French had helped the Americans to win had cost them dearly, and the Treasury was facing bankruptcy. On 1 January it had been announced that the French States General would be summoned to meet in May for the purpose of authorizing the Government to raise a loan.

Martin, for all his political sense, had no more reason than anybody else to suppose that this foreboded anything particular. But in April there were ugly outbreaks of violence in Paris, and when the States General met in Versailles the following month, things took an unexpected turn. It had been conceded that the Tiers Etat—the order of the bourgeois—should have double representation in parliament, and they now demanded that voting should be by individuals, and not by orders, which would give them supremacy. This was not granted, and they retaliated. Together with some of the nobility and clergy, they formed themselves into what they proceeded to declare was a National Assembly, and they demanded in particular the overthrow of the established privileges whereby the nobles and clergy were exempt from tax. Their cry was a reversal of that of the Americans; they wanted no representation without taxation. Their movement was against privilege, exclusivism and intolerance, and as such it appealed to Martin.

In July, still unsuspecting, the Martins moved to Paris. There they installed themselves in a hotel in the fashionable district of St. Philippe du Roule, beside the church where Martin's eminent cousin, Count Patrick D'Arcy, the great scientist, lay buried. The British Embassy, where the Duke of Leinster's brother, Lord Robert Fitzgerald, was Counsellor, was just up the road, and the area was shared by the aristocracy with the big bankers, including the Swiss, Necker, the financial wizard whom all looked to for the solution of the acute financial situation.

One day as Necker sat at table, a messenger brought him a note from the King. He read it, and with the *sang-froid* of his nation, put it away in his pocket and continued his meal. The bit of paper, however, was to have far-reaching consequences. It relieved him of his functions as Prime Minister. The masses immediately interpreted this as a victory for the Queen, who disliked Necker, and who was unpopular principally because it was believed that she ran the King. The removal of Necker at once brought about demonstrations in the city and calls for his return.

That day, Sunday 12 July, a former mistress of the Prince of

71

Wales, Mrs. Elliott, who had borne the prince a daughter, drove back to Paris with the French King's cousin, the Duke of Orléans, after fishing and dining with a number of his friends at his country place, the Château de Rainey. It had been a typical Sunday's outing, but when they reached Paris they found the city in an uproar. The Duke was credited with designs upon the throne, and the crowds were yelling, 'Long live the Duke of Orléans!' to his apparent astonishment, and 'Long live Necker!'.

The couple had been intending to go to the Italian opera, but on arrival there they found that it was shut. The Duke then decided that he would like to be dropped at his club, the Salon des Princes, but he found it closed also. They then drove through the Place Louis XV—the Place de la Concorde of later days—and found it full of soldiers. As the carriage worked its way through the crowds, the occupants were constantly questioned, and Mrs. Elliott repeatedly gave her name in order to conceal the presence of the Duke. It was all a far cry from the quiet day they had just spent in the country.

The confusion continued, and in the midst of it news penetrated the Bastille that the crowds were astir. An Irish peer, Lord Massereene, had been confined there for debt for thirty years, but that night he managed to break out and make his way to the British Embassy, just beside the Martins. When ultimately he got to England, he fell upon his knees on stepping on to English soil, exclaiming, 'God bless this land of liberty!' One of the most eccentric people of his period, he actually took his seat in the Irish House of Lords a couple of months later. He and his wife became known for their collection of cats for whom they established a feline cemetery.

Two days later, on Tuesday 14 July, while Mrs. Elliott was sitting with Talleyrand and Bailly, the Mayor of Paris, at breakfast, a meal which took place at mid-morning, at the Duke of Orléans' house in the Monceau district, they heard the firing of cannons. It heralded the news that the crowd had stormed the Invalides and seized twenty-eight thousand rifles and five cannons; on hearing that the major part of the ammunition had been deposited at the Bastille, they marched to the old fortress and seized it.

For two days the mob obliged everybody to wear a green cockade. It had become the symbol of the revolution when young

Camille Desmoulins, standing on a chair in the gardens of the Palais Royal, had plucked a leaf from a chestnut tree and, sticking it in his hat, had shouted, 'To arms!' But the green soon gave way to the red, white and blue of the Orléans family. In celebration, the Duke's mistress, the Countess de Buffon, danced a quadrille in the gardens of the Palais Royal with a fourteen-year-old girl called Pamela. Supposedly the illegitimate child of the Duke d'Orléans and Madame de Genlis, she was to become the wife of a famous and ill-fated Irishman, another brother of the Duke of Leinster, Lord Edward Fitzgerald.

By Thursday 16 July, good-humoured crowds were sightseeing in the Bastille and calm had been restored. The theatres were soon reopened, and on the 25th, the Baron de Staël, the Swedish Ambassador, was able to announce that his father-in-law, Necker, was returning. With their own National Assembly and Necker at the head of affairs, all the problems would be settled. So far as most people were concerned, the revolution was over and they could return peaceably to their good, solid, bourgeois lives.

The Martins had seen a world changing before their eyes and the society in which they now found themselves was a lively one. 'Never,' wrote Madame de Staël, Necker's daughter, 'was society as gay, but at the same time as serious as during the three years of 1788 to 1791.' The shouting of the mob and the firing of the cannon soon gave way to endless abstract discussion. The word liberty was on everybody's lips, and it was one which Martin was well accustomed to pronouncing, even in French which he spoke tolerably well.

With their gift for social life, the Martins were not short of salons to visit. There were the Tuesdays of Madame Helvétius, to whom Benjamin Franklin had proposed, the Mondays and Wednesdays of Madame Geoffrin, the Thursdays and Sundays of Baron d'Holbach, and the Fridays of Madame Necker, who had the tact always to serve an alternative dish without meat for practising Catholics. The philosophers and Encyclopedists met there, and Gibbon was a frequent guest. The economists and financiers went to Turgot's or to Madame Aurore Dupin's, the artists were to be found at Falconet's or Rameau's, and the aristocrats at Madame de Monesson's, while Madame de Beauharnais provided a temple for light and amorous poetry.

Animals were much in evidence in this highly sophisticated world. The Duchess de la Vallière, whom Swinburne described as 'looking like the mummy of an Egyptian queen', always received her guests seated at the end of a large room where she relegated the men to one side and the women to the other, while a little dog lay curled up on a cushion at her feet. Monkeys were popular pets, and Madame Helvétius had eighteen Angora cats which lay stretched on damask-covered armchairs where liveried servants served them with breast of chicken on silver salvers. And the principal decoration in the Princess de Chimay's drawing-room consisted of a large cage filled with a variety of singing birds.

The French did not share the English and Irish passion for amateur theatricals, but guests were often entertained to music. The harp was particularly popular, and Madame de Genlis, Pamela's so-called guardian, was accused of playing it uninvited. *Paul et Virginie*, which was to become one of the classics of adolescent love, had its first reading by Bernardin de Saint-Pierre at the Neckers' to the manifest boredom of the audience. Dinners where the guests had to dress up in some prearranged costume, such as Roman or Greek, were fashionable. Conversation was erudite or flippant, intellectual or wordly, according to the situation, and liberty was not the only theme. What the French call *conversation aimable* was general, and can be described as 'the language of inconstancy which was not spoken anywhere as lightly, as generally and as diversely as in France'.

Apart from this cosmopolitan society, the Martins had relatives and compatriots to meet. One of the Gormanstons was married to a Portuguese, Count Doria, and lived in Paris; Count Patrick D'Arcy's successor was Martin's cousin, Hyacinth; and the son of Lally Baron de Tollendal was briefly President of the self-styled National Assembly.

But in October Lally resigned. He had been proposing a Constitution on the English model, which was not popular. The American Ambassador, Morris, said that what the French wanted was an American constitution with a king instead of a president, and it is certain that at that stage what the nation wanted most was a stronger king. But now the revolution which had seemed ended burst out afresh. The crowds invaded

Versailles and brought back the King and the Assembly to Paris to reside among them, thereby nipping in the bud a counter-revolution which showed signs of starting among the royal guards. 'We have brought back the baker, the baker's wife and the baker's apprentice' was the popular saying. It was the bourgeoisie's victory, and the Assembly which in August had voted a charter for freedom, styled the Declaration of the Rights of Man, now produced a new constitution, and, as was to be expected, it was monarchist and bourgeois. Yet again, to all intents and purposes, the revolution was over, and few even of those who dropped in to hear the debates in the Club des Jacobins thought otherwise.

The Martins had lived throughout like other Parisians, but in March of the year 1790, their personal affairs took a new turn. Martin received news that an English company was interested in working the mines on the family estates to which they all now looked as a means of repairing their fortunes. It became necessary for him to go to London for discussions with the prospectors, which meant leaving the family. Reluctant as he was to go, he had no reason to expect any further disturbances, and he planned to return as soon as his business in England was completed, and then to take them all to Italy.

His wife accompanied him on the first stage of the journey as far as St. Venise. Separation was always hard for them to bear and they parted with their usual expressions of regret and affection. Martin then proceeded to London accompanied by Joseph Casteaux, the French valet who had been in his service since the third year of his marriage. They reached London on 26 March, and there followed a few weeks' negotiation. After much discussion, the deeds for the operation of the Connemara mines were at last drawn up, and Martin was impatient to receive them for signature. When they were finally brought to him, it was 10 o'clock at night, and he had a post-chaise and four ready at the door to convey him as fast as possible to Dover so as to return to France.

He read the deeds and they were executed on the spot, whereupon he was at last free to set out on his journey. But as he was coming down the stairs of his hotel to get into the chaise, he met an Irish friend who had been looking for him everywhere with the news that the Irish parliament had been dissolved. This faced Martin with an immediate change of plan. He had given an undertaking to stand for the town of Galway in the next election, and the news that he had just received meant that he had to return home immediately. Polling was to take place on 27 May, and he just had time to prepare his campaign. Reluctantly he ordered the post-chaise to turn around and make for the Irish packet instead of for Dover.

When in due course the election took place, it followed the familiar pattern. Denis Daly had a hundred and nine votes, Skeffington-Smith ninety-nine votes, and Martin only twenty-eight. Once again Martin accused the Sheriff of being biassed and produced after the election at least a hundred people whom he claimed were entitled to vote, but who had been refused the right. At the same time he objected to eighty people who had succeeded in voting for Daly, and in particular he contested the right of Skeffington-Smith to stand at all on the grounds that he was non-resident. He announced that he would send a petition to parliament when it reassembled on 2 July and would apply for a *quo warranto* for usurpation by several non-resident freemen.

With all this before him, he could not see himself returning to Paris and then setting off with the family for Italy. Moreover, after discussions with a Galway friend, Coneys, who had been with him in Paris, he came to the conclusion that it would be unwise to continue on the Continent, so he wrote to his wife telling her to return home with the children. He did not expect her to ask to defer her return; he was too accustomed to her ecstatic welcome whenever they had been apart, but the reason she gave was very understandable. She wanted to assist at what had been called the Fête de la Fédération. Still looking to the American as the model of a revolution, the French planned to celebrate the first anniversary of the taking of the Bastille on 14 July and all that it had come to symbolize with a festival grouping representatives from all the provinces. Martin acquiesced, and knowing that his wife would return as soon as the festivities were ended and being familiar with the many details such a journey with three children and servants involved, he despatched Joseph to Paris on 4 June to start making all the necessary arrangements and to accompany his mistress and the children home.

When Joseph arrived at their hotel he found his mistress in the company of a Mr. Petrie, a small, rather ugly Englishman, much her senior, to whom, it turned out, she had been introduced at the house of one of the big bankers shortly after Martin's departure three months earlier. The valet immediately handed Mrs. Martin a letter from her husband but was surprised to find that, instead of going through it with the usual affectionate concern, she flung it down on the table half-read.

Petrie then asked Joseph for news of Martin, and received the reply that he had been having some trouble with a Mr. Vansey.

'Oh, he's a violent man,' commented Petrie.

'In some affairs, yes, in some, no,' remarked Mrs. Martin. She then added the old proverb: 'The pitcher goes often to the well, but returns broken at last.' Petrie commented on the truth of this remark.

Preparations now started for the return to Ireland after an absence of nearly a year and a half. Petrie was constantly at the house, where he sometimes stayed alone with Mrs. Martin until 3 or 4 o'clock in the morning. She would give orders for the table to be laid for supper, and insist that none of the servants should come near her unless they were summoned.

Joseph could not fail to observe what was happening. Mrs. Martin's bedroom was connected by a door with the supper-room. One evening when Joseph was in her room, the door happened to be ajar. Candles were burning in the next room, and there he saw his mistress lying on a sofa. Petrie, kissing her, had one arm around her neck while the other lifted her skirts and was employed between her legs. Under the circumstances, the valet was not surprised when he saw the couple in bed together, but he did not dare to communicate anything he saw to his master because he knew that he would not be believed. Martin would not listen to an angel who said anything derogatory about his wife.

The Fête de la Fédération took place on 14 July on the Champ de Mars under pouring rain. Talleyrand said mass on the 'Altar of the Nation', La Fayette praised the Constitution, the King spoke, the Queen showed the Dauphin. And Mrs. Martin having had her wish of seeing this first celebration of what was to become the symbol of a republic, preparations for the return to Ireland were completed.

When at length the party set off on 20 August, Mrs. Martin did not travel in her own carriage, but in Petrie's chaise. Throughout the journey, the couple constantly separated themselves from the others and wandered off into remote parts of the country. On the night when they all stayed at Noyons, Joseph saw them once again in bed together. When they finally reached London, Mrs. Martin did not go, as might have been expected, to her aunt's house in Clarges Street, but stayed with Petrie at the Royal Hotel in Pall Mall.

Joseph, who remained in attendance, had no hesitation in remonstrating with Mrs. Martin. On one occasion he managed to take some compromising letters out of her dressing-box. Facing her with these, he undertook never to disclose what he knew if she would return to her mother, but she refused. At this time, her brother, an army officer, returned from America and she moved to Clarges Street. There she introduced her brother to Petrie, who invited them both to his country seat in Essex. He took little care to disguise the liaison, and introduced Mrs. Martin freely among his acquaintances. Major Vesey observed all that was going on and began to grow suspicious. Finally he resolved that his sister ought to be returned forthwith to her husband.

When Petrie realized what was afoot, he immediately hatched a plot: Mrs. Martin was to elope. He wrote to her telling her to leave the house in Clarges Street in the evening, and at the end of the street to hire a coach to take her to the Adelphi. On the way, she was to change her clothes and disguise herself by rubbing burnt cork on her eyebrows and putting rouge on her cheeks. At the Adelphi she was to discharge the coach and immediately take another to Westminster Bridge, where she was to alight, cross the bridge and take another coach to the appointed place.

It was no longer possible to conceal the situation from Martin; he had to be told. Any man would be shocked at the news that his wife had deserted him, but this came after years of domestic happiness during which there had never been a hint that a break of any kind could be remotely possible. The children were more than ordinarily cherished because they had been born after so many disappointments. Apart from the sentimental ties there were those which existed between the

Martin and Vesey families, and outside their own intimate relations there had been a theatrical partnership of which Martin was justly proud.

He could not be incredulous, as Joseph Casteaux had anticipated, because there were too many facts before him, and his first reaction was to try to save the situation: this was all a passing folly and his Elizabeth would come back to him. He would forgive her and everything would go on as before. The person who had been involved in these scandalous scenes was not the Elizabeth he loved, but some other person who would somehow disappear when all was set to rights.

But as time passed and none of this proved true, he had to find a cause for it, and that cause was Petrie. He was a rich seducer and adulterer who was capable of every form of duplicity to achieve his ends, and it was at his door that the full blame must be laid.

As hope began to fade and he started to face the great void that was opening before him, Martin was able to deal with dignity and compassion with two letters purporting to come from his wife which an intermediary sent him, and to whom he replied: 'The two letters you enclosed me did not give me as much pain as you supposed. My distress in this unhappy business arose if possible more from the situation of the unhappy person in question than from what I in my person suffered. I supposed Mrs. Martin had been betrayed into ruin by arts such as the weakness of humanity was unable to resist. I thought that the feelings of a noble mind for the loss of female honour would embitter the present and darken every future hope. I thought that the severity of self-accusation would anticipate or at least soften that of the world. I feared, yet I hoped, that by an open confession that she was undeserving of the love—the unexampled love—I for thirteen years bore to her that she thereby would have moved her title to my tenderest regard. If her letters prove those expectations to have been in vain, they yet leave to me the melancholy consolation that *no* possible act of mine could have restored her to her friends, to society or to herself. Of those two letters, she is only guilty of adopting the sentiments, for there is not one original idea of hers contained in them. The art is too apparent in those letters. While hope of amendment remained, Joseph never mentioned to mortal, but to the unfortunate lady in question, what he knew. Joseph on this occasion acted with a generosity beyond example. He told her if she returned to me he would quit my service if she feared his communicating what he had seen. I horror to name what that sight was. . . . Had the gentleman been wise he would have furnished hints and not have dictated verbatim the phraseology of those letters, much less would he have written with his own hand many words in both letters. When poor Elizabeth used to write to those dear and near connexions she wrote *from* and to the *heart*. Those enclosed to me neither manifest a feeling heart or a well organized head. . . . It was folly in the extreme to introduce the lady, who travelled without delay to Portsmouth, into such extensive mercantile connexions both in England and France, but the wanting money finishes the climax of folly. The riches of the *East* are at her command and if that can procure her happiness, may that fountain never be exhausted. The mention of one who for fourteen years lay constantly in her arms does not seem generous.

'Mrs. Vesey, I find, is not willing to take charge of Mrs. Martin's things, but I have ordered them to be forwarded with the greatest care. The particular friends of Elizabeth will, I hope, be charitable. I may add just enough to impute her strange conduct to a deranged mind. They will, I hope, manifest that they have compassion and not withdraw from her when she undoubtedly stands most in need of comfort. . . . When Mrs. Martin was what she ought to be, she was the ornament of every society and she made as many friends as she had acquaintances. Did mother, brother or aunts then do her honour when they anxious pressed forward to claim a separate kindred to so rare a being? Kindred was honour, was advantage to them. Now then let those dear and near connexions comfort her who did comfort them.'

It was as though there had been a death in the house, and now all that remained to him was to have his three small children brought home to him. But the world also had to be considered. He was a vigorous young man of thirty-six of considerable social standing, and he had been cuckolded. He could anticipate the astonishment the news would cause at home, but he also had little difficulty in imagining the reactions in Paris in those circles where his wife had heard infidelity talked of as an ambition and seen it practised as an art. He could hear his friends saying indulgently, '*Le bonhomme Martin est cocu,*' with the same relish as if he had just been ennobled. He was not vain, but he was a Martin, and natural pride made him loathe to be an object of pity. The only way of avoiding it was to be seen in high spirits.

By the end of September he was back in Paris, looking up old friends, going to the theatre, arguing in the salons, and gauging the progress of that strange revolution which he had seen born and which continued to advance by fits and starts. Another visitor to Paris at the same time was Erskine, who had defended Paine against the royal family and lost his post as Attorney-General to the Prince of Wales in consequence. He, like Martin, was well pleased with the strides being made by a revolution which, from being monarchist, was turning republican.

To crown his display of composure, Martin decided to give a large dinner party to the President and selected members of the Assembly and other notabilities. Even in Paris, well accustomed to show of every kind, the event made some stir. At home, the *Dublin Chronicle* informed the world of his progress: 'The entertainment consisted of every delicacy the season could afford or art produce. Dinner was served up under one hundred covers—in a sumptuous style of elegance and hospitality, which done honour to the character of an Irishman. These republican guests expressed the greatest happiness at their reception—where harmony and festivity went hand in hand. The dinner and wines, which were of the choicest description, it is said, cost Mr. Martin upwards of 600 Louis d'Or.' Martin no doubt considered it a trifle with which to bury humiliation, but insufficient to mend a heart.

Chapter Eight

MRS. MARTIN settled down to live openly with Petrie at his London house in Soho Square, and the world began to speculate on Martin's reactions. He had the kind of personality which creates legends. Among the tales now told of him was one according to which he had disguised himself as an Eastern pedlar selling silks and by this means obtained admission to the house where his wife was staying. There he found her in the arms of Petrie who almost died of shock, assuming that he was about to be challenged to a duel by the man who had earned himself the nickname of 'Hair-Trigger Dick'. But Martin preferred to resort to the accepted methods of the time; he brought a case against Petrie for what was called Criminal Conversation with his wife and claimed twenty thousand pounds damages.

The case was over a year in coming on, which left Martin ample time for reflection. Past actions of his wife's which had seemed innocent now acquired significance; men whom he had been proud to see admire her now appeared as potential seducers. He even began to examine his children's features and to ask himself questions. Was Laetitia's birth really premature? She had his mouth, but did it not also resemble Wolfe Tone's mouth? Nobody else had lived for the best part of two years at Dangan, and during his absence had Tone been fully occupied teaching Robert and Anthony? The young man had been fascinated by the theatre, but had he played his parts with more than an amateur's ardour? The field for conjecture was wide.

As for the theatre where he had revelled to see his wife display her talents, now that his 'fair penitent' would never again say, 'Is there yet some little dear remain of love and tenderness for poor undone Calista?' he threw in his hand and sold it.

Henry Flood, the man he most admired, died just before the case came on, and Martin was still mourning him when he appeared at the Guildhall in London in December 1791 before Lord Kenyon and a special jury. Petrie had chosen as his counsel a man who was a favourite with the judge, and who specialized in Criminal Conversation cases, namely, Erskine who had been in Paris during Martin's last visit. Yarrow and Bearcroft opened for Martin and among the witnesses they called was Martin's friend, Blake of Ardfry, one of the members for County Galway, who had sponsored Owenson's acting career. Sir Michael Cromie, who had witnessed Martin's marriage settlement and in whom the family estates had been vested, was also called, with another family friend, Coneys, who had stayed in the same hotel in Paris with the Martins.

They all attested to the Martins' reputation as a devoted couple whose life was a model for all others. Martin's counsel defied Petrie to attack Martin's character or to attribute any dishonourable behaviour to Mrs. Martin before she met Petrie. He maintained that Petrie was determined to debauch her. 'She must have been solely the object of his lust,' he declared; 'of his love she could not be.' Everything hung upon the evidence of Martin's valet, Joseph, and of Mrs. Martin's maid who both entertained the court with lurid details. The waiter of the Ship Tavern in Brightelmstone added to the general picture of concupiscence by stating that, although Petrie had a house in the vicinity, he always slept with Mrs. Martin at the tavern. He added that she looked pregnant.

The proofs of Petrie's culpability were blatant, but Erskine still did what he could to defend him by attacking. 'The best security for the honour of a wife,' he declared, 'is prudence on the part of the husband.' Yet what had Colonel Martin done? He had left his poor, innocent wife in times that were exceptionally eventful in a capital of the greatest luxury; 'I might almost say,' he went on, 'abomination.' The Colonel would have done better, in his view, to have allowed his wife to share in all the ups and downs of an election campaign instead of confidently leaving her at the mercy of every kind of dissipation. 'Had the husband been present,' he claimed, 'moral sense would have checked the vicious appetite.' Whatever the effect of such a statement on the court, it could only have filled Martin with dismay to hear it suggested that the exquisite and devoted creature in whose arms he had lain for so many years had all the time been the prey to a vicious appetite.

Petrie's entire fortune was invested in the West Indies, in Tobago, but as a result of the American war, it was the subject of tension between France and England, and he claimed that at the time of the case he did not know if he still had any fortune at all. He appealed to the mercy of the court. If they found against him, his wife and family would be made destitute and would suffer for his crime. But neither the ingenuity of Erskine, nor the pathos of Petrie, had any effect. After adjourning for only fifteen minutes, the jury returned a verdict in favour of Martin and ordered Petrie to pay ten thousand pounds in damages.

Although the sum was half that claimed, it was still too much in reality for Martin. A gentleman might feel obliged to vindicate his honour, but he could not be paid for his wife, and the money soon began to weigh upon him. He was returning immediately to Ireland, and before departure he handed Petrie's money to his coachman, Thady Harte, telling him to change it into small coin. He then proceeded to divest himself of it as fast as he could. He had his horses shod in silver shoes, and, as they set out for home, he ordered Thady to fling the money broadcast over the countryside along the way. A few weeks later, when Thady came for his wages, Martin asked him if he had not thought of keeping something of all the money they had brought back from London, but Thady was a typical west of Ireland man. If it had not been right for his master to keep it, he replied, it could not have been right for him.

The Criminal Conversation case filled a two-page centre spread in the *Freeman's Journal* which declared that the lady in question 'was possessed of the most exalted endowments, and esteemed to be one of the most amiable and accomplished women which this or any other country could produce.' Society was able to gloat over the full details. According to the paper, the court's decision gave general satisfaction both in England and in Ireland. Martin's children were only three, five and six years old at the time, but in later years they may have been less satisfied with the case than the rest of the world; the papers quoted their father's counsel as saying, 'The children have lost a protector, and, indeed, doubts may now be kindled of their legitimacy.'

At least one person did not agree with the verdict of the *Freeman's Journal* and that was Wolfe Tone. He felt that Martin had been treating his wife with the usual neglect, and wrote in his diary: 'I am satisfied from my own observation and the knowledge of the characters of both parties during my residence for many months in their family, that the fault was originally Martin's.'

Tone was twenty-nine. Since his youthful passion for Mrs. Martin he had passed through Trinity College, been called to the bar, and entertained briefly an imperialistic dream of conquering the Sandwich Islands for the British Empire. But his views had altered, and while Martin was preparing his case against Petrie, Tone had been producing a remarkable pamphlet. Entitled *An Argument on Behalf of the Catholics of Ireland*, and published under the pen-name of 'A Northern Whig', it urged the Ulster Dissenters to make common cause with the Catholics, taking up afresh the theme cherished by the notorious Earl-Bishop.

About the same time, Tone had taken the first step in the direction which was to lead him to be one of Ireland's great revolutionaries. He had helped to found in Belfast the Society of United Irishmen. Its objectives were those which Martin had long supported, parliamentary reform and Catholic emancipation. Martin's first cousin, Simon Butler, Lord Mountgarret's brother, was chairman of the Dublin branch. Martin may well have flattered himself that Tone had acquired his ideas under his influence, and he would have derived certain satisfaction from knowing that his former protégé was secretary of the Catholic Committee, which grouped together the Catholic leaders, and was energetically preparing for a great Catholic Convention to be held in December 1792.

But a disclosure of Fitzgibbon's the following year revealed a new Tone. It transpired that when the Society of United

Irishmen was being founded in 1791 Tone had addressed a letter to his friend, Russell, on the question of Ireland's relations with England. In it he had written: 'I have not said one word that looks like a wish for separation, though I give it to you and your friends as my most decided opinion that such an event would be a regeneration for this country. My unalterable opinion is that the bane of Irish prosperity is in the influence of England. I believe that influence will ever be extended while the connexion between the countries continues.'

The Castle had only discovered belatedly who was the author of the letter which reeked of sedition. Tone succeeded in explaining it away by declaring that his opinion of France had changed in the intervening two years and that he fully supported the English connection, provided it could be 'preserved consistently with the honour, the interests and the happiness of Ireland'. He had, however, already set his course.

Meanwhile, France, from whom the United Irishmen took their ideas, had put the final seal upon her revolution. By a majority of seventy-three, which included the Duke of Orléans, the Assembly voted that the King must die, and on 21 January 1793, his execution was carried out with all the trappings of a ritual murder. Torches flared, drums rolled, bugles blew, and the powdered head fell. Voltaire, who had been disgusted by the English habit of docking horses' tails, had written too soon:

> 'Vous fiers Anglois, et barbares que vous êtes,
> Coupent les têtes à vos Rois, et les queues à vos bêtes;
> Mais les Français plus polis, et aimant les loix,
> Laissent les queues à leur bêtes et la tête à leur Rois.'*

The world was shocked and Britain withdrew his credentials from the French Ambassador in London. France was seized by a messianic zeal for spreading her ideas, and on 1 February 1793, she declared war on Holland and England. The two great rivals were now locked in a conflict which was to last twenty-two years with only a brief respite.

This put Ireland in the position to which she had been

* Free translation:
    'You proud English, barbarians that you are,
    Cut the heads off your kings and the tails off your beasts.
    The French, more polite, and loving the law,
    Leave the tails on their beasts and the heads on their kings.'

accustomed whenever Britain was threatened. She was expected to subjugate her problems to the larger necessity of withstanding a common enemy. The old threat of a French invasion revived, but with new undertones, for France had not only staged a revolution, but given birth to new ideas embodied in the words liberty, equality, fraternity, justice, humanity, and they were fast gaining ground. Once again Britain was faced with the need to offer conciliation to the Catholic masses as a bait for their loyalty.

Within weeks a Relief Act got through the Irish parliament with comparative ease and speed. At last the Catholic tenantry were to be entitled to vote as forty-shilling freeholders. They could bear arms, take commissions in the army below the rank of general and get degrees at Dublin University. Most important, they could be admitted as grand jurors which involved them not only in the courts, but in many aspects of local government.

Yet this was not all the Catholics had sought. Under the influence of Luke Teeling, a prosperous linen merchant of Lisburn in Ulster, the Catholic Convention had declared that they would not be satisfied with anything short of absolute and total emancipation. An attempt to salvage the situation with a motion to allow Catholics to sit in parliament was roundly defeated in the House, and a lengthy list was appended to the Relief Act of spheres from which they were excluded and which debarred them from all offices in the Government and State.

The initial rejoicing over what had been achieved, soon gave way to bitterness when it was realized that the Catholics depended on the Protestant Ascendancy to give them access in fact to the rights which were now theirs by law; and it soon became plain that every conceivable obstacle was to be erected in their way. Once again a half-measure turned into a part insult what should have been a boon, and through the sense of frustration it fostered, it created the very circumstances Britain had set out to forestall. It left the mass of the people open to the persuasions of those who told them that France would regulate their affairs better, and when the French Directory sent an agent, Jackson, to Ireland the following year to test out the ground, Tone met him and handed him a memorandum to the Directory urging French intervention to separate Ireland from England. Agrarian disorders were rife among the Catholic peasantry under the leadership of the Defenders. In due course these identified themselves with the United Irishmen who were largely upper- and middle-class Protestants, thereby linking the two poles of discontent. Ireland, whose population had almost doubled in twenty years, became a country of latent strife which occasionally broke out on the surface.

In such circumstances, suspicion was widespread, and even the ordinary conflicts of daily life were given a political slant. One of the magistrates of County Galway, Mansergh St. George, had for long entertained doubts about the Martins. The year that the Duke of Rutland had been on his tour of the west, there had been a brief insurrection in Galway under one who signed himself 'Captain Right'. The rebels supported the Catholic claims and among their followers were the associates of Lord Louth with whom the Duke had stayed at Bermingham House. St. George maintained that the resolutions on which the 'Right Boys', as they called themselves, based their rising, had been drafted at Dangan and that Dick Martin had been one of the many who had tried to prevent his bringing the culprits to justice. His action in pressing the case had earned him permanent unpopularity among the Catholics of Galway and he dubbed the Martins who supported them 'Jacobites and Papists'. His animosity was now to have a fresh outlet.

The Martins' financial situation was now extremely embarrassed. Furthermore, all the time, energy and even money Dick Martin had put into his mining projects had produced nothing but disaster. He had been misled by those who were to exploit the mines. Meanwhile his debts had reached a point at which he considered it judicious to live as far as possible from the arm of the law.

He withdrew to Ballinahinch in the heart of the Martins' Connemara estate, a wild and beautiful tract of land lying to the north-west of Galway, cut off from the rest of Ireland by the twenty thousand acres of Lough Corrib on the east and bounded on the west by eighty miles of indented Atlantic coastline. Galway, the nearest town, was fifty miles away, and once it was left behind there was no road. A wag who once said of Dick Martin's stronghold that there had been only one house in the village, and it had been burnt down in a row, was probably exaggerating; it is unlikely there was ever anything resembling a village nearer than Oughterard, thirty miles away. It had grown up on the spot where Nimble Dick had established his manor of Clare and where Robert Martin had built the charming little classical house, Clareville. Behind it a track wound along the lower slopes of the mountains in order to avoid the bogs, and this was the only access by land to Ballinahinch. It took as good a horseman as Martin to negotiate it without mishap.

This was a setting fit to nourish the myths which always tended to surround him, and Maria Edgeworth whose work inspired Walter Scott's 'Waverley' novels, was to write: 'Smugglers and caves, murders and mermaids, and duels and banshees, and faeries, were all mingled together in my early association with Connemara and Dick Martin. . . . *Too, besides*, I once saw him, and I remember that my blood crept slow and my breath was held when he first came into the room. . . .'

Some aspects of the writer's fantasy were not far from the truth. Martin was ensconced in the house which his father claimed he had built at Ballinahinch as an inn, but it is hard to imagine what wayfarers could possibly pass that way. It is much more likely that the house was intended to be a base for the 'smuggling business', as it was openly called. All the gentry either participated in it, or connived at it, and it formed the main livelihood of the peasantry.

The house is remarkably finely situated. It stands by a little torrent running into Ballinahinch Lake which is dominated by a conical, quartz-studded mountain, Ben Lettery, one of the great range of the Twelve Pins which rise steeply above a chain of lakes and saffron-coloured bogs which the heather turns purple.

It was fashionable in those days to call every gentleman's residence a castle, even if it only comprised a plain farmhouse and yard. Ballinahinch Castle was such a house at the time, named after a small sixteenth-century castle which Donal of the Combats O'Flaherty had built on an artificial island in the lake. According to local tradition, it brought him bad luck because he had built it with the stones from a friary his ancestors had founded at nearby Toombeola, and it played its part in history. Grace O'Malley, a famous pirate chieftainess who was a thorn in Queen Elizabeth's side, married Donal of the Combats, and Bingham, the English Governor of Connaught, kidnapped their son from the little island castle. In Dick Martin's day it was destined to play a more important role.

'Connemara,' Mansergh St. George reported to the Government, 'is the asylum of outlaws, deserters and persons escaped from justice, the stronghold of smugglers etc. . . . There are at least 2,000 stand of arms dispersed in cabins and two battalions of deserters. Mr. Rich. Martin resides there and conciliates the garrison of Ouchterarde . . . by presents of liquor and provisions.' Into the bargain, he claimed, Martin had borrowed large sums of money from a man called O'Mealey, who was the acknowledged head of the whole smuggling business in the district. He lived in a state of permanent defence in a tiny peninsula between Great Man's Bay and Costello Bay, on Martin's estate, and ingratiated himself with the local people by dispensing lavish hospitality. On holidays he handed out casks of wine and kept open house.

Martin's habit of collecting lame ducks also did not recommend him to the magistrate. The porter at the lodge at Dangan, who had a pearl on his eye, was reputed to have deserted from several regiments. One of Martin's close associates in Galway was a merchant, Patrick Curly, who had been a servant at Dangan, and had been set up in business by Martin. According to St. George, he indulged in very shady monetary transactions, and had traded to Guernsey since the outbreak of war, slipping through both the French and British fleets. And at Ballinahinch Martin had a tenant whom he employed as a driver, and whom St. George claimed had been guilty of capital crimes.

Early in 1794, St. George decided that the time had come to break through Martin's defences; he despatched a process server into the wilderness to serve a Chancery Order on Martin. Having been on intimate terms with him for years before the 'Right Boys' affair, St. George should have known that things would not follow an orthodox pattern; in fact his action gave rise to a minor war.

St. George claimed that Martin wounded his constable, Car, in the foot with a sharp instrument concealed in a stick, and when a couple of days later Martin interrupted St. George in the court house in Galway while he was performing his duties as a magistrate, St. George was unwise enough to have him arrested and imprisoned. He quickly realized, in view of Martin's popularity, how imprudent this was, and, fearing a riot in Galway and an insurrection among the peasantry of Connemara as a result, he sent for a detachment of dragoons to preserve order.

But when they arrived at Dangan, where the constable, Car, was recuperating, pending St. George's receiving instructions from the Government on how to proceed, they were insolent and insubordinate, according to St. George, and some plotted to poison him, a fate he only escaped through fleeing to Galway, stripping as he went. The fact that St. George was in the habit of taking from four to six teaspoons of laudanum in twenty-four hours over a period of a fortnight or longer in order, as he himself confessed, 'to appease painful remembrances', may have lent some colour to his story. But it should certainly have warned him to think twice about despatching a process server into the Connemara wilds again.

Martin's creditors were many and varied, and his reputation as a duellist helped him to deal very satisfactorily with the unpleasant subject on one occasion. He owed money to Eustace Stowell who refused to accept the security Martin offered, and rashly asked for cash or personal satisfaction. Martin replied that 'though Solomon was a wise man and Samson a strong one, neither of them could pay ready money if they had it not'.

A duel was consequently arranged, but when Stowell found himself facing so renowned an antagonist at a distance of eight yards from muzzle to muzzle he took fright. Dropping his weapon he cried: 'Mr. Martin! Mr. Martin! a pretty sort of *payment* this! You'd shoot me for my interest money, would you?'

'If it's your *pleasure*, Mr. Eustace Stowell,' Martin replied, 'I certainly will; but it was not my desire to come here, or to shoot you. You insisted on it yourself, so go on, if you please, now we are here.'

But Stowell, no doubt wisely, thought better of the matter. He agreed to accept the security Martin had offered, principals and seconds stepped into the same carriage, all returned the best of friends, 'and I never heard any thing irritating about his interest money afterward', Martin told his friend, Barrington.

Yet, hard pressed as he often was himself for money and

regardless of the claims of his creditors, Martin never forgot his tenantry. No widow was ever asked for rent, he regularly paid out £800 a year in pensions to the widows and orphans on his estates, and evictions were unknown there.

Chapter Nine

ROBERT MARTIN died at Dangan on 7 August 1794 in his eightieth year, and Richard Martin came into a property which covered over a third of Galway, Ireland's second largest county. He was now forty, and his new estate, which was entailed, was encumbered with a debt of between £20,000 and £30,000.

There were good lands east of Lough Corrib, in Counties Mayo and Roscommon, and in east Galway near the Shannon. Between them they brought in about £3,800 a year. By far the largest part of the estate, however, was made up of the 200,000 acres of mountain, bog and water in Connemara. It extended over sixty miles and included countless islands, twenty good harbours and some twenty-five navigable lakes. There was a steady revenue from the excellent salmon fisheries, the best being in the river running from Ballinahinch to Roundstone, and from the proceeds of the oyster beds. In all the Connemara estate was bringing in around £10,000 a year, although this only represented a few pence per acre.

Arthur Young, the English agriculturalist, who had visited Ireland in 1779, had estimated that an average investment of £5 per acre would have been necessary to bring Irish land up to the standard of the English, but even had Martin had such a sum at his disposal, it would have been only a drop in the ocean in the wilderness of Connemara. Apart from the large area occupied by bog which the people cut to supply turf for fuel, it was principally a sheep-rearing area, although good corn could be grown in the small valleys. It was not unusual for a tenant to have nothing but a potato garden. The rent for this might be as low as half-a-crown a year, and as often as not that might end by being paid in kind. A present to the big house of a few score of eggs or a few pairs of fowl could settle everything. It was customary for part of the rent to be paid in labour, and people such as the Martins were used to having a large retinue of servants, a great many of whom were working off their rent. There were at the same time many other accommodations between landlord and tenant, and the landlord frequently paid for labour with what was termed a 'convenience'; he would give pasturage for a cow or a sty for a pig instead of paying for services. The Martins were traditionally good landlords, and when Dick Martin took over his father's estates, he was no stranger to his tenants. He had been on the closest terms with them since childhood, and, of course, with them he spoke Irish.

But when he came into the property he inherited something else as well, namely William III's patent to his great-grandfather, Nimble Dick. This entitled him to hold a court which would impose the law of the manor. In one respect that law was to prove unique, so that 7 August 1794 was not just the day upon which he inherited the largest property in fee simple in the British Isles; it was also a turning point in the social history of the world. But time was necessary for the full impact of Martin's law to be felt.

It happened that rabies was a greatly dreaded disease at the time. Every dog was suspect, especially in the summer months when the malady was most prevalent, and the peasantry made a habit of chasing dogs to death in the warm period of the year. The procedure was monstrous to a man who had risked his life duelling with the redoubtable Fighting Fitzgerald over a dog.

In general animals got scant notice among Martin's tenantry. The barbarous habit of making horses draw ploughs with their tails had more or less died out, but it was common to see oxen driven with a yoke and bow chafing so badly at the neck that the poor beasts walked with their heads almost on their knees in an attempt to avoid pain. Mercilessly beating and starving animals of all kinds was usual among people who themselves had little beyond what was necessary for subsistence, and there was no indulgence for sick animals.

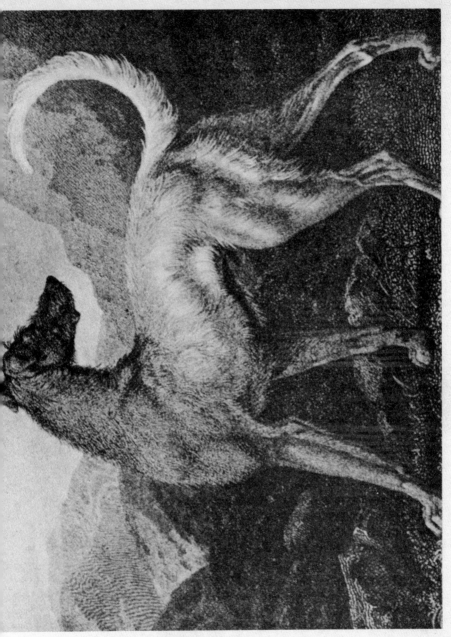

An Irish wolfhound
such as the Prime
Serjeant over whom
Martin fought a
duel with Fighting
FitzGerald

Fighting FitzGerald in the clothes in which he chose to be executed.
Published by J. Ridgeway, London, 1786

Ballinahinch Lake with the house on the extreme right. Drawn for Maria Edgeworth by Mr. Smith during their visit there in 1835

'Dick Martin's Prison' in Ballinahinch Lake where he detained those who were cruel to animals on his estates before there was an act to prevent such abuses

A Galway election as seen by 'Phiz', illustrating Charles Lever's
Charles O'Malley in which Uncle Godfrey, the Member for Galway, is
supposed to be Humanity Dick

Martin's whole nature reacted against these spectacles. His mother in his childhood and Dr. Parr in his adolescence had taught him that cruelty to an animal was often only the fore-runner of cruelty to a human being, and he now set his face against all such abuses. His tenants soon began to realize that their every step was being watched. Furthermore, if they were brought to court and it turned out, as was often the case, that they were too poor to pay the fine, Martin did not hesitate to turn to another form of punishment. Having acted as magistrate in bringing the culprit to justice, and as judge in condemning him, he would then proceed to act as gaoler and, taking up the oars himself, row the offender out into the middle of Ballina-hinch Lake. There he would deposit him in the little O'Flaherty castle on the island for a few days' contemplation which might convince him of the error of his ways.

The simple people involved in these strange proceedings in a remote corner of a small country had no idea that they were participating in something which was destined to develop into a world movement. They only knew that they had acquired a new and rather eccentric master. Had there been anything weak or effeminate about him, they would probably have scoffed at him behind his back, but he had 'blazed' his way through life and was known to be a lion in any contest, physical or verbal. This put a very different complexion on his admonitions. He was said to have replied to somebody who, commenting on his duelling career, asked why he cared so much for the lives of animals and so little for the lives of human beings: 'Sir, an ox cannot hold a pistol!' His immense territory and the absolute power he wielded gradually earned him the name of 'King of Connemara', and the countryman who declared that he was 'the best Martin that ever reigned' was only expressing the general feeling. As for the little island castle, it was to go down in history as 'Dick Martin's prison'.

While Martin was getting his innovations under way in Connemara, changes were taking place in England which were to have far-reaching consequences for him and Ireland. Differing attitudes towards the French Revolution had caused a split in the Whig party. As a result, the Conservative Whigs had joined in a coalition with Pitt's Tory Government.

A series of events immediately raised the Irish Catholics'

hopes. The Whigs had always been supposed to favour their cause. Then the Duke of Portland, who when Viceroy had supported them, became Home Secretary and, thereby, responsible for the government of Ireland. It was rumoured, and then confirmed, that another sympathizer, Lord Fitzwilliam, was to become Viceroy, and when he held consultations in London with Grattan and Ponsonby, both of whom stood for reform and emancipation, confidence was raised to the highest pitch. What nobody knew was that from the very outset there had been grave misunderstandings as to how independent a role the Whigs might play in the Government, and these now increased and transferred themselves to Irish affairs.

When Fitzwilliam left for Ireland at the beginning of 1795, he was instructed not to bring up the question of Catholic emancipation as a Government measure. Pitt, in fact, wanted it to be shelved until peace should be re-established, and then to be used as an argument in favour of the legislative union of Ireland with England which he regarded as the ultimate solution to all Irish problems. By it the Catholics would be transformed from a majority into a minority, the only terms upon which their emancipation could be granted without endangering the Protestant establishment in Church and State.

But by the time Fitzwilliam arrived in Ireland, the Catholic question had already been in agitation for several months and emancipation was regarded as a certainty, not only by the Catholics themselves, but even by the Protestants. Fitzwilliam had been instructed that if the matter was pressed so that he could not avoid it, he was to accept and support it. This he now proceeded to do, warning the English Government of the dire results of not now granting *'cheerfully'* what the Catholics asked. In the atmosphere that prevailed, refusal would mean losing the Catholics' confidence and giving rise to a Protestant cabal.

Meanwhile, he started to dismantle the junta which, under the leadership of Fitzgibbon, really ruled Ireland, resisting both the Government and the rest of the Irish parliament, and putting obstacles in the way of all progress. He asked for the resignation of Beresford, a member of Lord Tyrone's family and head of the Treasury and Revenue, whose relations, Fitzwilliam claimed, enjoyed 'more emoluments than ever was accumulated in any country upon any one family'. Fitzwilliam could not see his way to sharing the government with a man who had been responsible for the appointment of the Chancellor, the Chief Justice, the Attorney-General, the Commander-in-Chief, and almost the Primate, and he proceeded in a similar manner with the Attorney-General and the Solicitor-General.

When Grattan asked for leave to introduce a Catholic Relief Bill, the Viceroy assented, and soon support was coming in from far and wide, not only from Catholics, but from Protestants, including the Corporation of Derry. The old bigotry which had enslaved Ireland for so long appeared to have died, and the whole country was poised awaiting the final justice which would entitle the Catholic gentry to take their seats in their own parliament and thereby enter into the full enjoyment of their constitutional rights.

But the members of the junta were busy behind the scenes; they were not ready to let go their grip so easily. Beresford got to work on Pitt, who was not prepared under any circumstances to see such a friend sacrificed. Fitzgibbon went to work on the King, who had gone temporarily mad a few years before, and managed to persuade him that to allow the Catholics to sit in parliament would be contrary to his coronation oath, an idea which was to remain permanently rooted as a conviction in the deranged royal mind.

Then, when Catholic hopes were at their highest, Fitzwilliam, after only six weeks in office, was peremptorily recalled. The news caused a storm, and was interpreted as a rebuff to the Catholic aspirations. The new Catholic Relief Bill had not yet been introduced, and, in the universal consternation, the fear prevailed that it would not now be brought forward at all. Fitzwilliam himself attributed his recall to his dismissal of Beresford, but he knew that the general opinion was that it was due to his handling of the Catholic question; he was uncompromising as to the consequences of now withholding emancipation. 'The most serious calamities may arise to both nations,' he wrote to Carlisle. 'The prospect of having this plan defeated may and will plunge you and every well-wisher to his country in that affliction and consternation in which you say you are lost.'

After almost a month of wrangling, accusation and self-justification, Fitzwilliam finally left Ireland on 25 March 1795, before his successor had been appointed. 'Everything was perfectly quiet,' Fitzgibbon wrote to the former Viceroy, Westmoreland. 'Not even a hiss from the mob in the streets addressed to any of the men who followed him. At the college a set of fellows who had been planted there, took his horses from his coach and drew him from thence to the Pidgeon House, much to the annoyance of Lady Fitzwilliam who, I was told, got into histericks. After he had got into the boat which conveyed him to the yacht, he waved his hat and bowed most graciously to the ponies who had given him a set down to the Pidgeon House. And so the ceremony ended.'

Fitzgibbon could scarcely have imagined that Westmoreland would not hear the truth. All the houses along the route that the viceregal procession had followed were shuttered. The doors were hung with black crape, and Dublin and Belfast went into mourning for the man who, after centuries of strife, had so nearly brought peace. The ceremony might have ended, as Fitzgibbon said, but it had its aftermath. The arrival of the new Viceroy, Lord Camden, gave rise to widespread disorders in Dublin where the mob attacked Fitzgibbon, surrounded Beresford's house, and prevented all illuminations.

The Fitzwilliam episode brought about the polarization of opinion which the Viceroy had forecast, and from which Ireland was not to recover for centuries. The United Irishmen turned from constitutional to revolutionary methods, clashes between Catholic and Protestant factions became common, particularly in the North, and there the Orange Order was founded 'to maintain the laws and peace of the country and the Protestant Constitution', but it, too, contained the seed of sedition: it undertook 'to defend the King and his heirs as long as they shall maintain the Protestant ascendancy'.

Martin knew full well what good would have flowed from Fitzwilliam's policy, but he did not know yet the harm that would follow Camden's. He was prepared to serve once again as High Sheriff, and Trench, the independent member for County Galway, had written to the Lord Lieutenant recommending him; but Trench's letter had been superseded by one from Lord Clanricarde, a large western landowner, recommending a Mr. Burke, and, much to Trench's indignation, Martin was not appointed.

He had left Dangan to his stepmother and her two sons, and settled himself into Ballinahinch, an isolated place in which to bring up three children aged eleven, ten and eight. Whatever satisfaction his wife, Elizabeth, had derived from her relationship with Petrie, it had not lasted long. She had died, and Martin was free to think of remarrying. Once again he found a young woman of exceptional talent. The daughter of Hugh Evans, the senior surgeon of the 5th Dragoon Guards, and the widow of an English naval officer, Robert Hesketh, who had died the preceding year, the young lady, whose name was Harriet, had caused something of a stir by publishing a book called *Historic Tales*. An eminent Irish historian who was impressed with the work, decided to call on the author, and found himself with some astonishment in the presence of a girl of only seventeen.

Harriet was now twenty-seven and living at the family home in Cashel, County Tipperary. And there, on 5 June 1796, she married widower Dick Martin, fifteen years her senior. Few places could stand in greater contrast to her future residence than Cashel. In the place of bogs and lakes there was the rich pastureland of the Golden Vein which rolls away into the blue ridge of the Galtee mountains. In the place of the deserted wilds there was a small town clustered at the foot of a little acropolis surmounted by a fourteenth-century Gothic cathedral and a minute twelfth-century Hiberno-romanesque chapel. In the place of rugged peaks there were the remains of a glorious cultural past.

Before she had been settled many months in her new home in Connemara, Harriet was to have her first taste of what it was going to be like to be married to a man of benevolent temperament. Towards the close of the year 1796 violent anti-Catholic persecutions broke out in the North. Catholic houses were visited by night and the occupants ordered to leave immediately. Those returning to their empty abodes found notices telling them to go 'to Hell or Connaught'. Much of the violence was committed by lawless banditti rather than people fired with religious fervour or animosity, but the magistrates were so slack in dealing with the disorders that the situation soon became a scandal.

Those who fled because they had been turned out had only time to grab a few objects before taking to the road, and they were joined soon by those who had sold their properties and departed out of fear. They made for the region where they were most likely to meet with sympathy, namely the predominantly Catholic west, but there the Protestant and Catholic gentry were equally diligent in succouring them.

Dick Martin threw open his vast estate, and Harriet's introduction to his way of life consisted in dealing with a flood of refugees. It was mid-winter; food, clothing and shelter had to be provided in an outpost where provisions for the big house itself were often a problem. As for Martin, there was a fatherliness in his make-up which made him incapable of leaving the fugitives to work out their own destiny. He had to delve into all their problems, share all their misgivings and stimulate their hopes. He could not help making their predicament his own, and he ended by settling them free of rent for a number of years. They could build themselves houses and till the land, and in due course, when they were well established, he would require them to pay a nominal rent.

In the meantime, the young man who had worshipped at the first Mrs. Martin's shrine, the comic actor who had such difficulty pronouncing his 'Rs', was carving out a new career for himself far from the stage, which he had loved, and the bar, where he had practised. Influential friends had intervened to prevent Wolfe Tone being indicted when his treasonable dealings with the French agent, Jackson, were revealed at Jackson's trial; but he had been obliged to leave the country. After a brief stay in America, he had gone to France where he had now been living for almost a year under the name of James Smith.

He played a leading part in aiding the French to formulate plans for an invasion of Ireland, an event which he assured them would be greeted by a general uprising of the Irish under the United Irishmen. He advised the French to make their main landing in the vicinity of Belfast, the centre of the United Irish movement, and to make a second in Galway Bay with the objective of reaching the Shannon, demolishing its bridges and thereby controlling the whole country west of the river which, he claimed, was also the most discontented.

Various emissaries were sent to Ireland during the year to report on conditions and to make contact with the disaffected.

Invasion plans were suspended for a while during the time that Lord Malmesbury was in Paris trying to negotiate a peace between Britain and France. When in November his efforts failed, the plans were completed. Contrary to Tone's advice, the landing was to take place in the south. An expedition of 15,000 men was launched under General Hoche in mid-December, and on the Chief-of-Staff's ship, as an Adjutant-General of the French army, was Theobald Wolfe Tone.

When the expedition hove into sight off Bantry Bay in the south of Ireland on 20 December and the alarm was raised, there was a garrison of only 8,000 men in Cork. There was virtually no obstacle to a French force of twice the size marching the thirty-five miles to seize the second city in Ireland. But on 22 December a fierce easterly gale got up, and blew straight across the French fleet's path. It was accompanied by snow and continued to blow for six days, during which time the British fleet had hoisted sail and was hastening to rescue the situation. The French fleet was buffetted mercilessly in the bay, then was driven out, and finally was dispersed.

The danger which every British statesman had dreaded for generations had been averted, but not before the Irish people had presented the Government with a surprise. The general uprising which Tone had foretold had not taken place; on the contrary, the people had shown the most uncompromising loyalty.

The peasantry in the threatened areas had driven their stocks inland in order to deprive the invader of supplies and hastened to uphold all moves to check an advance. The Volunteers had been abolished a few years previously, but there were now yeomanry corps on foot throughout the country, and officers such as Martin, who was captain of the Ballinahinch yeomanry, rushed around in a ferment of activity, backing up the army. The Galway yeomanry announced that they were ready to fight anywhere, and that city, as well as Limerick and Cork, declared unswerving devotion to the Crown and the Government. Belfast alone of the major cities failed to express any sentiments of attachment.

The Martins' domestic happiness was increased by the arrival of a son on 25 March 1797. He was given the good Martin name of Richard, and to Harriet he was an addition to the family rather than the beginning of one; she had made Elizabeth's three children entirely her own. But these pre-occupations as well as the welfare of the refugees' families and those of the tenants did not entirely prevent her continuing to write. She was at work on a large novel which was growing into several volumes and to which the remoteness of life at Ballinahinch may well have contributed.

There later in the year the Martins were visited by a young French nobleman called De Latocnaye who was doing a walking tour of Ireland and who planned to write an account of what he saw. He was impressed with the Galway women's beauty, and with the gaiety which the ancient bye-laws had singularly failed to suppress. Outside the village of Oughterard, he was aston-ished at the sophistication and generally civilized air of Lemon-field, the seat of Sir John O'Flaherty, one of the ancient clan whose ancestors had managed to retain some property by the usual expedient of taking out a Protestant certificate. But when, greatly daring, he had decided to rough it and penetrate the depths of Connemara, there was something of a surprise in store for him. After Lemonfield, everything at Ballinahinch seemed rather haphazard.

'I have never in my life,' he wrote later, 'been in the house of a rich man who appeared to care so little for the things of this world as Colonel Martin. He is a man of the best intentions, and thinks of nothing more than how to improve the country which belongs to him. Unfortunately, some adventurers have abused his confidence, and have swindled him out of considerable sums under the pretext of finding mines on his estates, or of clearing land for cultivation. The kind of clearing done was clearing out, after they got the money. . . . The fortune of any private individual could not possibly suffice to people or cultivate a territory as large as Connemara.'

Despite the ramshackle state of the house, the young man stayed on for a few days to enjoy the Martins' almost proverbial hospitality. He also had an experience which proved that all Mansergh St. George's allegations about the lawless life at the big house were not true.

A vessel was wrecked on the lands of a neighbouring pro-prietor, and the local people, knowing that he was absent, boarded the boat and proceeded to pillage the cargo. The captain had heard of Dick Martin and his standing in the county, and immediately sent for his help. Martin promptly despatched one of his yeomen with a supply of arms, and the thieves were soon scattered and order restored.

The Irish parliament was dissolved in July 1797 and preparations started for the first elections in which the thousands of new freeholders who had obtained the franchise by the Catholic Relief Act of 1792 would vote. Martin decided to stand once more for Galway and to urge once more the parliamentary reform and Catholic emancipation which the last parliament had refused—a refusal which had resulted in Grattan, Ponsonby and a few of their followers withdrawing from parliament. The thousands of fresh tenants or freeholders he was able to bring to the hustings did not, however, assure Martin's success. St. George Daly and Martin's former friend, and later enemy, George Ponsonby were elected for Galway.

The country in which the sixth parliament of George III was elected was in a state of unparalleled tension. A further French invasion threat, this time launched from Holland, had been defeated by the British navy, but did nothing to diminish the chronic fears of a landing. The entire country, but particularly the North, was known to be ready for rebellion. The United Irishmen had spread the news among the peasantry that the French would abolish the detested tithes and that rents would be slashed, and these eventualities were talked of openly and hopefully.

Camden had been carrying out the disarming of Ulster with ruthless severity. The soldiery had been instructed to act without recourse to the civil authority, and the result was a succession of atrocities. Government steps to hush these up and prevent an enquiry only added to the general spirit of rebellion, while outrages committed mutually by the opposing religious factions continued.

One of those who suffered was Luke Teeling, the Lisburn linen manufacturer whose speech to the Catholic Convention in 1791 had established decisively the road the Catholics were to follow from then onwards. It was a friend who set in motion the chain of events which was to end in the persecution of an entire family. Lord Castlereagh, the cold, clever son of a big northern Irish land owner who had played a prominent part in the Volunteers, was a neighbour and intimate with the Teelings. But treachery came easily to him, and he personally arrested their eighteen-year-old son, Charles, and had him imprisoned for almost two years without trial on charges of sedition. A younger boy was arrested and marched seventeen miles in fetters to be confined in the vicinity of a furnace where leaden bullets were being cast, treatment which so undermined his health that he never recovered.

At a time when outrages in Belfast were widespread, Teeling's property in Lisburn was attacked and in a matter of a few hours was laid entirely waste. Mrs. Teeling was amazed at the tendency to play down the significance of what was happening, and wrote to her husband: 'Is it not surprising that not one of the Dublin papers mentions a word of the disturbances that happened there, but on the contrary say that the King's birthday was celebrated with the greatest peace and loyalty.'

As for themselves, after giving instructions about a few possessions it might still be possible to salvage from Lisburn, she wondered where they could go, and assured her husband that the smallest cabin would be better than a palace, so long as they were not separated.

Teeling knew of the magnanimity for which Dick Martin was renowned and his attitude towards the Catholics. He also knew of the immensity of the Martin estates and how well the earlier refugees had fared. Determined to seek an establishment for himself and his family and friends in a less bigoted part of the country, he got into touch with Martin. A correspondence followed which filled him with hope, and at the end of 1797 he set off for the wilds of Connemara to make arrangements with Dick Martin for starting a new life.

Chapter Ten

AFTER AN absence of fourteen years from parliament and despite his defeat in the election, Richard Martin was able to take his seat there once again on 9 January 1798. John La Touche, a member of the leading banking family, who had been returned for the freeman borough of Lanesborough, had opted to sit for Kildare, and he thereby vacated a seat for Martin to occupy.

Due to the Catholics now having the vote, the new House of Commons was the most representative Ireland had yet seen, but it was still a long way from expressing the mind of the majority of the people. The entire country was in a ferment, but the House preferred to ignore the fact. The repressive measures whereby Ulster had been subdued were being applied to the rest of Ireland. Floggings, torture and the shooting of men were daily occurrences, and the army, which was forcibly billeted upon the people at their expense, burned down whole villages on the suspicion of their harbouring a few rebels.

The misdemeanours of the soldiery were so notorious that Abercrombie, the Commander-in-Chief, had to issue general orders calling for discipline. The wording, which referred to the army as being 'in a state of licentiousness which must render it formidable to everyone but the enemy', immediately called forth a storm of protest in high places and led to Abercrombie's resignation. But it gave deep satisfaction to Martin and many others who could see in what direction things were moving.

In the face of all this it was remarkable that the House had time to debate such relatively innocuous things as the Press Bill.

In his speech Martin stoutly defended the printer and publisher of a paper against liability for any supposed libel the paper might carry. He argued that it would be contrary to the laws of evidence to make them responsible. But after almost two months of shutting its eyes to reality, the House was suddenly awakened.

The speaker responsible was Sir Laurence Parsons, the future Earl of Rosse. He shared many of the ideas of the United Irishmen, and had exercised some influence over Tone. He was one of the small minority in the Irish parliament who wanted its independence preserved so that the benefits of the Constitution might be extended to all the Irish people instead of, as with many others, looking to the independent legislature as a means of preserving Protestant oligarchy.

He now rose to chide the House for its silence on 'the alarming discontents of the people' which he attributed to the coercion to which the country had been subjected ever since the recall of Fitzwilliam. 'The instant that those who are in authority show a contempt for the law,' he declared, 'the people will imitate them. . . . Outrage will be retaliated with outrage, and force become the only arbiter between man and man.' He knew that there were those who saw the alternative as a compromise with rebels, but this was exactly the argument which had been used in the case of America. Then coercion had lost England the colonies while conciliation had preserved Ireland for her. He called for those in power to make way for others who would grant parliamentary reform and Catholic emancipation, and moved for a committee of enquiry into the country's wrongs.

The debate which followed revealed how many had been alive to the situation despite the inertia of the House. As the day wore on, member after member rose to speak, and Martin supported Parsons's motion. It was not until five in the morning that the discussion ended. In a division the motion was lost, Martin being one of the nineteen ayes to 156 noes. But the debate left its mark. The House could not return to its passivity nor those who spoke dissemble their sympathies.

The following week a new phase in events began. An informer, one of the *dramatis personae* of every rebellion, had been tempted. Named Reynolds, and something of a social climber, he was married to a sister of Wolfe Tone's wife. He had rented Kilkea Castle in County Kildare from the Fitzgeralds, and found himself in need of money to pursue his object of becoming a country gentleman. He was colonel of a regiment of United Irishmen and treasurer for County Kildare; as such he was in the know about the rebels' affairs.

While travelling to Dublin in the company of a merchant called Cope, Reynolds had begun to divulge information; he had been persuaded to continue doing so for the benefit of the Castle. When the Leinster Committee of the United Irishmen arranged to meet at the house of the national treasurer, Oliver Bond, in Dublin on 12 March, the Castle was already fully informed and the Government had conferred on the Lord Lieutenant the special powers for which he had asked. The entire Leinster Committee was arrested, including four members of the Irish Directory: Thomas Addis Emmet, M'Neven, Arthur O'Connor and Bond himself.

The rebellion had been planned to wait upon French aid, a necessity Tone had been driving home to the French Directory ever since he reached France. Now it seemed important to act before the whole United Irishmen's organization was itself wiped out. Talk of a rising was general, but what was involved was no revolt of the lower orders. The leaders were almost to a man members of the Anglo-Irish Protestant Ascendancy and the most respectable in the land were caught up in it. The Duke of Leinster's brother, Lord Edward Fitzgerald, was Commander-in-Chief, and it was he who had given Reynolds his commission and handed over to him as treasurer for County Kildare. And it was Fitzgerald's wife, Pamela, who as a girl had danced a quadrille in front of the Palais Royal in celebration of the taking of the Bastille, who actually transferred the funds to the budding informer.

Nobody was above suspicion. Sir Jonah Barrington, a member of parliament, found himself dining a few weeks after these events in County Wexford at the Colclough's, who were among the descendants of the famous Archbishop Vesey's progeny and thus connections of Martin's by his first marriage; one of them was a member of parliament. The following night Barrington dined with some of the same company at Bargay Castle, the residence of his old school friend, a large landowner named

Bagenal Harvey. The company was select, the bottle circulated freely, and inevitably the conversation turned to the themes on which the House of Commons had been so long silent. To his horror, Sir Jonah found himself in the midst of 'absolute though unavowed conspirators', and the next morning he wrote to the Castle that insurrection would break out at any moment.

At the Castle a change was in process which was to have a profound influence on the course of Irish affairs. Pelham, the Chief Secretary, was seriously ill, and Camden asked to be allowed to appoint Viscount Castlereagh temporarily in his place. He was aware that it could be objected that Castlereagh was unsuitable because he was an Irishman, but he pleaded that other qualifications counterbalanced this. 'I have absolute confidence,' he wrote to the Government, 'that his being a native of Ireland will neither sway his judgement nor his conduct.' It was one of the few of Camden's opinions on Ireland which were to be proved true.

A raid on the Duke of Leinster's house a few weeks afterwards produced incriminating evidence against Lord Edward. When later he was arrested only a few yards from where the Lord Lieutenant was attending the theatre, the latter did not leave his box when the news was brought to him for fear of causing a stir. The arrest itself was to do that. The Fitzgerald family was immensely popular and this was final proof, if any were needed, that the rebellion cut right through society. When Lord Edward died a painful death from his wounds in prison, consternation was universal. Only Castlereagh rejoiced. 'His death,' he wrote to the Government, 'it is probable will be of more service than if he had lived to be tried: his partisans would have retained the hope of rescuing him.'

A couple of days after Lord Edward's arrest, Castlereagh informed the Mayor of Dublin that the United Irishmen planned to seize executive power that week. The city was proscribed, all householders were required to post a list of occupants on their front doors, and curfew began at 9 p.m.

On 24 May hostilities began, and as the rebellion got into full swing it was concentrated in County Wexford. The weather was hot. The rebels were armed largely with pikes, although Westmoreland claimed that gunpowder had been smuggled to them from London in beer casks with false bottoms. For several weeks the insurgents carried all before them, town after town falling to them. The Lord Lieutenant pleaded for reinforcements. The King wanted nothing short of total victory. Camden, while sharing the sentiment, did not feel equal to the task. He asked to be replaced by Cornwallis who was appointed to the dual office of Lord Lieutenant and Commander-in-Chief while a violent battle was raging at New Ross which the rebels, under the command of Barrington's old friend, Bagenal Harvey, had captured.

The French invasion, for which the rebels hoped and which Camden feared might be commanded by Buonaparte, had not taken place. In the preceding February he had been stationed with his huge army at Boulogne, ready to invade England at the beginning of April after the spring equinox. Opinions varied as to why that invasion did not take place, but when the Irish rebellion had broken out, Napoleon wrote to the French Directory: 'What more do you want from the Irish? As you can see, from this moment their insurrection constitutes a mighty diversion.' Not long after he embarked at Toulon, and as the tide of events in the rebellion turned and New Ross fell to the Government, the news arrived that he had taken Malta and was sailing on to an unknown destination.

The Irish had not been thinking of creating a diversion for the French, but of gaining their liberty from the English. But without either their appointed leaders or the backing of French arms their purpose grew confused, and with the arrival of English reinforcements, their case became hopeless. From the outset the Orange yeomanry, who constituted a large part of the army involved, had given the fight a religious content, and as a number of remarkable priests, despite the protestations of loyalty of their bishops, became insurgent leaders, the conflict rapidly degenerated into a religious war. This ended by alienating the sympathies of the liberal Presbyterians of Ulster. They had been the backbone of the United Ireland movement; now they began to veer away from it.

Atrocities and rumours of atrocities in both camps were followed by retaliation, and the rebels succeeded in killing Lord Mountjoy, previously Luke Gardiner, to whom they owed the first Catholic Relief Bill. However, by early July after some five weeks' fighting, the rising was virtually quelled. A new atmosphere, suspicious and vindictive, then crept into affairs, and denunciations were frequent. Charles Tottenham, the member for New Ross, wrote to the Castle that he had the fullest information implicating Colclough, and demanded that he and his associates should be brought into the town 'when I have no doubt they will soon meet the fate that all traitors deserve'.

Colclough was a nephew of Cornelius Grogan, a former member for Wexford, who was summarily tried and condemned to death. He was so infirm he had to be led to the place of execution. Colclough and Bagenal Harvey met with a similar fate. Their heads stood side by side for months on very low spikes over the court-house door in Wexford. Of the entire company with whom Barrington had dined at Bargay Castle less than three months before, only he and one other survived. As for Luke Teeling who had expected to start a new life on Martin's estates, he was instead a prisoner aboard the tender *Postlethwaite* in Belfast Lough.

Richard Martin was among those suspected of sympathizing with the rebellion. He was known to have approved of the principles, though not of the outrages, of the French Revolution. He had supported Abercrombie in his stand on the army's atrocities, and had backed up Parsons's request for a committee of enquiry. Now he was foremost in constantly pressing for mercy.

One of Cornwallis's first acts was to issue a proclamation promising pardon to all rebels who surrendered, with the exception of the ringleaders, and Martin declared in the House that he hoped for the fullest measure of amnesty. It was, in his view, what was best calculated to achieve what every humane man must wish. He could not understand a policy which would refuse amnesty to 600,000 subjects, even if they were rebels; for what was the alternative except extermination? Surely, if humanity did not reject that, policy should.

A couple of weeks later he rose to complain that advantage was being taken of people's ignorance by those in various parts of the country who were averse to amnesty. Many who had surrendered, and who had a certificate of allegiance and the written protection of the Government in their pockets, had nevertheless been arrested and sent to prison or confined aboard tenders. He moved for a list to be supplied to the House of all people apprehended in these circumstances.

Castlereagh immediately took issue with him. The motion, he said, was 'highly premature, impolitic and most mischievous in its tendency'. He claimed that some abuses were bound to creep in, and had Mr. Martin made known his objections in the right quarter instead of ill-advisedly raising the matter openly in the House, he would have had immediate satisfaction. The fact was that there were people who had been granted pardons but who then proceeded to commit further crimes. He asked if Mr. Martin held that a certificate of absolution for past offences was licence for future misconduct. Behaviour such as Mr. Martin's, he declared, could only instigate to further rebellion. But Martin was not to be intimidated. He leaped to his feet and proceeded to explain, talking against the Speaker who constantly called him to order. Nobody seconded his motion and it fell to the ground.

When a few days later Sir William Newcomen called for a complete list of all who had surrendered, Martin again protested, claiming that it would neither fulfil the purpose of amnesty nor promote tranquillity if men's names were put on record as erstwhile rebels. Such an action could only, as he put it, 'embitter the boon of mercy'.

But it was on the case of Cornelius Grogan that his sentiments became most apparent. He objected to the whole manner in which Grogan had been tried, condemned and executed, and consequently could not agree to the bill which attainted him. The debate turned on the terms of evidence in the case—the kind of legal point on which Martin was a stickler—and the discussion went on until 5.30 in the morning. When it came to the division on the attainder, Martin was one of only five noes to forty-two ayes.

Meanwhile, it turned out that the rebellion was not over after all. On 22 August, Dr. Stock, the Protestant Bishop of Killala in County Mayo, had a visitation from his pastors. After dinner in his castle, a messenger suddenly burst in and announced that the French had landed and an advance detachment was a mile from the town. Within hours those in the castle were prisoners and the drawing-room was a detention centre. The fear that had dominated British policy in Ireland for centuries had at last been realized.

It was harvest time when the news of the French landing

arrived, and numbers of people working in the fields in the fine weather abandoned their crops, jumped on their horses and rode off to join the French. The sons of some of the principal county families, including Martin's two Jordan cousins, put themselves at the head of small bands of countrymen carrying green branches as emblems and preceded by the fife and drums. Trees of liberty appeared in the market places of little towns, and forges began working night and day to make pikes.

However, as the French advanced they could not fail to notice that this was not the general uprising they had been led to expect. In fact, for every countryman who marched with them there were as many more who took to the bogs to hide. The gentry of Connaught were as divided as elsewhere in Ireland, though for a different reason. Most of them in the western province were Catholics who had only recently acquired the right to purchase the estates which now made them landed proprietors. They wanted the full Catholic emancipation and parliamentary reform for which the insurgents were fighting, but they did not want a revolution, and still less the France of Robespierre to dominate them. While the Jordans marched with the invaders, the vast majority of Catholics hung back, and Robert French of Monivea, a Protestant, fortified his house. Lord Kilmaine, who was on a fishing holiday with his family on Lough Mask, took a philosophical view, and merely noted in his diary: 'Report of French having landed in Killala confirmed. Fish all day—good sport. Kill one pike of ten pounds and 3 small ones.'

By a clever ruse, the insurgents routed the King's forces at Castlebar on the morning of 27 August. In a panic the loyalist soldiers turned and raced through the town, discarding all they carried as they ran. The battle came to be known as the 'Races of Castlebar'. By the afternoon the temperature was 68°F, and when all was over, the insurgent soldiers lay down in the streets to sleep. Humbert's plan was to make eventually for Roscommon across the Shannon, there to join up with the rebels from the North, but for this he was impatiently awaiting reinforcements from the expedition due to sail from Brest under Hardy. Meanwhile, his despatches to the Directory giving an account of his victory were carried, it was rumoured, by smugglers waiting in one of the small inlets on Martin's estates.

Humbert made a determined effort to preserve order. Contrary to Wexford, not a drop of blood was shed by the Connaught rebels except on the battlefield. Looting, however, was general. The countrywoman who, when an exquisite little foreign clock taken from Lord Lucan's house began to chime, dropped it and ran across the bog shouting, 'The Divle, the Divle!' was not exceptional. Balls and banquets were held in Castlebar, French gallantry was much admired, and a Republic of Connaught was declared with John Moore of Moore Hall as President.

Meanwhile, Lord Cornwallis was on his way down the canal from Dublin. As the temperature climbed into the seventies, and the revelry continued, he approached at the head of an army of 16,000 men to encamp at Hollymount, only fourteen miles away. Hardy's reinforcements had not arrived, and Cornwallis's proximity was the signal for the French to move. The weather broke and they marched away in torrential rain. Just as an accident had won them Castlebar, another now lost them the war. While resting at a place called Cloone, they told a guard not to let them sleep more than two hours, but he left them for four. They had only seven miles to go in order to reach Granard where they were to be joined by thousands of insurgents. Instead they were overtaken and, after a march totalling a hundred and ten miles, were routed at Ballinamuck.

Five hundred insurgents in French uniforms were massacred, infinitely more were killed in pursuit, and lots were often drawn to decide who was to be executed. The French were taken prisoner, and the English garrison at Longford gave a banquet in their honour before they were embarked on canal boats for Sallins in County Kildare. From there they were conveyed to the Mail Coach Hotel in Dawson Street, Dublin, where they were treated as soldiers and gentlemen.

The rebellion continued sporadically for a while, bringing its toll of pursuit and execution, and Captain Hedges of the West Kent Militia, stationed in Dublin, said he had never seen so many people in mourning. But for Humbert the war was over. He had gallantly insisted on accompanying his Irish aide-de-camp, Luke Teeling's son Bartholomew, to prison, but floating up to Dublin with Captain Pack, a friend of Captain Hedges, he confided in him that the majority of the rebels were 'the most beggarly, rascally, cowardly scoundrels' he ever knew.

He did not forget his French manners, either, and upon departure wrote to Cornwallis: 'Sir, Allow me to bid you farewell on leaving your kingdom. The way in which you have treated me, as well as the officers of my suite, will always be dear to my heart, and rest assured that I shall endeavour by every means to show my warmest appreciation. My government will be informed of your generous conduct and, sir, will assuredly feel as keenly as I do that they owe you their thanks.'

The appeals for mercy made by Cornwallis availed little while martial law prevailed, and when parliament was prorogued on 6 October, men like Richard Martin hurried home to meet an unending string of people appealing for his intercession on their behalf. The black stumps of heads, many of them those of yesterday's leading citizens, exposed on spikes, and bodies hanging from trees for the birds to peck formed part of the landscape for months, and spread gloom over the countryside. Captain Hedges wrote in his diary in October of that fateful year: 'I am the first militia officer that ever sat in a general court martial on life and death *and trust shall be the last*', adding a few days later the comment of a jailer whose gallows could only hang three at a time. 'I hate this dribble drabble work. I shall soon have my new gallows and I can then hang thirty at least at a time.'

Behind the desolation ordinary life continued. The harvest had been interrupted in the west, but at the great annual fair of Ballinasloe Robert French noted that there was a 'prodigious quantity of cattle'. But one more eruption was to come. When all seemed over for the second time, the French made one more bid for a footing in Ireland. On 12 October, Hardy's expeditionary force, six weeks too late to join up with Humbert's, was engaged in battle in Lough Swilly in County Donegal, and defeated. On the day that Robert French, quietly tending his Connaught estates, received the news, he was also able to note in his diary: 'Buonaparte has taken Cairo and conquered Egypt.' The future master of Europe may have congratulated himself that the Irish diversion had lasted so long.

While the Bishop of Killala was still ruminating over a bread-and-butter letter written to him by Humbert while waiting at Dover on the last lap of his journey homeward, one of the captured ships of the French expedition was about to yield up Theobald Wolfe Tone. He was brought in irons to Dublin for a court martial. Attired in French uniform, he wore a large hat trimmed with gold lace, a tricolour cockade, gold epaulettes, gold garters and short boots bound with gold lace.

He was thirty-five, and it was fifteen years since he had worshipped at the feet of Elizabeth Martin. Had she eloped with him instead of with Petrie, had Pitt listened to his entreaties to be allowed to conquer the Sandwich Islands for the British Empire, had he settled down in America where he had contemplated farming in Rhode Island, had he taken any one of the turnings which his short life had opened up to him since he had left Dangan, all would have been different.

Powerful friends began to pull strings to save him, but now at last the die was cast. He was condemned to death, and true to the undertaking which he had given to himself and communicated to his wife, he eluded the hangman's rope. He chose the part he had played so convincingly on the little Galway stage: he committed suicide. He slit his throat from ear to ear and perished before his enemies could save him to die the ignominious death of a traitor.

Chapter Eleven

MERCY WAS the word predominant in Dick Martin's mind throughout the rebellion. Generations in the west were to remember him as the saviour of some relative from death or deportation. He applied all his craft as a lawyer and all his generosity as a human being to assisting even the least worthy, while he knew that the mountains around his home, with their perpendicular inclines and countless caves, provided refuge for the hopeless.

The attitude of the western gentry as a whole was the despair of men like the Honourable Dennis Browne, Altamont's brother, nicknamed 'Dennis the Rope' for the zeal with which he brought rebels to justice. Judges had great difficulty in getting juries, he wrote to the Castle, from the fear the loyal felt for their lives and property, but also from the disaffection of many leading people. 'They cannot be persuaded,' he complained, 'that assisting the French is any crime; they say that robbers ought to suffer; but the moment that you speak to them of rebels, they begin to plead for them.'

One thing which must have impressed itself daily upon Dick Martin was that Wolfe Tone, his wife Elizabeth's erstwhile admirer, had represented a turning-point in Irish history. For the first time the Irish Catholic people, traditionally monarchist and habitually loyal, who had struggled consistently to be admitted to the full benefits of British institutions, had been led to think of separation and a republic. After Tone, Ireland was

116

never to be the same again, and now total integration was being considered as an antidote.

The idea of a union of the two legislatures had been bandied about for years. Benjamin Franklin had suggested it at the time of the American war. Petrie and Adam Smith had written of its advantages, and ever since the Irish parliament had obtained its nominal independence in 1783, the notion had been nagging at British statesmen, including Fox. It had been a cherished idea of Chatham's, as it was of his son's.

Pitt had raised the question with Grenville on 4 June 1789 while the rebels were carrying off one victory after another in Wexford. By this time it was intended that Cornwallis should be appointed to Ireland, and on 10 June, the King wrote to Pitt: 'Lord Cornwallis must clearly understand that no indulgence can be granted to the Catholics further than has been, I am afraid unavoidably, done in former sessions, and that he must by a steady conduct effect in future the union of that kingdom with this.'

On the day that Cornwallis was actually appointed, George III wrote once again to Pitt, declaring that the Lord Lieutenant 'must not lose the present moment of terror for frightening the supporters of the Castle into an Union with this country, and no further indulgencies must be granted to the Roman Catholics.'

With such explicit instructions from his Sovereign coinciding with the departure of Cornwallis for Ireland, it seems unlikely that Pitt failed, as has been suggested, to transmit them to the Lord Lieutenant. The latter, in fact, started very soon to test out the ground with such members of the junta as Lord Clare, formerly John Fitzgibbon and now Lord Chancellor, and Beresford, the head of the Revenue. Cornwallis's own feelings about the Catholics pointed to the folly of any arrangement which did not take them into consideration, and Pitt was known to have long cherished the hope of offering emancipation as a bait for achieving the Union. Yet Clare, who regarded the Union as the best means of defeating the Catholics' aspirations for good, was able to talk Pitt out of his plan.

As a precarious peace was established and the Lord Lieutenant tested out more and more people on the Union, it became evident that there were as many opinions on its merits and short-comings as there were people. Each interpreted the proposition according to his own particular needs. There were those like the Duke of Leinster who were against it from the start. There were others who were doubtful and needed time to consider it. There were Sir John Blacquiere, Mr. Hare, Lords Ely and Kenmare and many others who were prepared to support it provided they were advanced in the peerage. George Ogle supported it because, like Clare, he saw in it the ending of all Catholic hopes, but Richard Martin saw in it the exact opposite.

When the Lord Lieutenant asked him his opinion on the subject he had replied that if the Union were to bring about emancipation, he would give it his strongest support, and he pressed Cornwallis to give an assurance to that effect in parliament. To this, however, Cornwallis objected strongly on the grounds that many votes in favour of the Union would be lost if any formal pledge were given to the Catholics. He did, however, undertake to give emancipation his most strenuous support in the United parliament, and guaranteed that the cabinet would do the same. Satisfied with these assurances, Martin called on the Lord Lieutenant at the end of November 1798 in order to convey his intention of supporting and his readiness to convince others.

It was twenty-two years since Martin had first taken his seat in the Irish House of Commons. It had been one of the proudest days of his life, but he was too realistic not to admit his disappointment with the Assembly to which he belonged. He had been steadfast in his aims of parliamentary reform and Catholic emancipation, but the Irish parliament had resisted them obstinately.

There was nothing to suggest that anything had changed for the better, but, rather, the contrary. The rebellion had stirred up latent animosities and served to harden attitudes. Martin resisted the suggestion that it had been a Catholic rebellion. Almost all the leaders had been Protestants, but it was undeniable that its main aim had been the removal of the penalties under which the Catholics suffered. The failure of the rebellion and its identification with separatism could, in his view, only set back the Catholic cause if its future remained in the hands of Irishmen. In an impartial assembly far from the influence of Irish prejudices, they would have more chance of a fair hearing. If they succeeded, the Protestant establishment would be safeguarded since instead of being in a minority of one to five, the Protestants would be in an over-all majority in the two islands of fourteen to three. This was Pitt's argument, and Martin's principal reason for supporting the Union.

He had, however, another. The corruption of the Irish parliament was due largely to the great borough owners who had, as Martin put it, 'substantially become the government'. It was proposed that at the Union they should be bought out, and this would guarantee that the Irish representation at Westminster would be as equitable as was possible pending the admission of Catholics to parliament.

By the time the Commons reassembled on 22 January, and the question of the Union was first officially raised, Galway Corporation had already petitioned against it, while Cork, hoping for advantages as a seaport, had petitioned in favour. The debate on the address lasted twenty hours, and the obvious virtues of a resident parliament were extolled, in particular by those who had been in opposition. But Martin was quick to pounce on them. Had they not, he reminded them, abandoned that very parliament for its 'incorrigible wickedness and corruption'?

When Sir John Parnell, the Chancellor of the Exchequer, an honest and disinterested man, enumerated the many spheres in which the economy had progressed since the Constitution of 1782, Martin replied: 'Since that period wealth has been more generally diffused through Ireland, than any other country; the poor have grown rich and there has arisen amongst us an agricultural yeomanry. If a country, sir, that was poor, is increasing beyond example in its agriculture and its commerce and yet becomes hourly discontented and at last breaks out into open rebellion against all its constituted authorities, what is to be done? Will my honourable friend propose to desolate the land and deprive them of all those benefits? . . . For those discontents we must look for some cause, and that cause is faction— the mischievous trade and speculation of parliament. . . . ' As a realist, he called upon the Opposition to suggest an alternative to union, and received no reply either then or later. At the same time he conveyed something of the regret he felt at the turn of events in declaring: 'Some things which at first blush appear bad, not only cease to be so, but even become remedies when compared with greater disadvantages.' Then, glad as always to air his classical learning, he threw out a quotation from Ovid:

Hic fitus est Phaethon, currus auriga paterni,
*Quem si non tenuit, magnus tamen excidit ausis.**

Yet, the misdemeanours of the Irish parliament and the advantages of a union were not so obvious to all. Thirty-four out of fifty-one county members opposed the proposition. When it came to the division, 109 voted for Union and 111 against. The Government, despite the immense majority it could normally control, had been defeated.

A satirical tabloid, the *Anti-Union*, referred to the opening debate as a performance at the 'Royal Circus'. 'Much more entertainment was given than the play-bill announced. A provincial performer moved *Martini's* minuet across the stage with rather an ill grace; however, he possesses the necessary assurance for the theatre, but we recommend it to the manager to be more attentive to *costume* and not to dress his first figurantes in Cunnemara stockings.'

Martin would, no doubt, have been pleased at this backhanded tribute to his patriotism; the Galway Volunteers' first resolution had been to wear nothing but Irish manufactures. But he would have had mixed feelings about what followed a few days later. 'The Cunnemara poney that was rode in the *Martingale*, will run against time from the Circus to the *Custom House*, and back again to the *House of Lords*, carrying a feather. Play or pay.'

It was true that Castlereagh, who had now succeeded as Chief Secretary, had offered him a seat on the Revenue Board, which had its headquarters in the Custom House, as a reward for promoting the Union; but the reference to the House of Lords was so wide of the mark that at the end of his days, if he remembered it, he must have smiled. A man who twice refused a peerage was unlikely to have considered one in the murky atmosphere surrounding the Union negotiations.

At the end of February 1799, County Galway declared against the Union, although it was the most Catholic county and the hierarchy, as well as some Catholic leaders such as the Earl

---

* 'Here, Phaethon, lies: his father's car he tried—Though proved too weak, he greatly daring died.'

of Fingal, were in favour of it. Castlereagh got to work personally on Trench, one of the County Galway members who had opposed at the outset, but had begun to reconsider his position. The *Anti-Union* made play with his semi-conversion. It had become popular for each of the two camps to hold dinner parties, and the paper described Trench turning up at the unionists' dinner by mistake, and, after some grumbling, being allowed to dine with them at a side table. On such occasions it was usual, after the cloth had been removed, to conclude the evening with songs, and these the paper selected appropriately according to the singer. Finally they came to: 'Mr. M – – t – n, who was dressed in Cunnemara stockings, as usual, insisted upon singing "God Save the King", but tho' he had got the words accurately by rote, he could not get out of the tune of Erin go Bragh.'

The quip got Martin's mood to perfection, for although he looked to the Union to bring about the great measure to which he was most committed, few could be sadder than he that it could not have been realized by the nation's own parliament.

The Government, determined to pursue its plan for a union, was not prepared to go to the country on the issue. Instead, they set about wearing down opposition by all means in their power. Sir John Parnell and Fitzgerald were sacked respectively as Chancellor of the Exchequer and Prime Serjeant for opposing the measure. So many promises of advancement were held out in exchange for support that anybody could see it would be difficult to fulfill them, and money was lavishly spent on bribes. The Opposition counteracted the latter move by themselves building up a fund from which substantial bribes were paid.

The only indications of public opinion came from meetings of freeholders who sent resolutions to the Lord Lieutenant, and Martin now devoted all his energies to undoing the damage done by the two Galway meetings. In particular, together with his old friend, Joseph Blake of Ardfry, one of the county members, he set about rallying the Catholics to the unionist standard. Meanwhile, he was preparing the ground for new meetings both of the town and county of Galway. On these he kept in close touch with Castlereagh, informing him, when the moment was ripe, that he would try to frame resolutions which would be 'a decided approbation of the measure and yet save the faces of those signatories who formerly expressed themselves against it', an aspect which principally concerned Trench.

True to his word, the first resolution he drafted for the meeting of freeholders in Galway town on 2 August 1799 admitted that when they had first heard of the measure, and before they knew precisely the terms upon which it was to be effected, it had made an unfavourable impression upon them, but that now, after 'mature and deliberate consideration', they felt that of all the systems it was the best calculated to give both countries 'the blessings of connexion' and defend them from the 'evils of separation'.

He had managed to convert some Galway Catholics who had previously declared against the Union, and he drafted the final resolution for the Galway town meeting to express the view he had held all along. It ran: 'Resolved, that we look with peculiar pleasure to this measure, as it promises an admission to our Catholic Brethren to the franchises of the Constitution— our most gracious and benevolent Sovereign, and a common and Impartial Parliament, relieved from the embarrassing dilemma of right on the one hand, and danger on the other, will, we confidently hope, extend to this class of the Irish people, those privileges which they may then enjoy with perfect security, to the privileges and property of the other.'

The resolutions of the Galway town meeting in favour of the Union were passed, and Martin was instructed to transmit them to the Lord Lieutenant. There remained the question of the county and Trench. It was decided to hold a county meeting on 30 August, and Martin and Blake were tireless in the preparation of what was aimed particularly at getting Trench now at last to declare formally for the Union.

But when the meeting finally took place in Loughrea, Bowes Daly, an active anti-unionist, tried to invade the hall with what Martin, writing to Castlereagh, described as 'a mob disposed to riot and break the windows of the hall in which we sat'. The Sheriff did not actually count the number who voted for the pro-unionist resolutions, because of Bowes Daly's attempt to wreck the meeting, but it was, nevertheless, considered a success by the unionists and managed finally to win over Trench. Martin claimed full credit for the advantages gained

122

and attributed them, among other things, to the fact that he had arrived at the gathering with some sixty gentlemen of property from Connemara.

As the year 1799 wore on, resolutions and counter-resolutions from every quarter followed each other speedily, many cancelling one another out. The Government sat anxiously counting the pros and cons with little certainty that their estimates approximated to Irish public opinion. The Catholics in general began to share Martin's opinion and to veer towards Union. Yet, no promise had been made to them, and Castlereagh and Cornwallis, both of whom favoured emancipation, had to perform a difficult feat in encouraging them sufficiently to gain their support while, at the same time, giving no positive understanding. But there were still many who held out, and, in the light of subsequent events, it was perhaps ironical that the man who declared most vehemently against a united parliament should be a young barrister called Daniel O'Connell. He announced at a Catholic meeting at the beginning of 1800 that he would rather see the penal laws re-enacted than the Irish parliament abolished.

By the time parliament reassembled on 15 January 1800, everybody had had time to say what he thought. Lord Clare, the Chancellor, was the foremost unionist, and Foster, the Speaker, the leading opponent. But the question was still so vexed that the Lord Lieutenant decided not to mention the Union at all in his address opening the session. Sir Laurence Parsons promptly moved into the attack. 'A set of English and Scottish journeymen politicians,' he said, 'get together in a corner of London, and project schemes for the settlement of this great nation which they know little or nothing about.' He produced all the familiar arguments, and concluded by a resolution affirming the blessings which the country owed 'to the spirited exertions of an independent resident Parliament, the paternal kindness of His Majesty and the liberality of the British Parliament in 1782.'

Martin was one of the first to speak. He argued that what the Opposition were saying was tantamount to, 'We are a discordant, disagreeing band, liable to perpetual desertion; we must, therefore, pledge ourselves by such a bond as shall secure us from abandoning each other.' Their behaviour reminded him of an old adage well known to doctors: 'Be as early in the field as the disease, but not before it.' Parsons, he claimed, was like a doctor, who, fearing that his patient would fall into a fever in six months' time, filled him with port, madeira and brandy, so as to kill him for a pure preventive. He then produced chapter and verse from the journals of the House of Commons for 1782 to prove that it was the British parliament which had then relinquished the right to legislate for Ireland, and that the Irish parliament had recognized the right up to that time.

The debate, which lasted eighteen hours, brought out the general confusion in people's minds. In fact everyone was arguing on a hypothesis—the value or weakness of a unified legislature. The alternative which the Opposition proposed was the continuance of the existing system, which was something they not only knew, but had themselves declared inadequate.

Martin's mind was made up that what was now facing them was the choice between separation and integration, a theory which had been put forward by the United Irishmen in one of their earliest pamphlets. He was among those who pointed out that the independence of the Irish parliament was at best nominal. It was true that when the King's mind broke down in 1788, the Irish parliament attempted to appoint a Regent for Ireland although the Prince was not to be appointed Regent for England, an event which had caused considerable alarm across the water. But so long as the Government was appointed by Westminster and the borough system enabled it to control the vote in the Irish parliament, that parliament could never be free. As for Pitt's assertion, adopted by Martin, that the Union would convert the Catholics into a safe minority, due to the subservience of the Irish Government they had in fact always been really ruled by the Protestant majority of the two islands.

The opening debate of January was enlivened by the entry at 7 o'clock in the morning of a frail, emaciated figure in Volunteer uniform. It was Henry Grattan, who had refused to stand at the last election due to ill health, but who now, in view of what was happening, had presented himself for the vacated seat of Wicklow and been elected at midnight. He had then hurried into town to defend the parliament which bore his name. He did so throughout the succeeding months with unrivalled eloquence often touching on the poignant, as when he quoted *Romeo*:

> 'Thou are not conquered; beauty's ensign yet
> Is crimson in thy lips and in thy cheeks,
> And death's pale flag is not advanced there.'

Dublin was a centre of anti-unionism. The commercial classes had gained greatly through the bounties and subsidies of the Irish parliament, and though the Union was to bring them the full trade of the empire and more or less equal rights with England—concessions which Pitt had offered in 1785 and then withdrawn under pressure from British commercial interests—they did not feel they would be amply compensated. Most of all, Dublin as a city stood to lose the standing and prosperity it had largely acquired through the wealthy, resident parliamentarians.

Feeling against the unionists ran high. One day a crowd swarmed into the parliament house and tried to rush those whom they thought were pro-unionist. Dick Martin found himself faced by a mob. He immediately whipped out a pocket pistol, and retreating backwards as he spoke, said that if anyone moved he would shoot them 'as dead as that paving stone'. The crowd immediately realized the absurdity of a man with a tiny pistol holding several thousand people at bay and cheered him, whereupon he made a rapid exit and ran for his house in Kildare Street.

The debates continued to take up half the night and more. One day Martin found himself leaving the House around 1 p.m. with the Town Major, Swann. They walked together until Martin got into his carriage and was driven off to cross the Liffey by Carlisle Bridge. Suddenly there was an outburst, and a mob collected and started to run after him. As they ran, they picked up stones and began hurling them at his carriage, and much worse in his eyes, at his horse. When Swann realized what was happening, he began himself to run after the crowd. On his way he came across a man who had just thrown a stone and was bending down to pick up another. Swann fired at him, and seeing the mob continuing to attack Martin's carriage, he fired at them and dispersed them. He then returned to the man

125

whom he had seen picking up a stone, and whose name was Brocas, and arrested him.

When parliament assembled the following day, there was a strong military guard around the buildings, and the Opposition was quick to suggest that this was intimidation of the members. But Castlereagh explained that it was necessary to protect them, as some had been attacked. Brocas was brought to the bar of the House, found guilty of a serious breach of privilege, although he pleaded not guilty, and committed to Newgate prison. But when he petitioned and others vouched for his good character, Martin was the first to ask for his release, and this was allowed, after Brocas had received the censure of the House.

On the day after the mob had attacked Martin, the session again continued throughout the night and at 3.30 a.m. the principle of Union was carried by forty-nine votes. Lord Clare, the Chancellor, had spoken for four hours, and justified the remark that Westmoreland had once made to Pitt about him, namely, that he had 'no other God but English government'.

Clearly, there had been some converts to unionism, but there had also been defections. Joseph Henry Blake's father, a practising Catholic, had been influenced by a theory of the Speaker's and decided that after all the Catholics would fare better under their own parliament. George Ogle also changed over to anti-unionism, but for the opposite reason. He now felt that the Protestant ascendancy could best be preserved by a resident Irish parliament; and his view was shared by the majority of Orangemen. Not a single Orange lodge voted in favour of integration.

The same ground continued to be gone over in parliament, and Martin was often on his feet. In fact, members were subjected to such lengthy attendance that many of them ended by taking to their beds. What was at stake, it was calculated, was £1,050,200 worth of property in favour of the Union, and £350,500 against it. Such computations were the nearest the Government could come to consulting the electorate.

Like everything that goes on too long, the Union debates gradually induced apathy. Considering that what was involved was virtually the signing away of a nation, it was remarkable that *Saunders Newsletter* at the end of April was able to devote the equivalent of a whole page and a half to a debate in the

English House of Commons on the abolition of bull-baiting. It would probably have had few more enthusiastic readers than Martin.

The bill was brought in by Sir William Pultney who claimed, among other things, that bull-baiting depraved the onlookers. Windham, the Secretary for War, and Canning, both ridiculed the bill on the grounds that it was beneath the notice of the House. Windham went so far as to praise the sport as being responsible for keeping alive the great race of British bull-dogs.

Dr. Parr's old pupil, Richard Brinsley Sheridan, brought all his dramatist's eloquence to bear upon the subject. He condemned the sport as one which was 'inhuman, cruel, disgraceful and beastly' and which could excite nothing but 'brutality, ferociousness, and cowardice'. He claimed that it must 'debase the mind, deaden the feelings, and extinguish every spark of courage and benevolence', and concluded by stating that a friend of his intended to bring in a bill to prevent cruelty to animals. He was, no doubt, referring to Erskine, who was giving much thought to the whole subject at the time, a fact which must have pleased 'the man for Galway' who, with his little prison in Ballinahinch Lake, had already stolen a march on history.

The mining prospectors for whom Martin had temporarily abandoned Elizabeth in Paris with such fateful results, had swindled him, and he had now had a survey of his Oughterard lands done by a Monsieur Subrine, one of the engineers to the late Louis XVI. Union business was sufficiently quiet in June 1800 for Martin to be able to arrange for the eminent Frenchman to read a paper on his findings to the Royal Irish Academy, then under the Presidency of his brilliant and exceedingly eccentric cousin, the geologist, Richard Kirwan. Subrine reported on finding lead, pink granite, quartz, copper ore and pyrites, and he conjectured that the head of the mountain rising from Glan, on Lough Corrib, must be very rich. He pointed out the mistakes of the earlier probes, and recommended fresh ones to be made. At the time Martin, with an estimated £7,000 a year, was the third richest man in County Galway, but his debts were always so enormous that no income was adequate. The mines were what he still looked to as a source of future wealth.

At length, on 7 June at 10 p.m. the Union bill passed without a division, after two thirds of the Opposition had withdrawn from the House. Castlereagh followed up with a masked ball and fête champêtre at his superb residence in Phoenix Park, with its spacious lawns and a view of the blue ridge of the Dublin mountains. Martin attired himself modestly. Similarly to half a dozen other gentlemen, he went in an elegant silk domino with rich plumes on his hat. In his heart there must have been a great mixture of feelings. What he expected for Ireland from the Union were Catholic emancipation and greatly increased trade, and the latter meant a growth in the cattle business to the advantage of western graziers. But few would have sensed more deeply than he who had been so alive to Dublin's charms that the Union would be the hand of death on a capital which had been one of the foremost in the world.

On 1 August the Lords assembled for the last time in their colourful robes beneath the tapestries depicting William of Orange's victory over James II at the Boyne. Elegant women mingled with them, and the gentlemen of the Commons were called to the bar to hear Lord Cornwallis give the royal assent to what was to terminate for ever the gay pageantry, the sublime oratory, the soaring hopes, but also the codified bigotry of the Irish parliament.

Cornwallis reported that it passed 'without a murmur in the City of Dublin, and without the smallest appearance of discontent or uneasiness'. But one young witness, Thomas de Quincy, was amazed that such a group of people could sell their birthright without obtaining even so much as a mess of pottage. 'The Bill received the Royal assent,' he wrote, 'without a muttering, or a whispering, or the protesting echo of a sigh. . . . All was, or looked, courtly, and free from vulgar emotion. One person only I remarked whose features were suddenly illuminated by a smile, a sarcastic smile, as I read it; which, however, might be all a fancy. It was Lord Castlereagh. . . .'

With Lord Clare, he was the chief architect of the Union. Yet, even they hoped for things which were diametrically opposed—Clare for the eclipse of all the Catholics' hopes and Castlereagh for their realization. Nobody could at that stage foretell what the Union would finally bring, although possibly

Charlemont, who at the end of his days was converted to the idea of Catholic emancipation, was the most far-seeing. He forecast that it would end by separating the two countries altogether. The most positive thing that could be said of it at that time was that it spelt the end of the Protestant nation.

Rewards to the supporters were distributed to the tune of thirty-one creations and advancements in the peerage. Even at that the Government had been hard put to it to meet all the demands. When Martin saw how hard pressed they were, he voluntarily relinquished any claim to a seat on the Revenue Board, leaving it to the Government's good faith to make him suitable amends in due course. Meanwhile he had been promised what he coveted most—the seat for County Galway. One of the two sitting members, Joseph Blake, had undertaken to accept the Escheatorship of Munster, whereby he would automatically vacate his seat; but now, at the eleventh hour, he changed his mind. This put Cornwallis in a very embarrassing situation with regard to Martin who had resigned his seat for Lanesborough in order to become one of the Gentlemen-at-Large to the Lord Lieutenant.

A request of Blake's made a month earlier finally provided the solution. He was married to the only daughter and heiress of Lord Louth and had requested to be granted a peerage with remainder to his heirs male. It was now decided to grant this. He became Lord Wallscourt, thus vacating his seat to which Martin was returned unopposed with Government support. At the same time, as a stop-gap, he was appointed one of the Commissioners for Stamps at the Board of Accounts during pleasure at a salary of £800 a year. The post was one that was tenable with a seat in parliament, and by the end of the year the Martins were packing their cases for the long trek to London from Connemara, where they had just buried their infant son, Charles.

Chapter Twelve

MOST OF the Irish members who were to take their seats in the new Imperial parliament at St. Stephen's Hall in Westminster were much travelled, but a journey for pleasure was a very different matter from what faced them now. From the outset it became plain that, whatever the political advantages the Union might be expected to bring, the practical difficulties were numerous.

Transport from Dublin to Holyhead or Liverpool was by sloop with room for only a few carriages. Sleeping accommodation was limited, and the ladies had to content themselves with just a curtain to screen themselves. Travellers brought their own provisions; the duration of the voyage depended upon the wind, and while at the best of times the crossing might take only a few hours, adverse winds might mean a journey of several days. Once landed on the other side, there were further difficulties. The English customs authorities were slow to grasp the fact that Ireland was now part of England, and 'the Irish Members' luggage' was a constant item in the correspondence of the Commissioners of Customs and Excise who received complaints about carriages and personal effects being delayed by red tape. Into the bargain, the journey had to be undertaken repeatedly so that, in the course of time, many saw no need for returning to Ireland at all and found it more convenient to become permanent absentees. Behind them, Dublin took on something of the air of a 'deserted mansion'.

The London to which they were travelling was the largest

city in the western world, with a population approaching a million. England, with almost eleven million inhabitants, had nearly double the population of Ireland. The industrial revolution was in full swing, and immigrant Irish labourers were helping to build cities which were to become the empire's commercial backbone. The war with France was stimulating the expansion of trade, new fortunes were being made, manners were becoming more refined, morals more staid and dress more simple. As a result of the tax on powder to raise money for the war, gentlemen had abandoned wigs, and the superstructures into which ladies had been erecting their hair had given way to a more natural style. Hoops and pads had disappeared, and the sobriety of Beau Brummel had set the vogue for gentlemen's attire.

The House of Commons was full of names which were to go down in history. Pitt had been at the helm for the whole of the seventeen years since the loss of the American colonies, and now the war with France was absorbing all his energies. Fox and Sheridan were the ornaments of the Opposition benches which they made famous for oratory, and Wilberforce was waging his long war against the slave trade.

The presence of one hundred new members in such an assembly of familiar faces was so strange that the newcomers' speeches were frequently reported with the words 'Irish member' after the name, and the son of one of the leading Irish anti-unionists, Bushe, satirized his countrymen:

. . . at St. Stephen's on a top bench waiting
In fretful doze while statesmen are debating,
Unknown, unnoticed save by some pert peer,
Who thus accosts his neighbour with a sneer,
'Who's that, my Lord? His face I don't remember'
'How could you? 'Tis a Scotch or Irish member.
They come and go in droves, but we don't know 'em.
They should have keepers, like wild beasts, to show 'em.'

The English members knew so little about Irish affairs that they tended to withdraw when they were being discussed, while in the course of time the Irish members became involved in the business of the larger partner to the exclusion of their home country.

131

But it was not only the faces of the Irish members which were unfamiliar; there was also the question of their accents. Nobody could be a gentleman in England unless he spoke standard English, but in Ireland it was possible to speak with a peculiar intonation and a particular emphasis which were clearly Irish, or even provincial, and yet to be refined.

Maria Edgeworth, who was exceptionally sensitive to accents, was to express the sense of the ridiculous which affected the native English on hearing the Irish pronunciation. In a telling portrait of the wife of an absentee Irish peer trying to make her way in London society, she was to write: 'Lady Clonburry was . . . in continual apprehension every time she opened her lips, lest some treacherous a or e, some stronger, some puzzling aspirate or non aspirate, some unguarded note, interrogative, or expostulatory, should betray her to be an Irishwoman.' But even a fellow Irishman, such as William Wickham when he was Chief Secretary, was prepared to be more English than the English and reported that some members of the House appeared 'to have been more astonished at the strength of Mr. Foster's *brogue* than convinced by his arguments'.

Martin was worldly enough to have acquired an English accent at Harrow and Cambridge and in the society he had frequented in his youth, but he was still Irish enough to betray his origins by certain tell-tale inflections, and more particularly by his individual and trenchant sense of humour, which fluctuated between dry understatement and flamboyant exaggeration. Unlike Castlereagh who, upon the passing of the Union, boasted that he had never felt himself 'so much an Englishman', Martin always felt and acted as an Irishman, and was proud of it.

His two sons by Elizabeth, Thomas and St. George, were now aged fifteen and thirteen, and he decided it was time for them to go to a boarding school. Furthermore, as a good Protestant himself, he wanted them to acquire a sound Protestant education. He sent them to a school called Redland, outside Bristol, run by the Reverend Mr. Jones. Then he settled with the remainder of the family in Cumberland Place, a fashionable district on the edge of Hyde Park.

Apart from their brogues, the Irish members brought with them their problems, foremost among them the Catholic question. Scarcely had the first united parliament assembled than Cornwallis wrote to Pitt urging him to bring up the subject as a matter of Government policy if he wished to avoid its being raised by the Opposition. Cornwallis believed implicitly in the promise of emancipation inherent in the Union contract, and the Irish Catholics awaited its fulfilment with a confidence not equalled since the arrival of Lord Fitzwilliam. But, as in the fateful sequence to that event, internal dissensions in England were to overrule honour as much as good sense.

As in the case of Fitzwilliam's viceroyalty, the cabinet was split. Loughborough, the Chancellor, who led the anti-Catholic faction, had once again incensed the King who obstinately clung to his conviction that emancipation would be contrary to his coronation oath. Pitt, on the other hand, not only urged the admission of the Catholics to parliament, but threatened as a matter of principle to resign if the question were shelved. But the King remained adamant, Pitt could not withdraw his threat, and when the King suffered a fresh mental breakdown he attributed it to Pitt's behaviour.

Pitt resigned on 14 March 1801. The war dragged on, and with Napoleon's army still staring across the narrow stretch of the Channel from Boulogne, invasion was a constant threat. In the circumstances, as on many previous occasions, it was essential that the Irish Catholics should be kept loyal. They had suffered what was probably their greatest disappointment so far, and the reaction must be controlled. Pitt took steps to diminish the effect of his own conduct. He wrote to Cornwallis that he should impress upon the Catholic leaders the importance of taking 'the most legal, dutiful and patient line of conduct', words which had a monotonously familiar ring in Irish ears. A resort to violence, the Lord Lieutenant was to say, could only lose them 'the aid and support of those who have sacrificed their own situation to their cause'.

Yet, having resigned, Pitt informed the King after a few weeks that he was prepared to resume office and would undertake never again to mention the Catholic question during the King's lifetime. When the anti-Catholic Speaker, Addington, formed a new Government, it was with the support of Pitt and half his cabinet. One interpretation of Pitt's resignation was

133

that, after seven years of war, he now favoured peace; but, as he had not the support of his cabinet, he preferred to withdraw and to put the onus of peace-making on another. Yet, the abiding impression left upon the Irish was that at the Union they had been duped and that now they had once again been betrayed.

Martin had arrived at Westminster full of confidence that all was to be changed by the Union. He defended it early in the session when he gave a taste of his logic to Mr. Jones who hoped that the Union would benefit both countries, yet doubted it.

'I can only thank him for the fervency of his prayer,' Martin said, 'for the speech which accompanied his prayer was very little likely to produce the consummation of it. . . . If he had given notice of a motion to have dissolved the Union, such a speech would have been relevant; because, if he would undo what has been done, it might be of use to demonstrate that what had been done ought not to have been done.'

He also believed in the unspoken pledge given to the Catholics, and went on to inform the Opposition, who were trying to monopolize the Catholic question, that the Catholics would not enlist under any party banner, but would willingly abide by whatever the Government should think fit to do. With such convictions, he was to suffer a bitter disillusionment over Pitt's behaviour.

At the same time he was sufficiently aware of the danger of fresh outbursts in Ireland to support both martial law and the suspension of the Habeas Corpus Act. He knew all too well that rebels still hid in the mountains around Ballinahinch. Only the previous year, Father Prendergast, who had taken a prominent part in the rebellion of 1798 and had been in hiding in Connemara ever since, had come asking Martin to obtain a pardon for him and one of the rebel leaders, John Gibbons, nicknamed 'Johnny the Outlaw', the son of the agent to the Marquis of Sligo, as Altamont had become at the Union. Although Martin considered Prendergast guilty of two murders, he agreed to intercede for him alone, but the priest had refused, and Martin had then told him to go away into hiding to the south of Ballinahinch. These were the kind of indulgences which made him constantly suspect, particularly with people like Sligo. He now emphasized in the House—and with an occasional

134

jocularity, for he liked to raise a laugh—that delay in applying the measures which were being discussed could be serious.

The first year of the Martins' residence in London was essentially Harriet's year. First of all, in July she gave birth to a daughter who was christened after her and was destined to be a writer. Next, the novel on which she had been working for years, and which had now reached a tremendous length, was published in London by Robinson in four volumes under the title *Helen of Glenross*.

Harriet, though more intellectual than mundane, shared cheerfully in her husband's active social life. She was no snob, and the fact that they were part of the circle of friends of the Prince of Wales would have impressed her less for its worldly significance than for the love of the theatre which they all shared.

She was immensely knowledgeable on theatrical affairs, and when towards the end of 1801 Kemble played *Hamlet* and *Richard III*, she was not only present, but undertook to write her impressions to a friend in Dublin. The result was some remarkable criticism, with enlightening comments on Kemble's technique and some acute observations on Shakespeare.

Of Hamlet she wrote: 'The single defect I perceived was when he imposed secrecy on Horatio and Marcellus. At such a moment Hamlet could not—ought not to be a mimic; but this fault is in the text itself. Kemble could hardly express it otherwise; but Shakespeare ought to have here conceived some of his fine imagined abjurations—he ought not to have put such sentences in Hamlet's way.' But for the performance itself she had unqualified praise.

As for *Richard III* her analysis shows a deep knowledge of feminine psychology. 'Being a woman, and not a very wise one, Lady Anne likes to be complimented precisely on the very qualities she is deficient in. . . . Richard knew too well he must steal the woman through the imagination; and Kemble conveys all that delicate, dangerous insinuation, most effectual for his purpose.'

Harriet also shows that she knows the world. Of Richard's ruling sin she writes, 'For a moment his audience are the dupes of his eloquence; and we admire ambition, even Richard's ambition, since he compels us to believe conscience is daily bartered, and obliges us to acknowledge ambition is the best exchange for its sacrificed scruples.'

Martin, with his own deep knowledge of the theatre, recognized immediately the grasp of theatrical techniques and the knowledge of Shakespeare, both as poet and psychologist, conveyed in his wife's letters. By the end of the year, Robinson had also published these in the form of a booklet.

Throughout this period Martin was also preoccupied with personal politics which were to absorb most of his energies for the next few years. The Act of Union had left it to the Imperial parliament to decide what offices it was possible to hold at the same time as a seat, and Martin had only been at Westminster a few months when it became clear that Commissioner of Stamps was not to be one of them. He wrote to Abbot, then Chief Secretary for Ireland, pointing out that the office had been given to him only because it happened to fall vacant just after his election for Galway, so that he did not have to relinquish his seat in accepting it; but, he pointed out, it was by no means sufficient recompense to him for the part he had played in bringing about the Union. In effect, an act of July 1801 made it impossible for him to continue to hold this office after the dissolution if he retained the seat for County Galway which was what he hoped to do.

He had been among the first people to declare their support for the Union, and he had lost no time in trying to persuade others. He had undertaken an even more difficult task in working to convert those in the town and county of Galway who had declared against the Union. In particular, he could claim a large part of the credit for convincing the Catholics of Galway, the most Catholic county in Ireland, that it was in their interests to support it. It was natural, according to the habits of the times, that he should expect to be compensated with an office other than one which was to be whipped away within a couple of years; and when he saw how well compensated people were who had done far less, and, later, to what high offices anti-unionists were appointed, he grew even more determined to claim his reward.

As the Government did not come forward with any offer, he broached the matter of office himself. At the end of 1801 he asked to be made a Governor of County Galway. This was refused on the grounds that sixteen Irish counties had only one Governor, and Galway already had two. The Lord Lieutenant wanted to keep as far as possible in line with British practice, and he could not, therefore, see his way to appointing a third for County Galway. Martin accepted this, and bided his time before asking to be made a member of the Privy Council.

A peace had meanwhile been concluded at Amiens and was greeted with mixed feelings. France was to retain a great part of her new conquests, a point Britain was prepared to concede because only shortly before, by the Treaty of Lunéville, France had undertaken to respect the independence of Switzerland, Holland—now the Batavian Republic—and the Cisalpine and Ligurian republics. But while London was being illuminated and the peace celebrated with masquerades, Napoleon started out on a new expansionist policy.

Addington decided it was time to test out the temper of the country; but before this took place discussion of the peace treaty caused several postponements of a bill in which Martin could not fail to have a particular interest—Dent's bill for the abolition of bull-baiting. Windham, the former Secretary of War, who had taken a leading part in defeating Pultney's bill in 1800, once more threw ridicule upon the bill. In April he asked Dent to adjourn it so as to allow one day to intervene between the discussion on the peace treaty, and that on bull-baiting, 'in order that gentlemen might be enabled to bring the whole force of their minds and their undivided attention to this important subject'. . . .

When it was ultimately discussed on 24 May, Windham revived all his old arguments, and accused the supporters of trying to put down the sports of the poor while condoning the equally cruel sports of the rich. Wilberforce referred to baiting as barbarian, and Sheridan once again rose to the occasion. If he wanted to give people a slave mentality, he argued, if he wanted them to watch with indifference their friends being killed off, or to oppress the weak and take advantage of their own power and superiority, he would teach them to be cruel to animals. Those who abused their own power, he declared, were always the most servile to others. But it was a northern Irishman, Sir George Hill, who invoked the name of Ireland. He had been a college friend of Tone's and had wanted the dying revolutionary's throat stitched up so that it could take the hangman's rope; but he was kind to animals. He reminded the House that the Irish parliament had passed an act abolishing bull-baiting, and he hoped that the Irish members who had been so favourable to their own bulls would not be less kind to those of England.

It was here that the clash between Dent's bill and the acrimonious discussions on the peace, which had led to its postponement, was to tell. Hill's appeal to the Irishmen in the House fell upon deaf ears, because by that time the majority of them, including Martin, were in Ireland electioneering, and the bill was lost by fifty-one votes to sixty-four.

At home people upon whose support in the elections Martin had thought he could count, such as Lord Clanricarde, whom he claimed owed much to his family, and Wallscourt, his life-long friend, were setting up an opposition, and Sligo continued to indulge an old grudge against him. Sligo wrote to the Castle claiming that the spirit of rebellion was not dead in Connaught and that it was even encouraged at election time by such as Martin who relied on people of unsound principles. Later, referring to the need to station a force in some of the wilder parts of the west, he gave the Castle the opinion that this would be necessary 'till Dick Martin's place is filled by a better member of society than is likely to be form'd from his precept and example'.

Martin represented to the Lord Lieutenant that the opposition to him was due to his support of the Union. But this could scarcely have been exact since Lords Clanricarde, Wallscourt and Sligo had all been supporters themselves. Rather it was due to the fact that more ponderous people always found it difficult to take Martin seriously. Even when he was most earnest he contrived to make a joke and in the most difficult circumstances his manner was always nonchalant. His determination to bring forward the Catholic question also led to misunderstandings, and there were people who attributed it to rapacity, presumably on the grounds that the Catholics being in a majority in Galway, they could guarantee Martin his seat.

However, despite all that Sligo and others could do to oppose him, one of the candidates, Burke, withdrew in his favour, and the clergy, gentlemen and freeholders of County Galway returned him for the second time unopposed. By the act of the previous summer, he was obliged now to relinquish his seat at the Board of Accounts and was allowed to sell it. He disposed of it to his own agent in settlement of a bad debt, and the £4,000 he obtained left some money in hand. But he had not been appointed to the Privy Council and was piqued.

He not only continued to press for office for himself, but made a series of recommendations regarding his friend, Mr. Coneys. In response, this gentleman was appointed Chairman of the quarter sessions. But as 1802 wore on, Martin continued to ask for offices for Coneys as Assistant Barrister for County Galway, as Commissioner of Appeals, and then to be used in Crown Prosecutions. Furthermore, he told the new Chief Secretary, Wickham, that his predecessor, Abbot, had undertaken to appoint Coneys as soon as a vacancy occurred for any of these posts.

All this set up an irritation in Wickham's mind which was to have serious consequences. He accused Martin of bullying. 'We shall not suffer ourselves to be frightened here,' he wrote to Abbot, who was now Speaker, 'and I hope and trust that all such attempts from whatever quarter they may come will be openly and steadily resisted. I am certain that Govt. will gain more credit by such conduct than it can lose of interest or influence by the loss of Mr. Martin's support.' His successors were to eat his words.

In the midst of this year of feverish political activity, family matters were also to occupy Martin. His youngest son, St. George, died at boarding school in Bristol. He was only fourteen, and Martin's last child by his beautiful and flighty Elizabeth. He had only just been born when they set off on their fated journey to Paris, and could not therefore, be said to have known any other mother than Harriet who loved Elizabeth's children as her own. Now, not only was the boy dead, but his brother Thomas had had to endure at close quarters all the lugubrious formalities associated with death.

Another family matter had to do with Martin's young half-brother, Anthony, who as a lad of sixteen had cut such a debonair figure in the little Galway theatre. He had grown up at Dangan, hunting, shooting and generally leading the life of a country gentleman. In his early twenties he had gone up to Brasenose College, Oxford, intending to take Holy Orders; but his patron died before he graduated, and he had come down and joined the East Devon Militia.

Now he had fallen hopelessly in love. The object of his affections was Marie, daughter of Jean Pierre de l'Espinasse, a former Director-General of the Dutch West Indies Company for Essequibo and Demerara. The family were a Dutch branch of a French aristocratic family with whom the Martins had been connected a century earlier; but this appears to have carried little weight with the young lady's parents. Whatever their sentiments about Anthony as an individual, the fact remained that the young squire of Dangan was thirty-one and Marie only seventeen. But the couple were not to be gainsaid. They eloped and got married at Gretna Green. Any parental authority Martin had exercised over Anthony would have been long since passed, and there was a panache about the wedding which would have appealed to him.

He also had a lot of new business on hand due to the death of Patrick D'Arcy, husband of his only sister, Mary; but it was not family matters which detained him at home. Extravagance which was phenomenal even in an extravagant age combined with bad management to make his financial situation so precarious that he could not afford to go to England to attend parliament. This did not, however, in any way diminish his political activities at home.

He claimed that Castlereagh had promised him the first vacancy on the Linen Board, but his request to the Lord Lieutenant to issue a warrant was refused. With a renewal of the war with France imminent, he asked to be given the command of the County Galway militia regiment which was about to be formed, and was particularly piqued to find it was as good as promised to his colleague, Trench, now Lord Dunlo, who he felt had supported the Government at the Union only because of his exertions.

When hostilities with France finally broke out, little more than a week elapsed before there was a fresh rebellion in Dublin where Robert Emmet, a young, romantic brother of one of the leaders of the 1798 rebellion, made a bid to seize power with a handful of desperate men whose violence Martin abhorred. At

140

this his patriotism made him swallow his pride, and he wrote from Ballinahinch to warn the Castle that arms had been landed in the west from Guernsey. Meanwhile Father Prendergast, who was trying to undermine the people's loyalty, was saying Mass twice a week in the house of one of Martin's Protestant tenants. Martin then offered to raise a regiment for the Government, but the Emmet rebellion was short-lived and nothing came of his offer.

James D'Arcy of Galway, writing to the Lord Chancellor, Redesdale, gave a lively description of the phoenix-like quality of Martin's temperament. 'So singular are his talents,' he wrote, 'so popular his manner and so fortunate his address, that without possessing an atom of public confidence, he at the very moment when he seems to have lost all public favour, and is actually without credit for a guinea, starts up to the astonishment of all with a greater command of influence than ever.'

In fact, at a county meeting Dunlo had summoned without consulting him, Martin had got the better of his colleague in debate, and, to the embarrassment of the Government, had raised the Catholic question. Then he had attended the great October fair at Ballinasloe, a favourite gathering place for country gentlemen, where a meeting took place with Catholics from different parts of the country. It was agreed that committees should be set up in each county, and they were to call public meetings supporting an application to parliament to be moved by Martin calling for complete Catholic emancipation.

None of his aspirations having been realized, he called on the Lord Lieutenant in the summer of 1804 and laid his grievances before him, complaining that in one instance he had received a reply from Wickham which was 'more than uncivil'. And when he asked for a seat on the Treasury Board, it turned out that at the head of the queue of those who were waiting was one of the leading anti-unionists, Sir Laurence Parsons. When finally he decided to go to London for the parliamentary session at the beginning of 1805, he called on Sir Evan Nepean at the Home Office in the hope of obtaining some redress, but was offered merely the Weighmastership of Cork at £600 a year, which he turned down, saying that he needed £1,000 a year.

The effect of all these slights was now to be seen in the House. Martin voted against the continued suspension of the Habeas

Corpus Act in Ireland, on the grounds that the situation had changed since his previous approval. He supported the Opposition call for a suspension of the Additional Forces Bill, designed to recruit extra men to fight the French. He voted with the majority for criminal proceedings to be instituted against Lord Melville, First Lord of the Admiralty, accused of interfering with Government funds. And he moved for a copy of the evidence and proceedings before the committee of the Irish House of Commons attainting Cornelius Grogan to be laid before the House with the object of obtaining a reversal of the attainder.

He was never so determined as when defending an individual, and this produced a sharp exchange with Castlereagh whom Martin accused of trying to shelter the Administration of which he had been a member. He quoted such eminent legal authorities as Coke and Hale for saying that a man may join rebels to save his own life until an opportunity arises for him to escape. Camden had, in fact, described to Pitt how the rebels gathered up people as they advanced, forcing them to join their ranks. Martin now maintained that Grogan's execution had been an act of murder. Both Fox and an Irish member, Sir John Newport supported him in attacking Castlereagh, and his motion was carried unanimously.

When the Irish Election Bill came up for its second reading, he objected to it on the grounds of 'unseemliness' because it vilified the country in stating that all vice was attributable to the poor, and all virtue to the rich. And when the evidence on Grogan's attainder was produced, he complained that it was inefficient and evasive, and said he would move for a committee to look into the question of the Irish parliament's records.

Practically the only thing he did not do to make his displeasure plain to Government was to raise the Catholic question, as Fox was to do this. But at the end of a heated debate, which lasted until 4.45 in the morning, Martin, of course, voted for the motion with the minority of 124 against 356. Twenty-nine Irish members voted for Fox and forty-four against, no doubt giving Martin grounds to ponder on how the question might have fared in an all-Irish parliament.

While he was thus expressing his feelings through parliament, he was causing a certain amount of uneasiness behind the

142

scenes. A by-election was about to take place in County Galway due to Dunlo's having succeeded his father as Lord Clancarty. Bowes Daly, the prominent anti-unionist with Whig sympathies, was standing for Dunlo's seat, opposed by a Mr. Charles Blake, and it was now vital that Martin should use all his influence to support Blake. As the Lord Lieutenant put it, his power in County Galway was even more important than his vote in the House. Yet nobody knew if he had, as he had threatened, committed himself to supporting Bowes Daly.

The Lord Lieutenant's private secretary, Marsden, wrote to Vansittart, the Chief Secretary, pointing out that Bowes Daly had no money and no particular influence in County Galway, that if Martin went against him and backed Blake, it would be decisive.

'It is greatly to be regretted,' he commented, 'that these matters were not arranged at an earlier period.' Nobody would have agreed with him more readily than Martin; it was certainly not for want of warning by him. In the event it appears he did not, as the Government hoped, back Blake; Dunlo's seat was won by Bowes Daly, a result Martin was to live to regret.

Chapter Thirteen

A GREAT sweep of events during the last part of 1805 radically changed Britain's relationship to the Continent. Austria's entrance, in the summer, into a Triple Alliance with Britain and Russia altered the picture for Napoleon, who suddenly dropped all thought of invading England and rushed his army towards the Danube to crush the Austrians. By early September the camp at Boulogne, which for more than a decade had been kept in readiness for action against Britain, was abandoned. The dream which for so long had nourished Frenchmen was to fade entirely with Nelson's successful exploit on 21 October at Trafalgar. Britain was now the unassailable mistress of the seas; nobody else could hope to patrol the Channel.

But the rejoicings were short-lived. Napoleon had already entered Vienna when the Russians decided to attack him without awaiting essential reinforcements. When Napoleon defeated them on the frozen lakes of Austerlitz at the beginning of December, a new order was established. Britain might reign at sea, but the French were the masters on land. Europe was to be carved up, parcelled out and reassembled in a series of alliances aimed at Britain, who was now faced with a constant search for a foothold on the European mainland. Pitt on his sick-bed, worn out in body and broken in spirit, could not have failed to see what was in store for his country. On 23 January 1806 he died at the age of forty-six.

A new cabinet was formed under Grenville, which came to be called the 'Ministry of all the Talents', and which included all the leading Whigs. In his first years in the Irish parliament, Martin had supported the Patriots, who had Whig tendencies, and more recently at Westminster he had been voting with the Opposition. Now at last he was shown a small mark of esteem in return for his recent support rather than for his approbation of the Union. On 1 May 1806 he was made a Commissioner for Hearth Money Collection, an office tenable at the same time as a seat in parliament.

When a couple of months later he was about to set out for the Galway assizes, he needed an introduction to the new Lord Lieutenant, Bedford, and he took the matter up at no less a level than Carlton House, the Prince of Wales's palace. In due course he received a letter from the Prince's private secretary, Colonel McMahon, which ran:

'Carlton House, August 11th 1806

My dear Sir,
    The Prince commands me to make you his best regards, and to assure you that he committed to the charge of Sir John Newport on the eve of his departure from London, a confidential request to the Duke of Bedford that His Grace should extend every service and attention to you, as "one for whom H.R.H. has entertained the strongest sentiments of friendship, and to whom he consider'd himself under very peculiar obligations, for the zealous, prompt, & most handsome support he had render'd the Government."
    The cadetship for your protégé is promised, & will be issued in the next batch, so as to proceed with the Sep^{tr} fleet.
        Believe me, my dear Sir,
          With the highest esteem,
            Most sincerely yours,
              J. McMahon.
R. Martin, Esqre M.P.'

It was proof of the Prince's attachment to Martin that he should have taken the trouble to deal with these matters just then, because he had weighty personal problems on his mind. His wife, Caroline, from whom he was separated and whom he detested, had not only been accused of loose living; rumour had it that she had given birth to an illegitimate son. The King had ordered an enquiry which came to be known as 'the delicate investigation', but this proved inconclusive—a fact which considerably vexed the Prince. In the light of Martin's later behaviour in regard to the royal couple, it can only be supposed that at this juncture he had not taken sides in the dispute.

According to the habits of the times, the Lord Lieutenant was probably not the slightest bit put out at receiving, on the heels of a recommendation from so exalted a person as the Prince, a memorial from a Mr. Duane protesting at the behaviour of Martin as a magistrate, member of parliament and captain of yeomanry. Duane held a farm adjoining Martin's lands from a Mr. Lynch at a rental of £300 a year, and he complained that it had been occupied by a force under orders from the member of parliament.

Duane maintained that he and some labourers were making some very valuable improvements on the lands when they were invaded by 200 members of the yeomanry and sea fencibles, and by servants of Martin's. The latter included a Frenchman who, Duane asserted, admitted to having landed with Humbert's forces in 1798 and to having fought against the King's forces at the Races of Castlebar.

The men were armed with muskets, bayonets, swords and pistols, were mounted on Martin's horses and were headed by a relation of Mrs. Martin's, a Lieutenant Evans of the Ballinahinch Cavalry. They entered in military order, with trumpets sounding, and proceeded to knock down walls, destroy ditches and lay the place waste. When Duane remonstrated with Lieutenant Evans he said there was nothing he could do; he was acting under instructions from Colonel Martin. He then took the bridles off the horses, turned them loose on the reserved grass, and sent for the cows of some of Martin's tenants which were put out there to graze. Duane claimed that the Frenchman was kept at Ballinahinch exclusively for the purpose of killing him, and on this occasion he had been so terrified that he had made for the coast where he had taken an open boat in which he travelled 100 miles to Galway in order to escape. In those days no method was too unorthodox for settling differences between gentlemen, and it is possible that Duane's landlord, Lynch, was a tenant of Martin's who was sub-letting but not paying his rent.

Fox, whose supporters predominated in the cabinet, had been in declining health ever since he took over the Foreign

Office in the new Government, and he died in September 1806. Grenville decided to go to the country, and the general feeling was that Martin and Bowes Daly would be returned for County Galway again unopposed.

In the meantime, Martin had another family wedding to attend. His eldest half-brother, Robert, a less impetuous character than Anthony, decided very suitably to marry a life-long friend. She was the sister of Thomas Henry O'Flaherty, Sir John O'Flaherty's son, who had been brought up with the young Martins at Dangan. Mary, six years Robert's junior, was living at the time with her parents at Lemonfield, a charming country house at the other side of the hamlet of Oughterard, formerly Clare. There the O'Flahertys were neighbours of the Martins during the winter months which they now tended to spend at Clareville, the small eighteenth-century house built by Dick Martin's father, Robert, at Clare. Set back about a hundred yards from a gushing little river and facing a small plantation, it is a perfect example of classical elegance standing at the entrance to Connemara where the rough mountain track in those days left Oughterard. As it was practically the last habitation before Ballinahinch, it came to be known as 'Dick Martin's Gate Lodge'.

When Mary O'Flaherty married Robert Martin on 5 October 1806, she went to live with him and his mother at Bushy Park, a fine property overlooking the narrower part of Lough Corrib and bordering on Dangan where Anthony and his Dutch wife were in the process of rearing a large family.

As election time approached it became clear that there would be a contest after all. The new candidate, put up by Lord Clancarty, formerly Martin's colleague, Trench, was Giles Eyre of Eyrecourt, the most dashing blade in County Galway and a famous master of hounds. Polling was due to begin on 24 November, and Martin no doubt awaited it with some apprehension; Harriet was once more expecting, and on the very eve of the opening of the poll she gave birth to a second daughter. She was christened Georgina, but for a second name she was given that of the Gormanston aunt who had cared so much for the welfare of young Dick and his sister Mary, and who had, also, been such an animal lover, namely Thomasine.

Martin's tenants had, as usual, a long distance to come to

147

vote, whereas the properties of Bowes Daly and Eyre were in east Galway, from which access to the city was easy, so they could bring in their freeholders early in the election. As a result, they were constantly ahead throughout the first ten days. Then Martin's freeholders began arriving in greater numbers and his prospects improved.

Standing at the hustings, he was able to create one of those ridiculous situations of which he was past master. Facing his opponent, Eyre, he offered to withdraw if Eyre would sign the resolution Martin held in his hand. The remark had its effect because everybody knew that, although Eyre was a member of one of the leading county families, he could neither read nor write.

When parliament finally reassembled on 15 December, there were not only no members from County Galway, but no returns. Questions were immediately raised, and there were suggestions that there had been some irregularity. This was just one more example of the anomalies resulting from the Union; nobody at Westminster seemed to know that the electoral laws in England and Ireland were different. Martin was to devote some of his energies trying to get them unified.

By the twenty-fourth day he was elected with a majority of 470, but it was estimated that this would have been 1,300 had the poll been kept open, as it had been insinuated had been the case, until every voter had polled. Even Eyre admitted Martin's superiority and declined to petition. A great dinner was given in Martin's honour, and he proposed the toasts of 'The Earl of Clanricarde', 'The Lord Chancellor of Ireland', who was his old friend and some time adversary, George Ponsonby, and, finally, 'Religious toleration!' the last being greeted with rapturous enthusiasm.

Wilberforce had been fighting for eighteen years for the slaves, and the new parliament was to make history by abolishing the slave trade. But the Catholic question was to be its undoing in more ways than one. By failing to take up emancipation as a whole, they lost the Whigs much support for decades, and by taking it up at all, they aroused a formidable opposition. It was proposed that the English Catholics should have the same advantages granted the Irish Catholics in 1793 when they were admitted to hold commissions in the forces; but when it became clear that it was also intended they should be allowed to hold staff appointments, a storm broke out, the most important aspect of which was the King's obstinate resistance. The Grenville cabinet, the last Whig cabinet of England, fell, a new Government was formed under Portland, and parliament was dissolved in the spring of 1807. In the ensuing election, Martin and Bowes Daly who stood as Independents, were returned unopposed to a House which had come in on a cry of 'No popery!'

Before the Government fell, Martin had been appointed to another sinecure as a gauger. His friend, Bedford, was replaced at the end of April by the Duke of Richmond as Lord Lieutenant; as his Chief Secretary he brought Arthur Wellesley; the leading anti-unionist, John Foster, once again became Chancellor of the Exchequer for Ireland.

Castlereagh had taken over the War Office and the year was marked by a series of military set-backs for Britain. The greatest by far was Napoleon's defeat of the Russians at Friedland, resulting in a Franco-Russian alliance against England who was already blockaded. The first minor French reverse came towards the end of the year when the Portuguese Regent managed to escape to Brazil with his navy before the French arrived to seize it. By the spring of 1808, the Peninsula had become the centre of attention. The Spanish King abdicated, and the French occupied Madrid and placed Joseph Buonaparte, Napoleon's brother, on the throne. It was one of Napoleon's most unwise moves. Spain and Portugal rose against the French, and provided Britain with the foothold on the European mainland for which she had been searching in vain. British troops were rushed to help the insurgents, and Wellesley abandoned his desk in Dublin to embark in Cork with an expeditionary force.

Martin's family was now partly grown up, and Laetitia, his first child by Elizabeth, a young woman of twenty-three, had fallen in love with a handsome Englishman a few years her senior. His father was Sir John Peshall of Hales Owen in Shropshire, and although the College of Heralds held that his baronetcy was extinct, he claimed direct descent from a certain Thomas in the lineage and clung resolutely to his title. His eldest son, Charles, was in the 88th Foot, or Connaught Rangers, and the marriage to Laetitia having been agreed, he

149

was invited to stay with Dick and Harriet Martin at Clareville. The two Martin boys were absent; Thomas who was twenty, was away at Cambridge, and rarely wrote, while young Richard, now aged eleven, was at the Reverend Mr. Jones's school outside Bristol. The whole Peshall family had, however, met him in London, and had been particularly charmed by his manners.

As always when he was at home, Martin was politically active, and he now took steps to further the affairs of the Catholics. It was known that Grattan, who had returned to parliament in 1805, was to present a petition from the Catholics of Dublin at the next session of parliament, and the High Sheriff of Galway convened a meeting to consider expressing support. This was agreed upon, and as people began to sign, Clanricarde first, Martin rose and, according to the *Freeman's Journal*, in 'a concise speech, marked by his usual pointed eloquence' requested that the signatures should be read out in order that the Catholics might know that the measure arose spontaneously from the Galway Protestants' feelings on the unconstitutional deprivations of their Catholic brethren. His words had the desired effect, and his motion was passed without debate.

After Laetitia and Charles Peshall had been married in Galway in May 1808, Martin proceeded to London for the parliamentary session, ready to support Grattan's petition. But it had scarcely been made before cold water began to be thrown on it from the Government benches, not only by Castlereagh, but by Canning, a future Prime Minister, who came to be associated with the Catholic cause, yet whose manner of speaking often gave the impression that he was not being sincere. They made a plea for moderation, and urged that, with the international situation as it was, this was scarcely the moment to raise the subject—an argument which, so far as the Irish were concerned, had grown hackneyed.

By the time Martin spoke, all the indignation of which he was capable had been roused. 'Notwithstanding what has been said about moderation and calmness, I have never heard more inflammatory language uttered with a calm voice and a sermonic tone, than what has come from the gentlemen on the other side of the House. Nothing like it has been uttered for a century within these walls.' He referred to Canning with contempt. He

150

foretold that the Catholics, seeing their petition rejected without even a discussion of their claims, would not trust the House with the bait of a petition again; they would no longer expose themselves to the mortification. He added one of his favourite arguments: that the Catholics would scorn to make their grievances a party issue.

'When the cry in Ireland was union or rebellion,' he concluded, 'I was in favour of the measure of union; but I have since learnt that it is very possible to have a rebellion after a union. The Catholics did certainly lend their aid to support the Union, which could not be carried without their acquiescence; and they as certainly did so upon an understood pledge of emancipation. It was strictly confided in by the Catholics, and even in some degree acted upon by those who gave it. If that pledge were now to be abandoned, the compact with the Catholics is broken, and they have a right to claim the restoration of their parliament. The consequence of this impolitic rejection will be, that the Catholics will join the Protestants, who were always averse from the Union, and with others who have since become equally so, and unite their endeavours in order to procure its repeal.' This was the first plea for the repeal of the Union. It was prophetic, and was soon being reiterated.

Meanwhile, the war in the Peninsula ebbed and flowed. The Peshalls were stationed in Maldon, but it was rumoured that Charles's regiment would be one of the first for service abroad; while in Galway the militia unanimously volunteered for Spain. By August 1808, the French had been defeated in Portugal, but Napoleon began to prepare for a decisive blow in Spain by withdrawing crack troops from Prussia and calling up 160,000 French conscripts. The challenge constituted Britain's first chance for fifteen years to end the French threat. By the spring Corunna was over, Sir John Moore was dead, and the Austrians were on the eve of inflicting a deadly blow on the French.

In the midst of it all, a proposal was put forward in the House of Lords which astonished many, but which would not have surprised Richard Martin. The mover was the former Chancellor, Lord Erskine, who had defended Petrie in Martin's Criminal Conversation case and who, like Martin, was a close friend of the Prince of Wales.

Erskine was an animal lover. He had a Newfoundland dog called Toss whom he had taught to impersonate the judge. Toss attended all the barrister's consultations, sitting with his paws placed before him on the table, and occasionally Erskine dressed him up in a full-bottomed wig. He also had a pet goose which followed him around his grounds like a dog, and two favourite leeches, kept in a glass, which he called Home and Cline, after two famous surgeons, and which had been used to bleed him.

Erskine was in love with nature in general, and had endeavoured to learn farming, not very successfully, from the agriculturalist, Coke of Holkham. He had, however, learnt a great deal about the habits of animals and insects, and was convinced of the superbly organized balance of nature. He had observed that when weasels were kept down to preserve game, rats increased; and while the wireworm would devour everything before it, a flock of rooks could destroy in a day several million of them. Trees produced a thousand times more seed than necessary for their reproduction, obviously being intended for animal sustenance. And he had seen Coke's method of dealing with the pest of the turnip fly which feeds on the first green leaves; he sowed twice as much as was necessary. Erskine was convinced that when man exterminated a living creature, he generally introduced something else more harmful.

He had been working on a bill for the prevention of cruelty to animals since, twenty years before, he had heard the story of a baker who, bearing enmity to another, put the man's dog in an oven and baked it alive. Now he introduced into the Lords a bill to prevent malicious and wanton cruelty to animals. The preamble ran:

> 'Whereas it has pleased Almighty God to subdue to the dominion, use and comfort of man, the strength and faculties of many useful animals, and to provide others for his food; and whereas the abuse of that dominion by cruel and oppressive treatment of such animals is not only highly unjust and immoral, but most pernicious in its example, having an evident tendency to harden the heart against the natural feelings of humanity. . . . '

He argued that cruelty to animals, as the law stood, could only be punished if the intention was to injure the proprietor; animals themselves had no rights. Yet, they had been endowed with the same feelings as man for their enjoyment and happiness—seeing, hearing, thinking, the sense of pain and pleasure, the passions of love and anger, sensibility to kindness and pangs from unkindness and neglect. They had been created for man's use, but not for his abuse. He quoted Cowper to explain his attitude:

'The sum is this—if man's convenience, health
Or safety interfere, his rights and claims
Are paramount, and must extinguish their's,
Else they are all—the meanest things that are
As free to live, and to enjoy that life
As God was free to form them at the first
Who in his sovereign wisdom made them all.'

But, in fact, he could not remember the final line. He argued that man's dominion over animals is a trust, and distinguished between wild animals and the reclaimed. It was plain that animals living in a state of nature would overrun the earth if not kept down by man and other preying animals; therefore he did not propose that the bill should apply to these.

After referring to the terrible over-driving of post-horses and chaise-horses, he gave a few examples of appalling cruelty. Some horses which were too exhausted to work any more had been brought up to London to be sold for the flesh and skins, but so that the market might be supplied gradually, they had been kept for days without food until they reached the point at which they ate their own dung and gnawed one another's manes in desperation. Their cries could be heard for miles around.

Dreadful cruelty was inflicted on horses by racing them against time, and overloading, particularly of asses, was a daily occurrence. He told the House of a case in which he himself had been involved. He saw a cart unmercifully laden with vegetables being drawn by a horse which was just skin and bones. There was no cart saddle to prevent the chain cutting, so that blood and matter were running down the animal's side; the fetlock joint was dislocated and the skin broken. He remonstrated with the man who asked Erskine if he would give him another horse; Erskine had replied that he would give him a guinea. But to that the man retorted that he could work the horse for another four or five weeks, and then get four or five guineas for him at the slaughter-house. Erskine admitted to their lordships that this was too much for him: he bought the horse.

As a lawyer he was able to counter in advance any objections which might be raised on the grounds that magistrates might find it difficult to decide what was wanton cruelty, and went on to refer to the revolutions which had 'destroyed the social happiness and independence of mankind, raising up tyrants to oppress them all in the end, by beginning with the oppression of each other'. All this, he claimed, had arisen 'from neglecting the cultivation of the moral sense, the best security of States and the greatest consolation of the world'. He concluded by declaring that his bill, if passed, would not only be 'an honour to the country, but an era in the history of the world'.

The bill passed the Lords in a modified form; it was agreed that it should apply only to beasts of burden. It was introduced in the Commons by Sir Charles Bunbury, and there Windham, who had already made a name for himself in opposing the bills on bull-baiting introduced by Sir William Pultney and Mr. Dent, took the floor. For one who considered the subject beneath the notice of the legislature, he spoke on it at great length. His main objection on this occasion was that the bill was confined to the drivers of horses and other animals. This meant that it was likely to penalize the lower orders of society, while the higher ranks were left free to pursue their cruel sports of hunting, shooting and fishing. It might be said in defence, that the animals which were hunted and shot would be liable to overrun the earth if not kept down, but the same could not be said of fish. It was argued that those which were hunted and shot would, if not killed in this manner, die or be killed by a worse death; but the argument for killing them because they would die anyway was an equally good argument for killing ourselves.

What was being proposed, he objected, was that legislation should effect something which fell properly within the domain of manners. Humanity could not be exacted by law. It could only be inculcated from the pulpit, recommended through the press and encouraged through the example of general morals.

Finally, he objected to the wording of the bill. Who was to judge what was wanton? Each individual could put his own

154

construction on an incident, and to pass such a bill would be a mockery of legislation. It would amount to giving way to a sanctimonious spirit of hypocrisy. It would be extraordinary if in the nineteenth century they were to adopt a principle of law which no human legislation had ever acted upon.

Mr. Steven countered the main trend of Windham's objections cleverly. The suggestion that the bill did not go far enough could equally well apply to the prevention of crime in general. No law could reach all dishonesty, but there was no reason why housebreakers, felons and others should not be punished. He furthermore denied that the bill marked a new era in legislation; humanity had always been a characteristic of British jurisprudence.

Mr. Steven's relative, Wilberforce, and Lord Erskine's friend, Mr. Jekyll, both argued ably in favour of the bill, and Sir Samuel Romilly, the law reformer, took Windham to task over his mistrust of the magistrates' powers of judgement. He pointed out that questions concerning an employer's treatment of an apprentice were of a similar nature, yet the magistrates had no difficulty in pronouncing upon them. It would be a strange thing, he felt, if the House were to forbear from making laws simply on the grounds that magistrates and juries might find them hard to interpret.

The House sat late into the night, but when the members were counted at three in the morning, only eighteen were found to be present, and the House adjourned. If Richard Martin was present, he does not appear to have spoken. But the reprinting of Erskine's speech to the Lords a couple of months later in Dublin as a pamphlet may have been his doing.

Chapter Fourteen

THE CATHOLIC question had now entered upon a new phase. Discussion centred less on whether or not to admit Catholics to parliament and the higher offices, than on the securities to be offered the Protestants in the event of emancipation. Predominating was the matter of the veto—the King's right to negative the appointment of Catholic bishops—and it found the Catholics themselves divided. The English Catholics and the Irish bishops were prepared to compromise, but the vast body of the Irish Catholics was not.

One of the effects of the Union had been to identify the interests of the English and Irish Catholics although their history differed. The penal laws, which Burke had described as being 'as well fitted for the oppression, impoverishment, and degradation of a people, and the debasement in them of human nature itself, as ever proceeded from the perverted ingenuity of man' had operated in a different manner in the two countries. In England they had involved something akin to a civil war in which the Catholics were all but eliminated, leaving a harmless minority living in peaceful isolation on their estates. The laws had not been an instrument of systematic plunder as in Ireland, where they had been imposed by an alien Government in the interests of a rapacious minority. In England the Catholics were now largely an aristocratic clique; in Ireland they were the great mass of the people. Before the Union, concessions which had been made to the Irish Catholics on grounds of political expediency, such as the Relief Act of 1793, had occasionally left the English Catholics lagging behind, but, by and large, they were sufficiently well established for such drawbacks to count less in the general scale of things than would have been the case in Ireland.

These disagreements between the Catholics tended to vitiate the question of emancipation in the years to come. At the same time, the proposal for the exercise of the veto by one who was incidentally already the head of another Church split the ranks of the liberal Protestants. It became something of a red herring to many who did not hold Richard Martin's view that emancipation must be full and unconditional, with no strings attached.

By the time Martin set out from Galway for Westminster after the Spring assizes of 1810, Portland had been dead several months. He had been replaced by Percival who, in search of a more widely based ministry, had made overtures to the Whig Lords, Grenville and Grey, but had been rebuffed. In the Peninsula, after the victory of Talavera which had won him his dukedom as Wellington, Wellesley was playing a waiting game, which dissatisfied the Opposition. And, persevering outside the main trend of events, Erskine had once again brought in his bill for the prevention of cruelty to animals, and had once again been defeated.

Grattan was due to bring up the Catholic question on 24 May, and Martin, as always when the subject was raised, was making a point of being present. But when he reached Dublin he found himself stranded by adverse winds. When at last they veered around and he was able to sail, he realized that it was now too late for him to arrive at the House of Commons in time for Grattan's motion; but he was too committed to the cause to be deterred. By taking post-chaises to drive him through the night as well as the day, he actually managed to reach London on the morning of the motion and was in his place to cast his vote that evening; but when the House rose at 1.30 a.m. the motion had been defeated.

Another vote which Martin cast shortly afterwards prompted the *Freeman's Journal*, aware of his close ties with the Prince of Wales, to make a shrewd forecast of his political behaviour. It was on a motion for parliamentary reform, and Martin voted with the governmental majority. 'We have some reason to conclude,' reported the paper, 'that this gentleman, except upon the question of Catholic emancipation, will seldom be found in the Opposition lists. Since the Prince of Wales declined taking an active part in the politics of Lord Grenville, Mr. Martin, we believe, although related to the Buckingham family, has not taken an active share in party questions. He has, it is said, attached himself particularly to the independent country interest except upon Irish questions, such, more especially, as are connected with the cause of the Catholics.'

The Prince's attitude to the Whigs was to be put more thoroughly to the test before the year was out. Princess Amelia had been ill for some time. She was now twenty-seven and her father's favourite child, and he was so affected by her illness that he was unable to open parliament on 1 November. The following day the Princess died, and the King's mind was once again unhinged. Nobody could tell how long the condition might last, and, following the precedent set by Pitt at the time of the King's previous mental breakdown, the Government proposed a limited regency. For a year the Prince was to take no long-lasting action of which the King might disapprove were he to recover his sanity. The Prince protested loudly against this indignity, and, as on the occasion of the previous regency crisis, the Whigs maintained that the Regent's powers must be absolute. But when the Regency Act was passed early in 1811, the Prince not only accepted the limitations imposed upon him, but, to the disappointment of the Whigs, continued to rule with his father's ministers.

Meanwhile, another daughter had been born to the Martins on 18 December 1810, and christened Mary Jane, and changes were under way at Ballinahinch. Thomas, who was now twenty-four, had come down from Cambridge, but without taking his degree, and at his request his father decided to make over the greater part of the estate to him. It was now bringing in around £12,000 a year, largely due to the kelp, or dried seaweed. About 4,000 tons of it were manufactured annually from what was gathered off the rocks along the wild Connemara coast, and at this time it was selling for as much as £13 a ton. At the same time, Harriet was planning to convert Ballinahinch Castle from a plain, glorified farmhouse into a stately mansion, all of which was to take time and money.

A period now began when the Irish Catholics found them-

Richard Martin, M.P. in Smithfield Market. A sketch by
Cruikshank

The Trial of 'Bill Burn', under Martin's Act. From an original picture
by P. Mathews

Robert Martin

Anthony Martin

Captain Robert Martin, Jnr.

Laetitia Martin, later Lady Peshall

Thomas Martin

Emily Martin, *née* Kirwan, wife of
Richard Martin, Jnr.

Martin's bill in operation

Martin addressing his constituents

selves being pursued in a new way. Martin had said that they were fighting constitutionally for their rights, and, in fact, they had found a valid counterpart to revolution in organization. Groups had been set up in each of the counties as long ago as 1803 when Martin had met the Catholic leaders at the fair of Ballinasloe, and they in turn were responsible to the Catholic Committee in Dublin on which Martin's Gormanston and Barnewall cousins sat. Now the Lord Lieutenant decided to put the Convention Act into effect against them. The act had originated with Lord Clare in 1793 and had been designed to prevent the United Irishmen from assembling and petitioning the King or parliament. It made all assemblies of people claiming to be delegates or representatives illegal.

The most serious consequence of this action was that it heralded a state of more or less open war between the Castle and the Catholic Committee. There was an outcry from the Catholics, Alderman Bradley-King and a colleague tried to break up a meeting of the Committee, and the Earl of Fingal and four of the Barnewalls were temporarily arrested. The Viceroy ultimately had to retract, but a final show-down between the Committee and the Castle was at best postponed.

As always with extremes, these events produced a counter-balance. A movement calling itself the Friends of Toleration grew up, and Martin was the guest of honour at one of its dinners where he was loudly applauded for declaring that the Galway Catholics had earned the gratitude of the country for the example they gave of 'affectionate and conciliatory conduct to their Protestant neighbours'. He attended a banquet for 400 people in London given by the Friends of Religious Liberty to the Irish Catholic leaders who were carrying an address to the Regent. When at another dinner at the Rotunda in Dublin one of the first toasts was 'Richard Martin and the Freeholders of Galway', he felt that he had been understood.

Thomas, now a tall, handsome young man, with his mother's delicate features and his father's powerful frame, was in love. The object of his attentions was the daughter of a man who had made a fortune as a chandler. Short of being a country gentle-man, there could be nothing in the social scale more desirable than marrying into a country gentleman's family. So enamoured was the chandler with the prospect of being the father-in-law of the heir to Ballinahinch Castle and 200,000 acres, that he offered to pay off all the very substantial debts on the property.

Martin's affairs were, as always, involved. He had inherited a highly encumbered estate, and had then proceeded through contested elections, lavish hospitality, general benevolence and chronic mismanagement to add to his liabilities. But the prospect of his problems being settled by a chandler and of his son being guilty of such a mésalliance was too disagreeable. He used every method he knew to separate the young couple, until at last he succeeded, though not without a bitter quarrel with Thomas. The young man had the fiery Martin temper and he found his own dramatic answer to the situation; he enlisted as a volunteer in the same regiment as his brother-in-law, Charles Peshall, the 88th, or Connaught Rangers, and soon he was on his way to the war in the Peninsula.

It must have been with a heavy heart that Martin set about the business which always came to hand around the assizes time before he returned to Westminster. At the beginning of April 1812 he attended a meeting of the Galway Protestants to whom he made a proposal. This was that they should undertake to withhold support in future elections from any candidate who had not taken a pledge of which he was the author. It ran: 'I do most solemnly declare, upon my honour, that until the Catholics are admitted to ALL the privileges of the British Constitution, by granting the prayer of their Petition, I will neither solicit nor accept any office, title or employment, nor will I solicit the same for any other; and it is in consequence of this solemn declaration, made as an Irishman to the Irish people, that I solicit the support of the Irish Constituents for my return to the Imperial Parliament.'

The meeting adopted Martin's proposition, and the *Freeman's Journal* referred to him as 'the never-to-be-forgotten author of the Pledge'. He also originated the practice of Protestants petitioning in favour of the Catholics, and when he set sail for England on 9 April, he was armed with an address from the Protestants of County Galway to the Prince Regent in favour of the Irish Catholics. Only one Galway gentleman, James Lambert of Cregclare, had refused to sign it.

Martin knew from the newspapers that Thomas and Charles Peshall were with the forces assembling under the Duke of

Wellington before Badajoz, the only one of the great citadels on the Spanish-Portuguese border still in French hands. With his affectionate temperament, Thomas could not now fail to be uppermost in his mind. He was quick to anger, but quicker to make amends. He could not bear a rift to last, and always hastened to wipe out its memory. Yet here was a quarrel he would give anything to make up, but he instead was faced with the possibility that it might never be possible to do so.

In fact, while Martin was proposing 'The Pledge', his son was preparing for battle. Wellington's task was to capture the citadel at the juncture of the rivers Guadiana and Rivella before the French armies of the Duke of Dalmatia joined those of the Duke of Ragusa to outnumber his forces in terrain favourable to cavalry in which the French had the superiority. It was the third time he had besieged Badajoz, and he planned that the old Moorish castle, which stood a hundred and fifty feet above the river, should be taken on the night of 5 April. He then postponed the assault to the 6th.

Thomas had arrived in time to participate in the twenty-one-day siege, during most of which the rain had been so torrential that the men preparing the ground for the attack had been obliged to work up to their waists in water. As a volunteer, Thomas messed with the officers and wore officer's uniform, but without epaulettes; but he stood in the ranks with a cross-belt and firelock, and took his turn in the trenches, six hours out of twenty-four, like the rest of the men, and he must often have seen Wellington, sometimes unshaven, moving about among the soldiers.

The attack was timed for 10 p.m. on Easter Sunday, and in the evening heavy green ladders were distributed among those who were to scale the walls of the castle. Apart from the croaking of the frogs in the marshes, the only sound came from the band of the Connaught Rangers playing Irish airs, particularly 'Savourneen Deelish'. Some wrote last-minute letters home, distributed little effects among their comrades, or bequeathed arrears of pay.

A thick fog hid the opponents from one another, but when the attack started, the advancing soldiers were suddenly lit up by fire-balls. The ramparts, ditch and plains were ablaze. Enormous pikes with crooks attached to them ranged the top of the walls, which were covered with rocks that a slight push could topple on to the besieging army. Entire sections were swept away by an incessant storm of musketry at a distance of fifteen yards.

The minute the ladders were erected against the thirty-five-foot walls and mounted, the men were shot down and fell back transfixed upon the bayonets of their comrades in the ditch below. After an hour no progress had been made and the Connaught Rangers alone had lost nineteen officers and 450 men. Their commander, General Picton, continued to urge them on. Then suddenly, two ladders were placed and mounted. A third was put in position by Lieutenant Mackie of the 88th, who managed to mount it. Immediately behind him came Thomas. He raced up the ladder, but as he reached the top he was hit in the shoulder by a bullet. Although severely wounded, he continued to press forward, but then was hit in the head by a fragment of shell and fell.

The main attack had failed, but this lodgement on the ramparts was decisive. Men began swarming up the ladders and on to the parapet, trampling on the dead and wounded as they advanced. They fought until 2.30 a.m. and finally routed the defenders, but 350 officers and 4,000 men had fallen. When Sir James McGregor, the Chief of Medical Staff, went through the breaches next day, his feet sank so deep into the mass of bodies that he could scarcely walk. The servant Thomas Martin had brought with him from Ballinahinch could be seen sitting on a height wringing his hands and moaning that fate had lured his master from the peace of Connemara to die in such a place. It was a decisive victory for Wellington, but when he heard what the cost had been, for the first time ever known he gave way to a passionate burst of grief and wept.

In London, where Martin was, all that was known was that an attack was planned, and like his daughter Laetitia, he had to face anxious days of waiting for news. It was 15 April before Wellington's despatch arrived and Liverpool was able to congratulate him on behalf of the Regent. The newspapers published lists lumping casualties together, such as '5 rank and file killed, 2 lieutenants, 24 rank and file wounded, 1 rank and file missing', and throughout it was clear that the heaviest losses had been in the 88th. Martin would no doubt have been able to use his influence to see Wellington's despatch before it was finally published in the *Gazette* Extraordinary on 24 April. Nowhere was there any mention of Thomas, but Martin had the unpleasant duty of informing Laetitia that Charles Peshall was slightly wounded.

Although he was a sanguine man, he must have been constantly nagged by the knowledge that the casualty lists were often inaccurate, so that it must have been with great relief that he received the news which at last arrived: Thomas had been badly wounded, but at least he was alive. Much later it became known that his behaviour had been heroic. Wellington had offered him a commission, but as he had no intention of continuing in the army, he had refused. It was years later that one of his companions wrote the true account of his action: 'Since the days of knight errantry, never has there been a parallel to his conduct.'

While things at the war front were improving, matters at home were hurrying towards a crisis. Martin claimed that he had not had the honour of taking off his hat to the Prime Minister, Perceval, more than twice, although they had once exchanged a few unforgettable words. Perceval had been impressed by some unexpected support from Martin and asked where he might meet the gallant colonel. Martin, leaning upon his reputation as a duellist, and with his usual trenchant humour, had replied promptly, 'Within pistol shot of the Treasury.' Now, on 11 May 1812, almost within pistol shot of the Treasury Bench, Perceval was assassinated by a maniac. This started a crisis which lasted several weeks and drove the final wedge between the Regent and the Whigs who, now that the period of limited regency was at an end, and the Prince had full powers, expected to be called to office.

The Regent, in fact, did not want the Whigs, but a broadly based ministry, and, unlike them, he approved of the way in which the war was being prosecuted. The Whigs were gradually ceasing to trust the Regent, and there was disagreement on the Catholic question. But more decisive in prolonging the crisis than any political divergencies were the personal animosities and jealousies which prevented men of substance from combining their efforts for the nation's good.

With a great war raging, the vacuum created a feeling of

163

despair, and on 20 May Martin gave notice that unless something was done, and unless somebody more competent undertook to do it, he would submit a resolution the following week. It would call for an address beseeching the Regent to take measures without delay to deal with the disorganized state of the country by appointing a more adequate Administration and one which had more of the people's confidence than the last. There was considerable support for Martin, and some thought his move might lead some of the aristocracy to approach the Regent individually in search of a solution. In fact, on the day following Martin's notice, an independent member, Stuart Wortley, moved for an address calling for a strong and efficient Administration, and after some discussions with him, Martin agreed to drop his own motion and voted for Wortley's.

The Catholic question became the crux of the negotiations for the formation of a new ministry, and Martin later claimed that it had been made 'the stalking horse for party views'. In debate Castlereagh had shown himself anxious to sidestep the issue. He had rather petulantly suggested that it was up to the Catholics to state precisely what it was they wanted; the Administration could not be expected to devote to the subject time and energy which should be concentrated on the war in the Peninsula.

This drew forth an attack from Martin and a reaction in parliamentary terms. The Catholics' claims, he pointed out, were clearly stated in their petitions; it only remained for the Government to announce on what terms they were prepared to grant them. He followed this by giving notice on 27 May that he would move on 12 July for the appointment of a committee to enquire whether the Catholics laboured under any, and what, disabilities, and whether it would be expedient to repeal the whole or any part of the laws now in force against them; and also to enquire whether such repeal should be accompanied by any, and what, securities for the further protection of the Established Protestant Church. He could scarcely have put the question more precisely. His reason for fixing the date so far ahead was that he wanted to ensure that his motion did not interfere with one of which Canning had given notice. Martin still hoped at this time that Canning, with his pro-Catholic views, would enter the Government, and he only intended to go ahead with his motion if Canning was prevented by office from bringing the matter forward. But Castlereagh put in a reasonable plea for not bringing it up until a new Government had been formed, and both Canning and Martin finally agreed to forbear.

Martin was, however, to be disappointed in that neither Canning nor the Marquess of Wellesley, both of whom could have been expected to be favourable to the Catholics, were to be in the Administration. The weeks of negotiation accentuated rather than diminished the differences between those who were consulted, until the Regent came to the decision which was the easiest, and, in the circumstances, probably the only one he could take: he invited Lord Liverpool, who could be relied upon to continue the existing war policy, to head a cabinet composed of the selfsame men who had been in office when the crisis began.

Since the Prince had chosen his father's ministers, the Whigs believed he must have decided to follow his father's policies. Into the bargain, Liverpool was known to be averse to the Catholics' claims. Now, although the Whigs had themselves totally failed to face up to the problem of emancipation when in office, they tried to make political capital out of the claim that, with such a ministry, the cause was lost for good. Replying to Sheridan, Martin took up the challenge in one of his best and longest speeches. It was significant that cries of 'Hear, hear' came equally from both sides of the House as he proceeded to demolish the argument that the Catholics would not accept emancipation from such a cabinet and to make a plea for granting them their rights. At the same time, possibly deliberately bearing out the forecast given in the *Freeman's Journal*, he outlined his future political conduct.

He started by deploring that the Catholic question had been dragged into what he called the 'paltry intrigues' of the recent negotiations. While admitting that the Whigs were friendly to the cause, he reminded them that they derived their importance from the Catholic question, and not the other way around. It was this question, which they clung to with convulsive energy, which prevented their popularity from drowning, but if that plank were removed, they would sink to rise no more.

This did not mean that he did not hold some of them in the highest esteem. For the greater part of his political life he had acted with them, and although never officially affiliated, he claimed that he had sometimes done more for the party than those who were. But it was measures, not men, that he supported, and above all that great measure which he had made the leading star of his political life, and without which, *unrestricted*, *unconditional*, unrestrained by any jealous provisos, by any foolish sanctions, by any absurd interference with the spiritual government of the Irish Church, no tranquillity could be expected, no salvation for the empire. This was greeted with loud cries of 'Hear, hear' from all parts of the House.

After warning Canning against the folly of introducing the measure on terms, and admitting that there was a feeling in Ireland that that was what the present Administration intended, he remarked that change was always possible, and that one of the most ardent supporters of the Catholics, George Ponsonby, was a convert to their cause.

At the same time he wanted it clearly understood that he disapproved '*in every and all its parts* the whole system of politics regarding Ireland'. He had no connection with the new Administration, but he felt that he of all men would be above suspicion if on some occasion he considered it right to support them—he might give them his vote. He wished to see the Administration strengthened, but he did not wish to see the kingly state humbled, he said, and took the opportunity of chastizing Lords Grey and Grenville for the demand they had made during the negotiations that the Regent should dismiss certain members of the royal household.

'To impute to any individual,' he declared, 'whether in or out of office, either directly or indirectly, the practice of using a private influence over the mind of the sovereign, so as to counteract the effect of the advice of his sworn counsellors, and to demand the dismissal of those individuals in consequence, was not alone a direct insult, but, in plain terms, signified that the illustrious person, whose feelings seem so little to be regarded, was so weak, that he had not the power to judge between right and wrong.' He thus made it plain that he was the Prince's man, and he was to remain so.

He concluded by reiterating that the Catholics were loyal

subjects demanding a fair and equal participation of the liberties of British subjects. If this were granted, they would not reject it because it did not come from an administration composed of individuals who were more favourable to them. 'The glory,' he declared, 'will be, in my mind, increased when even their oppressors could not longer resist the power of truth and justice.' But that year the Catholic Committee was suppressed under the Convention Act.

Among his activities during the remainder of the session, Martin sat on a select committee with Romilly to look into the condition of prisoners in Lincoln Castle. He was able also to amuse himself in a typical way over the Sinecure Bill to which he moved an amendment on the grounds that pensions should not be granted to relieve the needy, but to reward the virtuous. Was the recipient, he asked, 'to be put in the situation of the apothecary in *Romeo and Juliet*—was "his poverty and not his will" to be the actuating principle whereby he was to be guided?' After comparing the mover to a lover, he declared that he thought he would lose his mistress—the bill—and find it another Eurydice which would elude him at the very moment he was most sure of it, like another Orpheus. '*Te dulcis conjux,*' he quoted, relishing his Latin as always, '*Te veniente die, te decedente canebat.*'* This raised the laugh for which he was aiming, and his amendment was carried by 64 to 52.

Martin combined intense social activity with his parliamentary duties. His carriage was to be seen constantly drawing up to all the most fashionable houses, but the Martin coat of arms on its door was apt to cause a scene. The Calvary Cross on it drew forth from the crowd such cries as, 'Look at the papists!' followed by uncomplimentary remarks. That summer Harriet left little Mary with some of the O'Flaherty family in Connemara when she came to join her husband in London, while Harriet, now aged eleven, and Georgina, though only six, were both boarders at Mrs. Clarke's Free College in Bromley, Kent. There their mother kept them supplied with a commentary on the parties she attended, taking care to point out what was, or was not, desirable in the world for which she was preparing her children.

* 'You, sweet wife, . . .
  You at the dawn of day, he sang, at day's decline you.'

'I must tell you for your encouragement, my dear child,' she wrote to little Harriet, called Hatty for short, 'that I consciously compare you with all the young people I meet of your standing, and I have not yet seen any one whose manners and general deportment please me so much.'

A girl of fifteen who played Mozart at the house of the Dillons, a prominent County Galway family, obviously had the kind of manners which appealed to her and she hastened to praise the girl to Hatty.

'She was very modest in her air and deportment, 'tho perfectly at ease for she knew very well what she was about, and had confidence in her own possession of her subject. She was not, therefore, at all disconcerted 'tho perfectly free from presumption—nor did she seem at all abashed till on the conclusion the applause and bravos of the company called up her blushes.'

Hatty's youth entitled her to few concessions. She was expected to understand that Mr. Dillon's foible was love of ancestry, and that her father was more esteemed as Lord Trimlestown's grandson than as plain Mr. Martin. The eleven-year-old child was even informed that she was 'enough versed in *law* and politics' to appreciate the difficulties surrounding the morganatic marriage of the Duke of Sussex with Lady Augusta Murray. 'Pity for the sake of her own peace of mind and her children's,' wrote the mother, 'that she did not rather marry her equal.'

The two little girls in their boarding school were never left in any doubt as to the purpose of all their mother's party going; it was to prepare the way for their entry into society. Their father was even more tireless in the interests of his sons. Long after his wife had retired from the evening's social rounds, he could be seen flitting from one party to another, remembering that Richard, now a youth of fifteen, was already showing signs of worldliness.

As for Thomas, he had recovered and been repatriated, but for the rest of his life he walked with a slight stoop from the wound in his shoulder. He was already in County Galway before the Martins returned there after the dissolution of parliament, and there he found himself at the same time as William Poppleton, eleven years his senior and the husband of his cousin, Margaret Martin of Ross, who was home on leave from the Peninsula. They were both given the welcome of heroes, and the masonic lodge in Galway organized a big dinner in their honour.

Chapter Fifteen

'HIS STERLING qualities were so embossed with wild humour and fun,' wrote the well-known journalist William Jerdan of Martin, 'that it was no easy matter to form a correct judgement upon his real character.' Even if his children's interests had not been uppermost in his mind, Martin would have moved in the highest society; he had been accustomed to doing so since childhood. But the more discerning of those who knew him were aware that he was no common host or guest in the fashionable world. As one lady who viewed his idiosyncracies indulgently put it: 'He has so many strange notions.'

Wherever he was, he was perpetually on the look-out for the unfortunate. Some extra sensitivity in his nature made him aware of a slight where others would have overlooked it. The plain girl who was the wallflower at the ball could be sure of being the first to attract his attention. If somebody was passed over because of some social inadequacy, Martin would be bound to find the compensating virtues of good manners or charm. His own daughter was to paint in later years a typical scene in which he heard a young governess playing to a room full of people who then moved off to supper, leaving the girl alone. To Martin's enquiry, the hostess declared that the governess never took supper, but before many minutes had passed, she found that Martin had returned to the drawing-room to collect the girl and, bringing her to the supper table, had sat down beside her to give her his undivided attention.

Erring sons and daughters who had incurred the wrath of

170

their parents found in him a protector and a counsellor who restored them to the bosom of their families. He was notorious at interceding for young men who had fallen out of favour with their superiors, and his house was a refuge to the struggling while they tried to set themselves up in life. Out of delicacy he always tried to avoid their being embarrassed by his hospitality, and invented some small job for them to do. He could read hunger in a man's back, even if he had not seen the face, and, as with every waif he came across, it was his own house which supplied the want. He winced at others' physical or moral suffering and was no more capable of passing by their needs than a thief would be of passing by their riches. His general benevolence was a by-word in every circle, but it was the Prince Regent himself who was to establish it for all time. He nick-named him 'Humanity Martin', which became popularized as 'Humanity Dick' and abbreviated to 'Humanity'.

In the summer of 1812 parliament was dissolved and Humanity Dick decided to support the Government in the ensuing election. Before leaving London he set about pulling all the strings which were essential in any parliamentary contest at the time. Lord Sidmouth, the Home Secretary, had acknow-ledged the value of his services in the House, and Martin wrote asking him to drop a hint to Lord Clancarty, the former colleague in whose conversion to the Union he had helped, to support him. The new Chief Secretary for Ireland was Robert Peel who was to find the country uncongenial except for the opportunities it afforded for shooting and who considered the Catholic claims incompatible with British interests. Martin now sent him a list of people whom the Government could influence to stand by him, and before Peel left for Dublin he called on him to emphasize his point. When he felt that Peel was not taking the matter sufficiently seriously, he wrote again to Sidmouth asking him to impress upon Peel the need to act at once, and reminded the Home Secretary that his principal service to the Government had been to reconcile the Galway Catholics to the new ministry.

He left for Ireland on 26 September, and after spending ten days in Dublin, he called again on Peel before leaving for the west. But by then the die was cast. Although Liverpool had personally asked Clancarty to support him, his lordship had already decided to back James Daly and Colonel Eyre, and would not hear of Humanity Dick under any circumstances. Peel did what he could to influence various people in his favour, but when he reached Galway a shock was in store for him. It turned out that 2,300 of his freeholders were not eligible to vote because they had registered too late. Apart from this, there were influential people, including Clanricarde's father-in-law, Sir Thomas Burke, who had promised him support but now let him down. In the circumstances an election would be an exceptionally difficult and costly business, and he was not in a financial position to go through with it. He had no alternative to declining to stand, and from Dalgin Castle, his Kirwan cousins' house in east Galway, he wrote to inform Peel. He declared at the same time that he would throw all his weight into supporting Eyre in order to keep out Bowes Daly, the representative of 'the Talents', as he still called the Whigs who were now the Regent's enemies.

There were, however, other circumstances surrounding Bowes Daly and the election. Humanity Dick claimed that an agreement had been made between them some time previously that, if necessary, Bowes Daly would relinquish his stand for the county in order to ensure Martin's return. Bowes Daly admitted the agreement, but refused to submit the interpretation to the arbitration of friends, as suggested by Humanity. As a man of honour, Humanity had felt obliged to challenge him, but Bowes Daly, instead of fighting, had claimed that his life was in danger and had had Humanity arrested and bound to keep the peace.

All this was discussed with some warmth at a county meeting where, to emphasize his point, Bowes Daly said that Humanity had stated publicly, when asked who would win the election, that it would be 'the survivor'. It was even rumoured that the remark had been made to the Prince Regent. Bowes Daly as an Irishman should have recognized this as typical of Humanity Dick's exuberant sense of humour, but when he did not, Humanity played mercilessly upon his failure to understand. He entertained the meeting in his own inimitable way with an outline of what had occurred, and by his gestures and the ludicrous way in which he described the state of Bowes Daly's nerves, he kept the meeting in peals of laughter.

Meanwhile Thomas was following the family tradition and becoming involved in politics; he had decided to stand for the town of Galway. His object was the same as that which had led his grandfather, Robert, to expend large sums of money: namely, to limit the influence of the Daly family who, through packing the Corporation with their friends and relatives, and creating non-resident freemen, had established a monopoly over the town.

The freeholders and inhabitants of Galway met on 16 October to nominate candidates, but Thomas had to come from the depths of Connemara, and arrived late. By that time, Valentine Blake of Menlo, the nearest neighbour to Dangan, had been nominated, and Thomas, feeling that Blake had the support of the meeting and not wishing to cause a scene, relinquished all claim to stand. The meeting was so appreciative that it passed a resolution thanking him for his 'manly and disinterested conduct', but his stepmother, Harriet, felt that he had thrown away his opportunity. She consoled herself by admitting that as he had escaped from Badajoz, she should not complain of any worldly losses.

Humanity Dick had suggested on the occasion of his long speech in the House on the Catholic question that the Liverpool Administration had experienced a change of heart on the subject, and he evidently had sufficient confidence in this to back Eyre as a Government candidate against Bowes Daly for the Opposition; his most ardent support for the Prince could not have led him away from the cause he had made his own. With the campaign in full swing he still saw ways of aiding Eyre, and, characteristically heading his letter 'The Hustings', wrote to Peel telling him what influence could still be canvassed.

As always, he went about his business with energy and determination, but emotional strain could get the better of his robust frame. After so many years in parliament, it was a bitter experience to have to relinquish his candidature, and however lightly he treated the Bowes Daly incident, he could not ignore it. The combination of fatigue and anxiety at last overcame him, and with the election still in progress, he collapsed into bed at Clareville with a fever, while in another room young Richard lay ill with scarlet fever.

None of this prevented Harriet's dutifully sitting beside

Humanity Dick's bed, and, under his direction, writing a full account to Peel of how the withdrawal of support by one person and then another had forced him to forego the contest. Little Hatty was also kept fully posted at school where she was told she would shortly receive for her mistress, Miss Clarke, her father's printed version of what had happened between himself and Bowes Daly whose 'petty conduct,' wrote her mother, 'has made him very ridiculous among men . . . but I know I rejoice at his cowardice since it saved us from a dreadful shock'. A couple of weeks later the election results showed that all Humanity's exertions had been in vain. James Daly and his cousin, Bowes Daly, were elected for County Galway.

For the first time in twenty years, Humanity Dick found himself in almost uninterrupted residence on his estate. Most of the winter was spent in what Hatty had christened 'pretty Clareville' and when the weather got better they moved to join Thomas in what she called 'grand Ballinahinch'. Some improvements had been made to the smaller house, while the enlargement and general refurbishing of Ballinahinch which Harriet had undertaken were sufficiently advanced by the summer of 1813 for at least half of the family to gather there. The exceptions were the two little girls, Hatty and Georgy, still at Miss Clarke's school, and Laetitia and her four-year-old son, Charles, who were in England, while Charles Peshall himself was aide-de-camp to Lieutenant General Chown in the Peninsula.

Harriet had just sailed across the fifteen miles of Lough Corrib in order to go to Dalgin. There she was to see her dearest friend, Miss Kirwan, who had just visited the two little Martin girls in their Kentish school, and was able to give Harriet a detailed description of her two small daughters singing one of their mother's favourite songs as a duet. Harriet held that Miss Kirwan had kept all the details of her visit to the school in order to lure her across the lake, and now she in turn tempted Miss Kirwan to sail back across the water to spend a night at Clareville, which she greatly admired, before setting out across the mountains for Ballinahinch. This wild and majestic stretch of country, with its broad horizons and racing clouds, was what Martin had in his mind's eye when the Regent was showing him the avenues at Hampton Court and he, evidently with his tongue in his cheek, had boasted that the approach from his gate lodge to his hall door was thirty miles long.

Miss Kirwan, coming from the flat country east of Lough Corrib, found the beauty of the Ballinahinch countryside sublime. Although still only scantily furnished with things brought from Clareville, the house was comfortable, and Thomas was tireless in planting trees and making other outdoor improvements. The party made an expedition to Derryclare Lake, and climbed the shining quartz-capped peak of Ben Lettery which falls steeply into Ballinahinch Lake, and there were boating trips winding in and out of the long chain of lakes which adjoins the house.

Here the Martins' youngest child, Mary, made her first public entry at the age of three into the long drawing-room overlooking the water. She was in full dress for the arrival of Miss Kirwan who thought she was the image of her sister, Georgy. As for Humanity Dick, Harriet wrote to his little daughter that he was 'in high health and spirits seeing us all around him in his favourite residence'.

Within the next year Thomas was to show he had fully forgotten his heiress. Following the western tradition of not going beyond the Shannon in search of a bride, he had fallen in love with Julia Kirwan, daughter of the late Patrick Kirwan of Dalgin, niece of his mother's best friend, and a relation of his own through his great-grandmother. Beautiful, accomplished and accustomed to the best society, she was on her mother's side a niece of the 4th Countess of Buckinghamshire.

The entire arrangement was highly satisfactory to all concerned, and when young Richard, now rising seventeen, was studying at Ballinahinch to enter Trinity College, Dublin, it was natural that he should be invited with Thomas to Dalgin for Christmas. Richard, who was an excellent horseman, knew that if he went he would not be able to resist the hunting, which was particularly good in the area. That would interfere with his working for the exam he was due to take a week after Christmas, so he refused. His mother felt that such virtue should be rewarded, and rather than leave him alone at Ballinahinch, she went there to join him before Christmas, even though it meant cutting herself off from her daughter's correspondence,

175

as at Ballinahinch there was no post. A couple of months later Thomas and Julia were married and settled into Ballinahinch where Thomas dispensed the proverbial Martin hospitality even in excess of his father's.

Although he had given up active politics, Humanity Dick had plenty to do. He lost his only sister, Mary, in 1813, and had to settle up her affairs as she was childless. He had succeeded in getting his mines reopened and spent many hours in all weathers trudging around observing the work that was now going on underground by day and night. He also had some disagreeable legal business on hand.

In the first place, Bowes Daly decided to bring a case against him for challenging him to a duel. It was heard in Galway before Judge McClelland, and Humanity was neither allowed to speak nor to cross-examine Bowes Daly. The case went against Humanity, but it was not so much on account of this, as because he felt that he had been treated unfairly that he bore a grudge against the judge who was later to be involved in another case concerning Humanity.

He had discovered that a solicitor named Edward Burke had cheated him of £420 by forgery as well as being guilty of perjury. He had trusted Burke, as he trusted almost everyone, and his anger was aroused. He resolved to prosecute, but, as always, the processes of justice were slow. When at last the case was due to come on, he suddenly realized that forgery was punishable by death; this would be Burke's fate if he were found guilty. The thought of being responsible for a man being put to death in cold blood filled him with horror, and the benevolence which led him to collect lame dogs came into play. Burke was as good as a thief, but was it right that he should pay for a moment of temptation with his life? To Humanity Dick the idea was monstrous. He rushed messages to his counsel to withdraw the charge, and was just in the nick of time. Burke was saved. Humanity made up his mind to campaign for the abolition of the death penalty for forgery. That did not, however, prevent his pursuing Burke relentlessly for perjury, sometimes with amusing overtones. On one occasion he proceeded to conduct the case himself, and there was such pandemonium in the court that the judge had to bring in the military to clear it.

Another incident which was to affect his parliamentary

conduct occurred during this period. On the shores of Clew Bay, in the region of Westport, there lived a man who had a tame seal which he claimed was 'as fond as a dog and as playful as a kitten'. In the summer it liked to bask in the sun, and in winter to lie stretched before the fire or in the big oven in the kitchen. When the man's stock started falling ill and dying, he consulted a wise woman who told him it was because he kept an unclean animal as a pet. If he wanted to save his stock he must get rid of the seal. In Irish folklore seals are frequently human beings who have been transformed and it is considered unlucky to kill one. Therefore, the only way in which the man could rid himself of his pet was by having it taken out to sea and dumped. This he did, but the next day the faithful creature returned to its home. The man had it carried out to sea once again, this time much further, but once again the devoted animal returned.

He then consulted the wise woman again, and she said there was only one thing left that he could do: he must blind the seal so that it would not be able to find its way back to his house. The seal had been a household pet for four years. Yet the man found it in his heart, if he had one, to perform the dreadful deed, inflicting terrible agony on the harmless creature, and once again the seal was taken out to sea and dumped. A week passed without its reappearing; then a terrible wailing was heard in the night. Next morning the affectionate animal was found outside the door where it had perished from starvation; deprived of its sight, it had not been able to fish for its customary food. Nothing but disaster followed the man who was responsible. Not only his stock, but all belonging to him died. The man who had been punishing crimes against animals on his own estates for more than a decade was outraged. Such barbarity, he was convinced, must be made punishable by law, and he determined that if ever he got back into parliament he would make it his business to fight for legislation on the subject.

His period of retirement from politics coincided with one of the great turning-points in world affairs. Napoleon had retreated through the snow from Moscow, surrendered and been imprisoned on Elba, escaped after a hundred days and renewed the fight. But he had lost the magic touch which for years had brought him victory. Defeated by Wellington at Waterloo in 1815, he had once again surrendered and was now a prisoner on St. Helena. The Martins occasionally had news from there, for the orderly at Longwood where Napoleon was detained, was the husband of Margaret Martin of Ross, William Poppleton. When he left St. Helena in 1817, he incurred the displeasure of the Governor, Sir Hudson Lowe, by accepting from Napoleon a farewell gift of a snuff-box which he brought back to add to the bibelots at Ross House.

By the time the rumour got around in 1817 that parliament was about to be dissolved and Humanity Dick began to think about standing in the next elections, he had seen one part of his family growing up around him. Little Mary now seven, was wild and clever; Thomas had not succeeded, as their mother had feared, in corrupting her language. Thomas had a three-year-old daughter, also called Mary, whom he idolized. His door was always open and his sideboard always groaning.

As for Richard, the Martins had seen more of him than at any time since he was a small child. He spent long vacations at Ballinahinch, where he loved to walk and shoot over the Connemara bogs, and he cut a dash in society. His mother wrote to the two girls at school in England that he had been to a ball in Galway where 'his deportment and dancing were much lauded by the genteelest and best bred of the ladies. He soars high as to partners,' she added, 'and as he has very gay spirits and a talent at a good style of flattery to the fair he was in great favour.' Yet, he was serious-minded enough to write to Hatty that she could not do better than to read history.

Hatty and Georgy were now sixteen and eleven, and although Harriet had the utmost confidence in Miss Clarke's school, there had, nonetheless, been occasions when she would have wished to be able to correct her daughters other than by letter. Laetitia often visited the girls with little Charles, now eight, but remarks such as that Georgy spoke too fast and indistinctly made Harriet wish that she could have her daughters at her side. She had written off immediately urging the child to repeat some lines of prose or poetry slowly twice a day, and after imploring Hatty to help to correct her younger sister, added, 'It is a great blemish to have bad articulation.'

So Harriet rejoiced as much as Humanity Dick at the prospect of returning to London where they would be nearer the girls. But the financial situation, pending the great revenue which was expected from the mines, was far from satisfactory, and certainly not such as to warrant the expenses of an electoral campaign. Yet, Humanity Dick was determined to return to parliament if he could. He had both the question of the death penalty for forgery and legislation for the prevention of cruelty to animals to take up. But most of all he needed to be in parliament to pursue his life's work for Catholic emancipation.

While Martin was in retirement Grattan had made another attempt to get through a bill in favour of the Catholics but Canning, with the best intentions, had tagged on to it a string of 'securities' which forced the sponsors to withdraw it as being unacceptable to the Irish Catholics themselves. Humanity Dick must have asked himself constantly where the Catholics would now have stood had there been no Union, but it was a question that it was impossible to answer.

Now in April 1817 he took the first steps necessary for his return to Westminster. He was on intimate terms with Martin Joseph Blake, a big landowner of Ballygloonin, near Tuam, in east Galway. He wrote asking Blake for his support in the next election, but this was not to remain purely political. Blake was committed to Catholic emancipation and trusted most completely in Humanity's zeal and ability in bringing it about. He was, also, rich, and he agreed to back Humanity Dick financially.

Chapter Sixteen

HUMANITY DICK had boundless confidence in the Prince
Regent's friendship, and with an election in sight, he could
think of no better place to begin his canvas than Carlton House
itself. Sir Benjamin Bloomfield, the Prince's private secretary,
met William Gregory, Under-Secretary at Dublin Castle, in
London one day in June 1818 and told him that the Regent had
received what he termed an extraordinary letter from Humanity
asking the Prince to procure support for him in the election. It
was, in fact, only a couple of months since the Regent had
appointed young Richard, who had taken his B.A. the previous
year, to a cornetcy in the 3rd Dragoon Guards—his grandfather
was in the 5TH—where he could not fail, with his dashing
ways, to cut a fine figure. But whatever bonds united the
Prince to Humanity Dick, Bloomfield did not feel that they
extended to political patronage.

He told Gregory that he had decided to reply that the
Regent could not intervene in any election; but, nevertheless, as
if interested in the issue, he enquired how the Irish Government felt towards Humanity Dick. Gregory was an ardent
supporter of the Orangemen and had no reason to like Humanity
Dick. He replied unhesitatingly that it would not be in the
Irish Government's interest to support Humanity for Galway,
and, reporting his conversation to Peel who, he believed,
shared his views, he wrote: 'I said . . . that I knew how revolting
it was to the feelings of the gentlemen of that county to be
represented by him, and that if he should unfortunately be

returned, I could not suppose the Ministry to have a more troublesome supporter.'

In fact, Peel had probably not changed the opinion he had expressed in 1813 when he had declared: 'Martin, I know, is a very uncertain friend, but at any rate a less uncertain enemy than Bowes Daly', and he now gave him the Government's support. As for the gentlemen of the county to whom Gregory had referred, it was two leading Catholics who proposed and seconded Humanity Dick at the county meeting, despite his declaration, which surprised some, that he intended to support Liverpool, and far from being revolted at being represented by him, that gathering of county gentlemen adopted him as their candidate.

James Daly was also standing for the county, and was putting up a Mr. Prendergast for the town. The crux of the campaign, so far as Humanity Dick was concerned, was to ensure that James Daly adhered to an undertaking given a year previously to support him in the county rather than Bowes Daly, James's wife's uncle and his own cousin. But Humanity Dick, true to the family tradition of trying to wrest Galway from the domination of the Daly family, was actively opposing James Daly in the town. Daly resented this and threatened to resist Peel's pressure to win him for Humanity Dick. The most he could offer, he said, was neutrality. 'The contest will be an extremely stiff one', he wrote to Peel, 'if all your applications in favour of Martin are attended to', and Humanity Dick, with his usual wry humour, wrote to his sponsor, Martin Joseph Blake: 'I beg you will send me a case of pistols to remain with me until the election is over.'

As polling proceeded, Daly forecast to Peel, 'Your protégé will be beaten in this county', and in the first days this seemed likely. It was not until the nineteenth day that Humanity Dick's votes began to catch up on Bowes Daly's until finally they surpassed them, and he and James Daly were elected for the county, while in the town, Daly's candidate, Prendergast was beaten.

'I acknowledge I am tired of the rascality of elections and electioneering,' Daly wrote to Peel. 'I wish you would get me an Irish peerage which would enable me to give all up without giving up my interest. . . . No person with any ounce of principle can contest an Irish town or county.'

True to the usual form at election time, Bowes Daly accused Reddington, one of Martin's supporters, of causing a riot, and Reddington in turn accused Bowes Daly of trying to organize his assassination at a race meeting at the Curragh, an incident which provided Humanity Dick with an opportunity for writing a long and well-phrased letter to the *Freeman's Journal*. Among other things he said: 'Mr. Daly compliments himself upon "the conduct of his long life" and assures you that it places him "above every insinuation" of error. So lovely a picture of the beau ideal in moral perfection cannot be contemplated without some regret, that the happy original, whilst it indulges in the self-approving retrospections of such age and innocence, does not evince for others any of those placid and benign feelings, which should be the desert of either, and especially of both.'

In the interval between the elections and the reopening of parliament, there was a change in the Irish Government which could not fail to give hope to such as Humanity Dick. Robert Peel, the known enemy of the Catholics, was replaced as Chief Secretary by Charles Grant, the friend of emancipation. A county meeting was to be called to address Peel upon his departure, and Humanity wrote to Martin Joseph Blake: 'I see no kind of objection to a complimentary address provided there be a strong expression of our entire dissent and protest against the line of conduct pursued by Peel on the Catholic question.' As events turned out, he had to fight to make his opinion prevail, and writing an account of the meeting to Blake, he said: 'I am glad I was present for I prevented an affront intended as I believe to be given to Mr. Grant, the strenuous friend of Catholic Emancipation, in order to pay an awkward compliment to his predecessor in office.' When the Friends of Independence of Galway held their quarterly dinner at Kilroy's hotel at the beginning of November, where they were served in the greatest style with 'every delicacy the country could afford', Humanity Dick started his speech by welcoming the appointment of Grant and paying tribute to his devotion to Irish interests, extensive knowledge, powerful eloquence, liberal sentiments and enlightened mind.

What neither Humanity Dick nor the rest of the Irish knew were the terms upon which Grant was to serve. The Lord

Lieutenant, Talbot, had only just written to the Home Secretary, Sidmouth: 'Mr. Grant, our new secretary, is, as I dare say your Lordship is aware, friendly to the granting the Catholic claims. I am happy, however, to state for your private information that he has assured me, that he will take no steps whatever, nor lend himself to any measure, *on this side the water*, to the furtherance of their views.' Grant himself was worried on arrival in Ireland lest he should be compromised due to his known sympathies with the Catholics, and he was relieved to be able to write to Sidmouth that, contrary to his expectations, the Irish had treated him with 'consideration and delicacy'.

When Humanity Dick returned to Westminster at the beginning of 1819, he had been six years out of parliament. He was sixty-five years of age and his most important work still lay ahead. Since he had first entered parliament Britain had emerged from battling to retain her American colonies and then, licking her wounds after their loss, to being the leading world power after Waterloo. The problems of war were now over, but peace was to present others which were new and disturbing. Even prosperity, it became apparent, had to be controlled, and when it admitted sweated labour and excessive poverty it bred a new kind of social unrest deriving inspiration from the French Revolution. The moment when Humanity Dick returned to parliament coincided with the beginning of the struggle for economic equality within the institutions of a parliamentary democracy which was to characterize political life for generations.

The Martins took a house in Manchester Buildings, a street right beside the Houses of Parliament. By Dickens's day it had become the seedy dwelling place of the lesser members of parliament, particularly the Irish, and figured in *Nicholas Nickleby*, but in the Martins' time it was still the essence of elegance and respectability. From the moment Humanity Dick re-entered the House of Commons he tended to make the members laugh whenever he got to his feet. It was so usual for him to be entertaining that they sometimes misunderstood him and laughed when he was not even joking. When in the course of a debate Castlereagh referred to his years of absence and congratulated all present on once more having the benefits of his talents, the whole House cheered.

Martin was ready with a quip on every occasion. Whether the

debate was an acrimonious one on the Duke of York's allowance, or a solemn one on the appointment of Brougham, a very ambitious lawyer and future Lord Chancellor, to the Committee of Secrecy of the Bank of England, he managed to introduce some light relief and to raise a laugh, and on one occasion when he was interrupted by loud cries of 'Order' as he rose, he remained obstinately standing while he declared that it would take less time to hear him than to put him down. But it was when he was personal that he was at his funniest, and when he complained of Judge McClelland's handling of the cases in which he had been involved with Bowes Daly and Burke, and compared the learned judge to a hare for timidity and a tiger for ferocity, his detailed description of all that had occurred kept the House in convulsions. And he was as ready with an answer in social life as in parliament. On one occasion when a particularly sharp argument had broken out at the dinner table, he was seen to turn to the servant who stood behind his chair and heard to say dryly, 'Melt the lead, John.' He did not allow parliament to interfere with what he considered a social obligation; shortly after his return to the House he absented himself for a few days in order to go to Calais to act as second to his cousin, Kirwan, in a duel.

The debates in the House dealt principally with English domestic affairs, and Humanity voted with the Government whilst manifesting his usual independence of spirit. Catholic affairs were at a low ebb, but Grattan persisted in the fight, although he had lost the support of a large section of the Irish Catholics through having accepted the idea of the veto. Nevertheless, a motion he brought in during May 1819 for relief for the Catholics was lost by only two votes and saw the greatest attendance of Irish members of any debate since the Union.

Interest in the international field was focused on South America where the rebel forces under Bolivar were trying to oust the Spaniards. The American and French Revolutions guaranteed support for popular causes, but here another factor came into play. There were a great many half-pay officers and others trained in warfare in both England and Ireland who, since the ending of the Napoleonic wars, had time on their hands, and they now began to join up for service in South America.

The principal recruiting agent in Ireland was a certain John Devereux who had fought for the Irish rebels at the battle of New Ross in the rebellion of 1798 and then fled to America, and one of his main aides was Daniel O'Connell's son, Morgan. Acting on the authority of a letter he carried from Bolivar, Devereux was selling commissions in the South American insurgent army. Country gentlemen of the highest standing, among them an Eyre and a MacDermott, near neighbours of Humanity Dick's, were busy raising regiments many of which were to serve under the command of a Scot named Sir Gregor McGregor.

Devereux held levees attended by recruits resplendent in brilliant, specially designed uniforms, many of them wearing the Waterloo campaign medal. When he received an invitation from O'Connell, he replied as 'Juan d'Evereux de la Orden del Libertador, Mayor General de la Republica de Venezuela y Nueva Granada y Commandante de la Legion Irlandes.'* His acceptance, fortunately, was signified in English. Drilling in full uniform was going on all over Ireland, which alarmed the Lord Lieutenant who wrote to Sidmouth at the Home Office asking what he should do. And San Carlos, the Spanish Ambassador in London, protested that Spain, who was Britain's ally, had put up all too patiently with these hostile manifestations from a supposedly friendly power.

The British Government had tried to get around the problem by declaring that nobody could leave for South American service without the special permission of the Prince Regent; otherwise they would be punished by law. In fact no law existed to prevent people volunteering. To rectify this, the Government introduced the Foreign Enlistment Bill. The Opposition claimed that instead of preserving neutrality, as it was intended to do, it would operate in favour of Spain by denying the insurgents support, and Humanity Dick was with them in spirit in that he declared that he prayed day by day and night by night for the success of the rebels. Despite that, he said he would vote for the bill because members had a duty to prevent their fellow subjects from ruining themselves by going abroad to be executed as rebels. The Opposition argued that volunteers would be

* 'John d'Evereux of the Order of the Liberator, Major General of the Republic of Venezuela and New Granada and Commander of the Irish Legion.'

185

treated as prisoners-of-war if captured, but the truth of the matter was that only a few months previously the King of Spain had decreed the death penalty for foreigners found with arms or supplying the insurgents.

Although the bill passed, volunteering continued, but gradually doubt began to be thrown on the authenticity of both Devereux and Gregor McGregor. People who had got as far as South America and returned, brought back tales of men abandoned without pay, rations or clothing. By the time the summer came, thousands had died of hunger and exposure crossing the Andes, and those who were captured, including Eyre and his entire regiment, were put to the sword. Nonetheless the volunteers played a decisive role in the war, and the battle they won at Boyaca placed Bolivar within two days' march of Bogota and victory. In time both McGregor and Devereux were exposed as cynical adventurers. The latter had sold himself to Bolivar as the leader of the Irish Catholics in their struggle for emancipation; the letter from Bolivar authorizing him to sell commissions was forged. Within a decade he had been found guilty of passing false cheques and McGregor was involved in another fraud.

The ordinary life of the Irish countryside was meanwhile disrupted by agrarian unrest which had been growing in the west of Ireland and which now reached an alarming pitch. Members of the peasantry calling themselves Ribbonmen had been infiltrating County Galway from the North of Ireland where they had been protesting against excessive rents. Now they were forcing the Galway peasantry to take oaths and organizing them against their landlords, many of whom lived in a state of siege or had to move to the town for safety. There were no disturbances on the Martin estates, where none of the usual abuses of landlordism existed, but Humanity Dick was one of the grand jurors at the spring assizes which condemned some Ribbonmen to death and others to transportation, while members of the gentry, not content with this, were pressing for a revival of the Insurrection Act.

At this time, 1820, George III died. Parliament was dissolved, and Humanity Dick was re-elected unanimously for the fourth time. As soon as the results were known he made a declaration which showed clearly how he felt about the disturbances and the further remedy being sought. He was, he declared, an enemy to what he called the 'sanguinary temper' of the criminal code in Ireland.

Back at Westminster he was as good as his word. Speaking against the renewal of the Insurrection Act, he pointed to the folly of attempting to govern any country through such an instrument, and he put in a plea for the Ribbonmen.

'The object of those deluded peasants,' he said, 'was doubtless criminal, but let us see what that object was. To pay but a certain sum per acre for tithes, and not to pay more than six guineas per acre for land, in which the poor man, finding seed and labour, is to plant his potatoes. To English landlords, this would appear but a very low rent, yet the Irish peasant asks, in mercy, not to have this exacted from him. Administration looks to this effect, and extorting oaths was the crime for which seven or eight poor wretches suffered death, and fifty or sixty were transported. After such examples we may surely be allowed to pause.' His speech was constantly interrupted by cries of 'Hear, hear'.

The state of Ireland would have been a constant theme of conversation at the Martins' table, and Hatty, now nineteen, was expected to express her views on this and similar topics. She was qualified by her upbringing to do so. Like her father, she was a good Greek and Latin scholar and spoke several languages. She held firmly to the conviction that the French Revolution was one of the greatest events for good in the history of mankind. She had grown up an intellectual, and her parents no doubt hoped that she might now reap the benefit of some of their party-going.

Thomas, on the other hand, had given some cause for worry. Mining prospectors were carrying out apparently successful probes on one of the islands of the estate, and Humanity Dick, who, as usual, followed all the operations in detail, felt the expectations had gone to Thomas's head. 'From this out,' he complained to his solicitor, 'he looks to immediate wealth. Now, this it is that renders him so culpable for as to my purpose of reopening the mine is certain and with this certainty of immoderate wealth his is more turbulent and outrageous than ever.'

The imperfections in his English may have been an indication of his agitation, which was increased by the fact that Martin Joseph Blake, quite understandably, as Humanity himself pointed out to his solicitor, now wanted to be repaid the money he had laid out on the election. The fact that the loan was secured on the estate made it the more pressing that it should be settled, but much as he wished it, Humanity could see no immediate prospect of being able to repay Blake or any other of his creditors. Had he not been protected through being a member of parliament, some of them would undoubtedly have pursued their claims in court.

Now he was also to have young Richard on his mind. He had just taken his M.A. from Trinity College, Dublin, and had fallen in love. Emily, the young lady in question, was a year younger than Richard, who was twenty-three, and she was the daughter of a Mr. Kirwan, King's Counsel. Rumours of Richard's reputation as a gay blade had, unfortunately, reached the girl's father, and he refused to give his consent to the match. But Richard was nothing if not resourceful: he asked Mr. Kirwan if he were to become a clergyman would he then approve, and, somewhat surprisingly, visualizing his future son-in-law in such a serious calling, Mr. Kirwan agreed. Richard forthwith settled down to becoming a parson, and his father began to worry about the financial outcome.

It was now eight years since Humanity Dick's famous pledge not to accept any office, or to ask for it for another, until Catholic emancipation was granted. Either others had broken their word, or he considered that the statute of limitations had come into operation, for there was nothing covert about his request the previous year that the Honourable Martin French should be appointed as Distributor of Stamps for County Galway. He had at the same time asked for offices for two other people and requested that he himself might be made a Commissioner of Fisheries. Now he asked for a better post for Martin French; he himself had already been appointed a Commissioner of Fisheries; and, although Richard was barely in Holy Orders, he set about preparing the way for him. He asked Peel for preferment for him in the Church.

Chapter Seventeen

ENGLAND WAS now to witness one of the most extraordinary events in the history of any nation: a Queen on trial by the representatives of the people for immorality. Ever since Caroline had gone to live abroad in 1813, rumours had been constant about her loose behaviour. The Regent, with a view to divorce, had set spies to keep a continual watch on her, and the results had not been edifying. But it had been impossible to distinguish between her natural inclination to indiscretion and an actual transgression.

The confidential servants of the Crown were sensitive to this uncertainty, and in the summer of 1819, Liverpool had written to the Regent saying that they advised strongly against any steps being taken, among other things because of the 'evil effects which might be the consequence of any proceedings against the Princess which in its result should prove abortive'.

Now, however, George III being dead, Caroline was Queen, and she had decided to hasten back from Europe to be crowned. Brougham, who was to be her legal adviser, was one of the messengers sent to waylay her with offers of money if she would agree to stay away. In despatching him, Liverpool emphasized that if she were to land a message would go at once to parliament asking for an investigation of her conduct, and all were agreed that this must be avoided. Meanwhile, her name had been removed from that part of the liturgy in which prayers were offered for the Royal Family.

But for reasons he never explained Brougham failed to

convey the Government's financial offer, and this, combined with Caroline's strong will-power and general gift for indiscretion, led to her landing at Dover on 4 June 1820. Almost immediately a Queen's faction emerged, led by the Whigs, the champions of the common man now became more monarchist than the monarch.

Confusion was general. Was it advisable to have an enquiry or not? Was it possible, or desirable, to bring about a reconciliation between the royal pair? Was Caroline entitled to demand that her name be restored to the liturgy? Amidst it all, Caroline alone was beset with no doubts. Legally she was Queen of England, and her people would support her in claiming her rights and privileges.

In the acrimonious debates in the House of Commons which followed Caroline's return, Humanity Dick was not only constantly on his legs, but on his toes. He gave an admirable display of his legal capacities and, knowing intimately both parties concerned, managed to present both sides of the case as fairly as a judge. Repeatedly when the discussion was getting off the rails his intervention righted it.

Great hopes hung upon Wilberforce's attempt to bring about an understanding between the King and his Consort which would enable them to live amicably apart. But Caroline insisted first and foremost on her name being reintroduced into the liturgy, and negotiations broke down.

Meanwhile, preparations were going ahead for an enquiry into her conduct with her Italian Chamberlain, Bergami, whom she was said to have laden with gifts bought with the English people's money, and *The Times* in a quip described him dining with Benjamin Constant in Paris wearing huge diamond drop earrings. Arrangements were being made for witnesses to be brought to England, and the green bag containing the accusations which was to be laid on the table of the House of Lords was christened by the Opposition 'Pandora's Box'.

Humanity Dick believed that, if some compromise was to be reached, the Queen must first leave the country. Her presence, as he put it, was 'pregnant with mischief'. As for her name being restored to the liturgy, when Brougham, her counsel, moved for it, Humanity Dick replied ably from the gallery. The agreed basis for negotiations, he pointed out, had been that the Queen must not be required to admit anything, nor the King to retract anything. But if the King were now to reintroduce the Queen's name into the liturgy, it would be admitting that he had calumniated her. Could any individual, let alone the Sovereign, be called upon to take such a step?

'Wishing to credit all that can be said of the unspotted, unstained character of the Queen, I dissent from the proposition which has for its object to introduce the Queen's name into the Liturgy. I am free to grant, that omitting to name the Queen is more or less a disrespect, and, without casting any blame, I lament that it occurred. But is it now possible, recollecting the reasons assigned for excluding the Queen, to call on Ministers to recommend to his Majesty, under all circumstances to correct—for argument sake, say—an original error? Can any man really disposed to support the dignity of the House expect from us the entire formal recognition of the innocence of the Queen, knowing that certain charges, all false, if you will, but as yet unexamined, have been prepared against her from the highest quarter?'

Humanity Dick felt that, once the Queen had been accused, it was essential in her own interests to proceed with an enquiry; she must be acquitted on the merits. In a closely reasoned speech in which he was loudly cheered, he declared:

'... The Defendant has many advantages over the Plaintiff, and one of those advantages is, that the Plaintiff has the burden of proving his case imposed upon him. Now, the legal advantage which the Traverser has, should, in all fair dealing, be secured to the Queen, and this advantage would be lost to her if the Government did not proceed. If Government did not proceed, the Queen must, for it would not be for her honour to leave anything to doubt.'

Whilst the Commons was debating, the House of Lords was being got ready for the trial. There was accommodation for only about half those expected to attend, and a special gallery had to be erected to take the surplus. Peers were to be fined £100 for each of the first three days' absence, and £40 for every succeeding day, and the only accepted excuses were ill-health, being over seventy or having suffered the death of a parent, wife or child.

The Queen arrived when the trial opened on 17 August dressed in black with white crape trimmings, and wearing a large white veil thrown back from her face. Until 3 October the nation was entertained to the meanderings of witnesses, most of them servants, from which her guilt was to be adduced. Then there was an adjournment in order to allow time for the defence to be prepared. But by 10 November that possibility against which Liverpool only the year before had so aptly warned the Regent had happened: the proceedings proved abortive. The majority for the Bill of Pains and Penalties was so slender that when Liverpool moved that they should consider the bill 'this day six months', which meant that it should be shelved, there was not a dissenting voice.

There was a burst of triumph from the Queen's supporters. They illuminated their houses to show their sympathies and the Opposition press gloated. The King was outraged, not only at the turn of events, but at the behaviour of some of his friends, among them Humanity Dick. Anybody who had heard him in the House knew that he had defended the ministry tooth and nail, while adhering to the strictest legal arguments; but the King thought differently.

Had not Humanity Dick said that he regretted the decision to omit the Queen's name from the liturgy? Had he not declared that he believed all that was said of her unspotted character? Had he not said, 'as the Queen's friend, if I may be so bold' and implied that the charges against her were false? He had even foretold that if she were tried she would be acquitted. To George this was tantamount to desertion. He and Humanity Dick had been friends since youth, but now their association came to an abrupt end.

When Humanity Dick returned to Galway after the session, the good effects of the previous spring assizes were still noticeable. All had returned to peace and industry, and he did not wait at home as usual for the next assizes, but went back to Westminster early in the new year.

When he had referred after his election to the 'sanguinary nature of the criminal code' he was already formulating a plan to do something about it, and on 26 February 1821 he was granted leave to bring in his Capital Crimes Defence Bill. At that time, a man on trial for his life, except in cases of treason, had no counsel to defend him. He could, furthermore, be hanged for petty larceny, sheep stealing and some hundreds of

192

equally minor offences. Humanity Dick considered this an absurdity. He could see no reason why the indulgence granted those on trial for treason should not apply to those accused of other crimes, and he referred in particular to cases where it was necessary to prove imbecility.

The argument used against him was that the judge was counsel for the accused, and that no cases were known of the prisoner having been at a disadvantage as a result. Surprisingly, some of the leading legal brains in the House maintained this attitude; but Humanity Dick was adamant. The judge, he claimed, must be neutral. He quoted the principal legal authority, Blackstone, as stating that 'it was irreconcilable with the humanity and benignity of the criminal law of England to refuse counsel to a prisoner'. The subject was a solemn one, but in his usual manner he managed to have the House in convulsions whilst he told the tale of an accused man who was an imbecile and who, when asked if he understood the meaning of the oath, merely wanted to know if the judge had any plum pudding in his pocket.

The bill got as far as a second reading when, feeling that it would be defeated, Humanity Dick decided to withdraw it just as there was about to be a division. But there was another aspect of the criminal code which had been worrying him ever since his case against Burke, namely the imposition of the death penalty for forgery. It was not difficult to imagine circumstances in which somebody might be pushed into such a crime, and death seemed an unwarrantably heavy price to pay. Apart from this, there was the fact that the law as it stood operated against its own interests, since a great many people like Humanity Dick, as well as many banks, were so loath to prosecute for forgery that it went altogether unpunished.

He spoke twice in support of the Forgery Punishment Mitigation Bill brought in by Sir James Mackintosh, the Scottish Whig philosopher and friend of Coleridge, and when it was defeated, Martin brought in a bill of his own. But this also was lost.

While he was thus engaged with the problems of his fellow men he had not, however, forgotten the case of the blinded seal or the determination with which he had returned to parliament to get legislation introduced to outlaw such barbarities. He was working on the whole problem of cruelty to animals and in the process had become friendly with Dr. John Lawrence, philosopher and farmer, now living in London.

A year Humanity Dick's senior, Lawrence was at Colchester Grammar School when Humanity was at Harrow, and at the age of fifteen he had written an essay in favour of kindness to animals. From the time he first took up writing while farming in East Anglia, his main interest, apart from politics, had been nature. He was widely known as the author of the annual *New Farmer's Calendar* which was full of practical advice and found its way into every farmhouse.

His *Philosophical and Practical Treatise on Horses and on the Moral Duties of Man towards the Brute Creation* had come out in 1796, and like Erskine's, his ideas were based on recognition of the balance of nature. Like Erskine, he believed that the possession of intelligence and feeling implies the existence of rights. There cannot be one kind of justice for man and another for the beast whose 'body is nourished by the same food, hurt by the same injuries; his mind actuated by the same passions and affections which animate the human breast'.

But nature, he claimed, has established an order to which man himself is subservient. Just as she has created one set of animals to keep another in check, and the carrion to dispose of the corpses, she has created man carnivorous. Were it not for such dispensations of nature to man, animals, many of which proliferate at great speed, would overrun the earth and starve man out of existence.

'By the scheme of universal providence,' Lawrence wrote, 'the services between man and beast are intended to be reciprocal.' If it were not recognized that nature had rendered it necessary for man to kill animals, it would ultimately become a moral obligation to build hospitals for lice and fleas. As for those who were vegetarian on principle, he compared them with the saints of Butler's days who were for 'abolishing black pudding and eating nothing with the blood in it'. Hunting he judged by the hunted, and condemned the pursuit of harmless, herbivorous creatures such as the hare or deer, but would raise no objection to hunting a predator, such as the fox.

While he and Humanity Dick were collaborating, Lawrence took his arguments a step further in *National Sports of Great*

Britain which he published in French as well as English under the pen name of 'Henry Alken'. He described all the well-known field sports, but he also gave an account of the horrors involved in deliberately maddening a bull in order to bait him, of setting sixteen cocks to lacerate one another, of baiting such wild animals as the bear, and of drawing the badger. When he was ten years old, Lawrence had seen a man roasting a live rat over a fire, and he had never forgotten the wretched creature's shrieks. He denounced everything which had torture as its object, but he did not condemn the badger being fairly hunted in the field with vermin dogs. 'These natural antagonists,' he wrote, 'would fight, did they meet in the desert, unaccompanied by man. It is then a lawful, and may be a useful sport.'

There was one activity indulged in purely for the sake of money, which he considered extremely cruel, namely, racing horses against the clock. He told of an old flea-bitten gelding so brutally whipped while being raced over a hard road that his entrails were visible and ultimately hung trailing on the ground until he died. He had seen another horse in such a race flayed until he was cut from the shoulder to the flank, his sheath in ribbons with the testicles laid bare.

In 1796 Lawrence had advocated in his treatise the introduction of legislation to protect animals, and in 1818 a correspondent in the *Monthly Magazine* had proposed the establishment of a society for the prevention of cruelty to animals. The idea was now revived in the same magazine, and Lawrence involved himself in the correspondence. He confessed that he had as yet met nobody with whom he could fully agree. The people proposing the measure seemed to be immensely confused. Most of them lacked the necessary practical knowledge of nature and animals. They were vague as to the real grounds and principles of what they wanted to do, and they ignored the compromises and limitations which nature has imposed.

Now Lawrence had found in Humanity Dick somebody with whom he could co-operate. Since his childhood Humanity had been in close touch with nature. Though he could not have the detailed knowledge Lawrence possessed, as a good classical scholar he would have known his Aristotle. An expert horseman, there was little about the horse he did not know. And he was probably the first man in the world to have had the practical experience of trying to curb cruelty to animals by punishing the culprits on his own estates. He agreed with Lawrence that whatever was attempted, in order to be successful, must be based on rational and practical grounds.

The two men now collaborated to frame a bill which would, for the first time in history, establish animals' rights. Humanity Dick consulted Lawrence because he had already made a study of the question, but what Humanity had to hand to Lawrence with regard to nature, Lawrence had to concede him on the question of law.

They set about doing something that was a legal innovation—legislating for the dumb, for while they admitted that animals were capable of the same sensations as man, they also had to admit that the one thing animals lacked was speech. How, then, were their assailants to be apprehended? An animal could not go to a police station and declare that he had been assaulted. The two men had to evolve something entirely new to the law and suited to the peculiar circumstances. The words which both Lawrence and Erskine had used, and which were perpetually on Doctor Parr's lips at Harrow, described the principle upon which their design was based—*wanton cruelty*.

Chapter Eighteen

WHEN HUMANITY DICK went down to the House on 9 May 1821, it was with a proposition which could not fail to attract sympathy. It concerned the owners of the stage-coaches which every member knew well. He was armed with a petition which he could claim plausibly enough had literally been put into his hand. A group of highly respectable individuals, the stage-coach owners, were complaining that valuable horses were constantly being ruined by grooms and other servants from whom, due to their circumstances, no damages could be recovered. He read out the petition asking for a remedy. Then, while sympathy was still alive, he announced that the following week he would move for leave to bring in a bill 'pursuant to the prayer in the petition'.

'Irish drollery predominating,' Jerdan was to write of Humanity Dick, 'it cropped out most luxuriantly in his sayings and doings, and begat the absorbing opinion of his being a sheer madcap, a blundering blade without rational aim, conduct or capacity. This was, however, a great mistake. No madness had ever more method in it.' The House was to discover over the next few years how much truth there was in the remark. Humanity was perfectly conscious that what he had just done was to insert the thin end of the wedge, and a man with his sense of humour could scarcely have failed to have his tongue in his cheek when he rose again in the House on 17 May.

Members had shown that they were moved by the plight of the stage-coach owners. It was plain that something must be done about their horses; and now, almost before they realized what they were doing, they had granted Humanity Dick permission to bring in a bill 'to prevent the ill-treatment of horses and other animals'.

He threw in 'other animals' hopefully, but he had the example of Erskine's bill to follow; the former Chancellor had been obliged in the end to limit its application to beasts of burden. At the same time, Humanity Dick was deeply conscious of the magnitude and infinite variety of the animal kingdom and knew that it would be impossible to legislate for the whole. Any attempt to do so would throw him open to ridicule and lead either to Lawrence's proposition of hospitals for lice and fleas or to an outright rejection of the principle. He decided to start by confining himself to the most obviously abused of animals—the horses, upon whom daily life depended as much at the time as it came to do on the motor in later days. The cruelty inflicted on horses in the hubbub of city traffic was visible to all.

The bill he and Lawrence had drafted provided that if any person should 'wantonly and cruelly beat, abuse or ill-treat' a horse and a complaint were made on oath before a magistrate, the party complained of could be brought to court and charged.

When the bill came to the Committee stage on 1 June, the opposition was of two kinds. Some considered the subject beneath the dignity of the legislature, others could not see why the bill should be limited to horses. But in fact it provided for 'other animals' and those now inserted by name were 'mares, geldings, mules, asses, cows, heifers, steers, oxen, sheep and other cattle'. It became known as the Ill-Treatment of Cattle Bill, and in the small hours of the morning it scraped through by three votes. It was a meagre beginning.

When not in the House, Humanity Dick was roving the town, alert for any sign of cruelty, and this occasionally put him in strange situations. On one occasion when he saw a man beating a horse mercilessly, he gave two men £5 to chastise the fellow. A few days later it happened that the offender was watering his horse right beside the spot where Humanity was recounting the episode to a friend. He very shortly received an invitation from the magistrates at Bow Street to give bail for an assault, but managed to settle the matter by a compromise: he gave £5 to the man who had been beating his horse.

He enlivened the discussions in the House by reporting the incident; he always enjoyed telling a story against himself. But when the report of the bill was brought up on 4 June, he met with serious opposition on much the same grounds as before. There were only fifty-two members present, and when finally it was put to the vote, half were for the bill and half against. The Speaker had the casting vote, and declared that he would follow the example of his predecessors on similar occasions and vote so that the bill could be further considered.

Once again it was a narrow shave, but it did not prevent Humanity Dick confidently appearing the next morning at the Guildhall police court. Upon his complaint, two men had been summoned for cruelly beating a horse in Giltspur Street, but only one appeared. Humanity Dick gave the magistrate a description of what had taken place. He had never, he said, seen such barbarous treatment inflicted on a horse in his life. Despite the man's protestations, the magistrate was more inclined to believe Humanity. But what was he to do? As the law stood, he could not convict. No man knew this better than Humanity himself, but he had achieved something. He had brought to court the first man charged with cruelty to a horse, and *The Times* had reported it under the heading, 'Cruelty to Animals'.

He continued to do the groundwork outside parliament, and soon members were arriving with petitions from their constituents in favour of his bill. Wilberforce produced one from Hull, Sir James Graham brought one from Peckham, Charles Grant, the Chief Secretary for Ireland, presented one from Christchurch in Surrey, and Sir W. de Crespigny had one from Camberwell. When at last Humanity Dick moved the third reading of his bill on 29 June, the House proceeded to a division without a discussion, and he had a majority of twenty-four.

There could have been no prouder man than he on 2 July 1821 when his bill was taken up to the Lords, but its initial success was not to be repeated. The Lords rejected it, and any intention he may have had of starting the whole process over again, was to be overtaken by events. The coronation was to take place on the 19th, the King was to pay a state visit to Ireland immediately after, and that was to be followed by an official visit to his Kingdom of Hanover. Parliament was prorogued and Humanity Dick's campaign for animals was cut short.

The King was to be crowned without the Queen; that was explicit. When the day came, he was somewhat indisposed but went through with all the ceremonies. He was dressed in the kind of clothes that delighted him. He wore a silver dress à la Henri Quatre, with a crimson velvet surcoat embroidered in gold. Over this there was a sword-belt, the buckle, scabbard and hilt entirely studded in diamonds. The whole was covered by a scarlet velvet robe nine yards long, lined with ermine, with an embroidered border nine inches deep studded all over with the rose, the thistle and the shamrock. The eldest sons of seven peers bore the train.

After the ceremony 354 peers, bishops, Privy Councillors and knights sat down to a banquet prepared for them at Westminster Hall by 130 cooks, and all members of parliament were presented with a commemorative medal made of one ounce of gold.

On Tuesday, 31 July, the King left for Portsmouth where the royal squadron was waiting to take him around the south and west coasts of England to Holyhead, whence he would sail for Dublin. This was the first time an English king had visited Ireland except in conquest and the natural ebullience of the Irish had the capital in a state of anticipation for weeks ahead.

The scramble for honours was almost equal to the days of the Union. Everybody wanted to be knighted, viscounts wanted to be earls, and earls marquises. People who had been absentees for decades planned to return, and country mansions were refurbished in the hope that the King would visit them. Lodgings doubled in price and every hotel room in the city was booked by the gentry coming up from the country for the event, or by those, like Metternich's son and the Easterhazys, who were coming on to Dublin for the celebrations following the coronation. Pleasure boats were being hired at vast sums, and many people planned to take their yachts to Holyhead in order to accompany the royal squadron back to Dublin.

At the King's express wish, everybody was to wear garments of Irish manufacture, and the streets were thronged with people attired in the 'Welcome' uniform of blue and buff, with gilt buttons depicting the union of the crown and shamrock. A special medal was struck bearing the words, 'Advenit Rex concordat civitas' and the Aldermen all got new scarlet robes trimmed with ermine. Religious bitterness thawed in the general warm-heartedness, a Conciliation Dinner of prominent Catholics and Protestants was held, and O'Connell declared of the King, 'the sound of his approach has allayed the dissensions of centuries'.

As the King was progressing around the coasts of England, out of communication with London, Caroline lay in a serious condition. She had been taken ill at the theatre on the eve of the King's departure, and three days later it became known that she was suffering from an obstruction of the bowel. It was a week before news of her illness reached Dublin and created uneasy forebodings. People crowded around the mail packet to learn the latest bulletin, genuinely concerned for the Queen, but more anxious lest the royal visit should be cancelled.

On the night of Tuesday, 7 August, Caroline died. No account of the progress of the royal squadron had been received since it sailed from Cowes on 2 August. The Prime Minister, Lord Liverpool, who had no direct contact with Caroline's residence, Brandenburgh House, had not attempted to send the King bulletins which were appearing in the press. On the night of the Queen's death, he sent the first news of her to the King at Milford Haven; but the royal squadron was already at Holyhead and planned to sail for Dublin the next day.

The weather was to intervene. The wind shifted so as to make departure impossible, and the royal yacht had to ride at anchor, awaiting a lull. News reached Liverpool that the King had sailed for Dublin without knowing that the Queen was dead, but in fact on the 9th a messenger bearing a duplicate of Liverpool's letter to Milford Haven arrived at Holyhead. Londonderry, as Castlereagh now was, received the box on deck, and, having read the letter, went below to communicate the contents to the King.

The news had not yet reached Dublin and nobody knew that, despite it, they could now heave a sigh of relief: the King decided not to alter his plans. He ordered court mourning for as short a period as might be 'consistent with decorum' and gave instructions for the Queen's body to be transported privately to her home in Brunswick. As soon as the storm abated, he intended to leave for Dublin, but instead of making an official entry he would remain in privacy for a brief interval at the Viceregal Lodge.

While the royal yacht remained at Holyhead with the flag at half-mast, the tempest continued to rage and the steam packet *Earl Moira*, on its way from Liverpool to Dublin with 155 people, struck the Wharf Bank, filled with water and sank. By the time the King reached Ireland on 12 August, having had to abandon his yacht and take the postal steam packet, there were still no details of those who were lost. All that was known was that a great number of important people were on board on their way to Dublin for the royal visit, among them Humanity Dick. When the news reached Connemara there was consternation among his tenants, but one old woman was heard to remark: 'No one need be afeared for the master; for if he was in the midst of a raging sea the prayers of widows and orphans would keep his head above water.' But for a man as sentimental and as capable of compunction as George, the wreck of his friend, more particularly in the circumstances in which he had severed relations the previous year, could provide food for thought during his retirement in Phoenix Park.

When he emerged, wearing a black crape arm band, he was caught up at once in the whirl of gaiety and hospitality for which Dublin was justly famed. On 22 August there was a levee at Dublin Castle which was the largest ever known. Over two thousand people were present, the men in full court dress and their ladies with lappets, feathers and trains, but, in view of the crush, without hoops.

During the course of the evening, the King graciously recognized various people who came before him. Then suddenly he found himself face to face with Humanity Dick, a man who always sought to make up a quarrel and was incapable of bearing a grudge against its instigator. All George's natural spontaneity came to the top. He immediately seized Humanity Dick's hand and hastened to tell him how distressed he had been at the news of the wreck, and how delighted he now was that Humanity Dick could contradict in person the rumour of his death. The quarrel was well and truly over, and in due course the King sealed the renewed friendship with a peace offering. Two Arab stallions, Mirza and The Shah, part of a gift from the Shah of Persia, arrived at Ballinahinch.

To the disgust of the English Opposition, Dublin did not allow the Queen's death to dampen the city's ardour. Despite pouring rain, the capital was brilliant. There was a triumphal arch across Sackville Street; a round room, a hundred feet in diameter, was built on to the Mansion House for the Lord Mayor's dinner to the King; the *Dublin Patriot* opened a fund to build a palace fit for such a sovereign, suggesting that a few decayed mansions in St. Stephen's Green could be pulled down to provide an admirable site with views of Dublin Bay and the Wicklow Hills. The watchword the King gave was 'Religious Conciliation', and when Alderman Darley—the man who had tried to break up the meeting of the Catholic Committee—gave the Orangemen's toast to King Billy, with its implied affront to the Catholics, Dublin passed it over with its native discretion and infuriated *The Times*.

When the royal visit was over, the Martins had their hands full with family matters. The gay young Richard, true to his pledge to Mr. Kirwan, was about to be ordained as a prelude to marrying Emily Kirwan. His future mother-in-law was a grand-niece of the Earl of Aldeborough, and through her Emily was heiress to certain lands in County Wicklow and a small sum of money which her father had undertaken to augment by £2,000 on her marriage. But the problem of what the young people were to live on remained acute.

Humanity Dick's own affairs were far from prospering. Although marble had been discovered in Connemara, the quarries were not bringing in what he and Thomas had expected of them. But Humanity was the first person to have the marble polished, and he derived great personal satisfaction from a superb pair of oval-topped tables Thomas had had made for Ballinahinch and a fine fireplace which he himself presented to the King.

The portion of the estates which he had retained after Thomas's marriage was in the hands of agents and he was spending the proceeds faster than they accrued; but he had to do something for young Richard. Under Thomas's marriage settlement, Humanity Dick was entitled to an annuity of £5,000 a year. He now arranged to pay Richard £200 a year out of the latter and to give him £3,000 out of the £10,000 he had allotted for his children on marriage.

But this was only a beginning and the question of Richard's livelihood, which had been worrying him for some time, continued to do so. Nothing had resulted from his request to Peel to find Richard a living in the Church, and now young Richard had been trying himself to use the family influence with Lord Downshire to obtain a commission in his regiment. But, after being ordained by the Archbishop of Tuam, he was married on 6 December without as yet having achieved anything in the way of a position, and the young couple proceeded to Clareville.

The wedding was barely over when the conciliatory spirit in which the King had visited Ireland began to bear fruit. On 10 December the Marquess of Wellesley was nominated Lord Lieutenant of Ireland. Brother to the Duke of Wellington, he was in due course to marry a Catholic, the grand-daughter of an Irishman, Carrol, who had signed the American Declaration of Independence. His pro-Catholic views were as well known as his love of show, and he was to have himself crowned as Viceroy with as much pomp as if he were to rule a vast empire. Except for the appointment of Cornwallis at the time of the Rebellion, the British Government considered this the most important appointment they had ever made to the Government of Ireland. It was, nonetheless, essential to preserve the balance. As always with British policy in Ireland, something had to be sacrificed to keeping the extremists among the Protestant minority happy, and Goulburn, whose views were known to be the contrary of Wellesley's, was appointed Chief Secretary.

With young Richard very much on his mind, Humanity Dick did not waste a minute in availing himself of the happy circumstance of having a friend and kindred spirit coming to the Castle. As soon as Wellesley's appointment became official, he wrote to Liverpool at Bath, where the new Lord Lieutenant was visiting the Prime Minister, asking for Richard's preferment in the Church to be put before Wellesley.

Humanity Dick was not the only person to approach the Lord Lieutenant early; his clerical brother was already pressing him embarrassingly, whilst Liverpool was anxious not to make any applications to him for patronage until he had assumed office. He did, however, promise to make the recommendation for Richard with the first of the same kind.

Meanwhile, Richard's immediate problem was suddenly solved and Humanity Dick's mind set at ease. A letter arrived at Clareville for the young man from Lord Downshire giving him a commission as an ensign in the Royal Downshire Regiment, with a promise of a promotion within a couple of weeks when a lieutenant was due to be promoted. He instructed Richard to join him at once at his base in England.

When the spring assizes were over the following year, Humanity Dick returned to Westminster to present his Ill-Treatment of Cattle Bill again. He decided to prefix it with a word on baiting which he had already tried unsuccessfully to have brought within the purview of the Metropolitan Police Bill in the preceding session. He gave the House an account of a fight which had taken place at the Westminster Pit between Jacco, a famous monkey and a white bitch called Puss. Puss tore away the whole of Jacco's underjaw, and Jacco lacerated Puss's windpipe and arteria carotis. As he told the story he presented a petition from the inhabitants of Camberwell requesting that measures be taken to protect animals from such atrocities.

It was a far cry from stage-coach horses, but it stimulated sympathy for the animals. Several members expressed disgust, and though Humanity Dick did not intend to pursue the matter immediately, it helped to create the kind of support he was trying to raise on a variety of levels.

The clergy were among his most valuable adherents. Like Doctor Johnson, they believed that pity is not natural, but is acquired by the cultivation of reason. Whilst he was starting afresh on his efforts to get his Ill-Treatment of Cattle Bill through, the Reverend Henry Crowe, Vicar of Buckingham, was preparing for republication his book *Zoophilus*.

Like Lawrence, he gave a shocking list of the cruelties to which animals were subjected, from horses kept for weeks at the knackers without food, to dogs used as turnspits, enclosed in a wheel from which they could not escape, burned by the heat of the stove and lashed constantly to keep moving. Like Lawrence, he told stories of cock-fighting and bull-running, including one of a bull who had had his horns sawn off, his ears cropped, his tail cut short, his body well soaped to make it slippery, and pepper then blown into his nose to make him furious.

He decried the killing of young animals in particular, because of the strong maternal instinct in the animal world, and quoted a touching example from Doctor Thomas Percival's *Moral Tales, Fables and Reflections,* of a mother bear in the Arctic who was attracted by some blubber thrown on the ice from a boat. She collected it and apportioned it carefully between her two cubs, keeping only a small piece for herself. Then the men in the boat shot the cubs. The mother had been walking away, and when she saw the cubs lying down and not eating, she came back and started pushing the blubber towards them, trying to make them take it. It took her a little while to realize that they were dead; then she put her head down beside them and moaned in the most heart-rending way. At last she stood up and shook her paw at the boat—when the men shot her dead, also.

But contrary to Lawrence, Crowe condemned all hunting, and reminded his readers that Arthur Young had called fox-hunting 'the cricket of savages'. Yet he admitted the superior skill with which animals killed one another relatively painlessly. As for Lawrence's theory that if man were not carnivorous the world would be overrun by animals, Crowe asserted that animals being carnivorous also, they would keep one another in check.

All animals, he pointed out, prey or are preyed upon. 'The musca aphidivora feeds on the tree louse, the hornet and wasp on the musca aphidivora, the dragon-fly on the hornet and wasp, spiders on the dragon-fly, small birds on the spider, and the hawk on small birds.' He had performed the same exercise which years before Erskine had undertaken with the wire-worm.

Humanity Dick was very conscious of the support he was receiving from the clergy when he moved the second reading of his Ill-Treatment of Cattle Bill on 24 May 1822. When the Attorney-General moved for it to be thrown out, Humanity accused him of flying in the face of public opinion. The Magistracy of London and Middlesex had spoken unanimously in its favour; what was more, there was not a pulpit in London from which the same had not been done.

The suggestion that a spiritual construction could be put on his campaign for some reason caused laughter in the House, but did not impress Humanity Dick. He called those who opposed the bill 'the abetters of cruelty' on the grounds that those who were not against cruelty were for it. The difficulty of legislating for the dumb was emphasized by one criticism: the bill did not define properly in what cruelty to an animal consisted. Plainly, an animal could not explain what it suffered, but Humanity evaded the difficulty by asking another question. Could anybody, he asked, define in what excessive correction of an apprentice consisted? Yet it was forbidden by law. It was a comparison Romilly had made at the time of Erskine's bill.

The Attorney-General continued obstinate, but the bill got through the second reading by twenty-nine votes to eighteen. Once again Humanity Dick had shown himself to be the astute parliamentarian. He had brought up the bill towards midnight when there was a thin House containing a good number of his friends. And on 2 June, once again at the very end of the day, he brought it up for the third reading and it passed without a division.

Humanity Dick's next step was to get to work on the House of Lords. The bill was to be introduced there by Erskine who was the author of an apt piece of doggerel:

> 'Our keepers of a livery stable,
> Get rich as fast as they are able,
> No fraud in them, when beasts are thin,
> They write up *Horses Taken In*.'

Humanity approached the Duke of Buckingham, as well as Downshire and Ormonde, and he made a point of canvassing Liverpool personally, while he asked Erskine to try to procure the support of some of the bishops.

Within six weeks the bill had passed through the Lords, and on 21 July the King, who had always been sympathetic to Humanity Dick's exertions in favour of animals, gave it his assent. Known as Martin's Act, it was the foundation of all legislation anywhere in the world for the protection of animals, and Humanity was determined it should not be forgotten for a day.

Within a couple of weeks of the act becoming law, he brought two men before the magistrates at the Guildhall. One had beaten a horse so violently that the animal was covered with weals. The other had been showing a horse for sale in Smithfield Market. He had the horse's head fixed in a certain position by a rope under the bridle, in order to make him carry his head properly, and every time he deviated from that position, the man hit him across the head with the butt end of his whip. When the man, replying to a question, said that he was a butcher by trade, Humanity Dick replied: 'I perceive that—a horse butcher.' The men, Samuel Clarke and David Hyde, each had to pay twenty shillings and were the first people to be fined for cruelty to animals.

Meanwhile the recognition which was Humanity Dick's due, but which he never sought, was beginning to come his way. He negotiated with Erskine to reproduce his great speech of 1809 on cruelty to animals, and the elder statesman insisted on adding a preface declaring how deeply the public were indebted to Richard Martin for originating the measure and 'for the skill, patience and perseverance with which, amidst many difficulties, he succeeded in giving it effect'.

The Reverend Arthur Broome, who was foremost in the campaign for animals, now brought out a new edition of Dr. Primatt's *The Duty of Mercy and Sin of Cruelty to Brute Animals* and dedicated it to Richard Martin and his benevolence of heart.

Lawrence approached the problem of cruelty as a naturalist and philosopher, but Primatt viewed it as a theologian. Because of man's higher station, he claimed that the cruelty of man to animals is worse, in point of justice, than the cruelty of man to man. Furthermore, animals having no concept of a hereafter only know the present: present pain is the only evil and present happiness the only good. The creator, he asserted, never made a single creature to be miserable. Sin alone brought misery into the world; therefore man alone could inherit misery as his birthright.

As Crowe had done, Primatt before him had quoted from *Measure for Measure*. With Cowper's lines recited by Erskine

208

when presenting his own bill, they became those most often repeated by the people fighting for animals' rights:

> 'The poor beetle that we tread upon, in corporal sufferance, finds a pang as great
> As when a giant dies.'

Chapter Nineteen

THE HOUSE had long since made a habit of laughing even when Humanity Dick was being perfectly serious, but the press began inserting laughs in their reports where there had been none. This was something he was not prepared to abide, and on the evening that his bill was given the royal assent he presented himself in the gallery and asked for the reporter from *The Times*.

'I come, sir,' he said to him, 'to request that you will never in future, upon any occasion, attribute a single syllable to me in your paper. I know that, when you choose, you are able to do full justice to any member who may speak, but somehow or other, it happens that whenever I rise to address the House, you take the opportunity of putting something foolish or ridiculous into my mouth. Now I promise you, upon my word, that if I ever find myself in print again in your paper, I will complain of it to the House, and bring to the bar all the parties concerned. I will, therefore, thank you not to report me in future, and to tell the others to do the same.'

Somewhat abashed, the reporter claimed that he was sure Humanity Dick had never been intentionally misrepresented, and assured him that, so far as he was concerned, he would never appear in print again.

'I am glad to hear you say so,' Humanity replied. 'If you say any more of me than that Mr. R. Martin spoke, or Mr. R. Martin voted, on such or such a side—for you may say that, as I am not ashamed of my party—I will bring you before the

House, depend upon it; and I will also put a stop to reporting altogether.'

At this the reporter of the *Morning Chronicle* intervened to say that Humanity had no power to stop reporting.

'I forbid you also, sir, reporting me,' retorted Humanity.

The reporter then having declared that he would not accept any dictation from Humanity Dick as to how he was to perform his duty, Humanity asked for his name and, without another word, marched away.

Fortunately for posterity, the press ignored his commands, and he had his own way of dealing with what he considered transgressions. On one occasion the *Morning Post* incurred his displeasure over the report of a speech, and he called on the editor to ask for an explanation. The editor, an Irishman named Byrne, protested that the report had been made by one of the most reliable members of his staff. Humanity Dick replied to this defence by pulling a copy of the paper out of his pocket, holding it up and demanding: 'Sir, did I ever speak in italics?' Both men immediately burst into a fit of laughter and a compromise was reached.

It would, in fact, have taken a good reporter to keep up with all Humanity Dick's activities. Despite his support for the Foreign Enlistment Bill, he was one of the distinguished people on the platform when the Friends of South American Independence gave a grand dinner to Zea, the Plenipotentiary of the recently formed Colombian Republic. He was at a special meeting of Lords and M.P.s with interests in Ireland to discuss a solution to the eternal tithe problem. He made a valuable speech at a meeting to open a subscription to relieve distress in Ireland, and he was on the Committee of the British and Foreign Philanthropic Society with Chateaubriand, Count Lieven, Baron de Staël, Coke of Holkham and a number of other eminent people. The society aimed at putting into effect the theories of Robert Owen, and had already started, with his support, a model community in Lanark where conditions somewhat similar to those of a modern welfare state prevailed.

Owen was shortly to make a tour of Ireland and to suggest his own remedies for conditions which were now disquieting. A couple of years previously the Lord Lieutenant, Talbot, had written to Sidmouth at the Home Office, 'The potatoe ground, which the poor people must take, or starve, is let at a price which no man can pay or earned by labour, at a rate at which no man can subsist.' This dependence upon the potato, in a country which was agriculturally potentially rich, was one of the anomalies arising from the abuses of the landlord system, aggravated by the general economic conditions which prevailed in Ireland after the Union. Instead of bringing the promised benefits of English capital investment and enlarged markets, it had caused industrial collapse, unemployment, a glut of English goods and general stagnation.

Distress now reached the proportions of famine. People were eating the bark off the trees, the young wheat in the ear, and primrose leaves. Those trying to collect shellfish and seaweed to eat were often surrounded by the sea and drowned because they were too weak to save themselves, and many of those who received relief were so unaccustomed to eating that they died from the effect. The living were too enfeebled to bury the dead, and fever was widespread. Connemara was inevitably one of the hardest hit areas. People were crowding into Galway by boat in order to qualify for residence, and thereby relief, and the hospital was so packed that patients were sleeping between the beds and in tents pitched in the grounds.

While Humanity Dick was busy in parliament, where he was later to bring in a bill for the improvement of waste lands in Ireland, Thomas was actively engaged in relief measures. Humanity's hope of providing employment for his poverty-stricken tenantry through the mines had not yet been realized, and Thomas, one of only two resident landlords in Connemara, was providing relief out of his own pocket.

In the summer of 1822, Castlereagh committed suicide. Humanity Dick had been on close terms with him, dining with him as constantly as he did with his arch-enemy, Canning. Now Wellington persuaded the King to appoint Canning to the vacant post of Foreign Secretary. The King had always objected to him because there had been a suspicion that he had had intimate relations with Caroline about the time of the 'delicate investigation'. Now that the King had given in, he wrote to Liverpool: 'This is the greatest sacrifice of my opinion and feelings, that I have ever made in my life.'

Grattan, the great defender of the Catholics was now dead,

but with both a Foreign Secretary and a Lord Lieutenant known to be sympathetic to their cause the Catholics, whose new and supremely eloquent spokesman in parliament was Plunkett, a future Lord Chancellor of Ireland, renewed their hopes. But every advance in their affairs seemed doomed to meet with a check.

It had been the habit for many years for the Orangemen to decorate the equestrian statue of William III in front of Trinity College in Dublin, on William's birthday and on 12 July, the anniversary of the Battle of the Boyne. The performance had become the act of defiance of a triumphant minority and, as such, could not fail to irritate the population at large. It was annually associated with scenes of violence, sometimes ending in bloodshed, and the preceding Lord Lieutenant, Talbot, had already been looking for the means of imposing a ban.

On the eve of the 12 July celebrations in 1822, Wellesley appealed to the Orange party agents, in view of the general distress of the country, to avoid anything which could threaten public tranquillity. They replied that they could not forego the customary demonstrations because they were under orders from the Orange Lodges, thereby admitting that they were a 'representative' body, liable to be proscribed by the Convention Act, and the decoration proceeded with the usual outbreaks of lawlessness.

A few days later the question of Orange processions was raised in the House by Tone's old enemy, Sir George Hill always an upholder of the Protestant cause, and he accused the Catholics of being as guilty as the Orange party in promoting unrest in Ireland. Humanity Dick could not let this challenge pass. He bided his time, then rose to his feet to issue what he termed an unqualified contradiction of Sir George's statement. The processions, he pointed out, usually took place in the Protestant north where they were a source of provocation to the Catholic population. He went on to contrast this situation with that which prevailed in County Galway. There the Catholics outnumbered the Protestants by fifty to one. Yet, no toast was ever drunk and no demonstration ever held which could in the slightest degree cause offence to fellow subjects.

By the end of the year this conflict took an unpleasant turn. After consulting the Attorney-General, Wellesley found that he could legally prevent the decoration of King William's statue on his birthday in November on the grounds that it was public property with which nobody had a right to interfere, and that, the decoration having caused a disturbance in the past, 'the King's subjects have a right to the protection of the magistrates against the recurrence of such scenes and the continuance of such apprehensions'. Wellesley therefore decided to ban the decoration of the statue, and, although attempts were made to break the law, the day passed off peacefully. But a group of people formed a deputation to protest to the Lord Mayor about the prohibition.

Humanity Dick at the time was in the west of Ireland where, as usual, he found endless requests for assistance. On this occasion he found one which outraged him. A Catholic named Dolphin, who he had been instrumental in getting appointed to the Commission of the Peace nineteen years previously, was now to be excluded. In his typical indignation he wrote promptly to Goulburn, the Chief Secretary, saying that the news had almost turned Dolphin's mind. 'He feels this degradation as a stain upon his honour and character,' he wrote, 'and from my knowledge of the man and my friendship for him, I would rather hear of his death.'

But by the time the letter reached the Castle, the Lord Lieutenant had other matters on his mind. While he was at the Theatre Royal in Dublin on 14 December he was attacked by armed assailants, pieces of metal and glass bottles were hurled at him, and three thousand handbills were showered upon the audience, proclaiming 'No popery!', attacking him and the Lord Mayor, and demanding the return of Talbot. For an hour Wellesley was hissed and booed, and when ultimately ten men were arrested, some of them turned out to be people who had been on the deputation to the Lord Mayor to protest against the ban on dressing King William's statue.

Yet, when the case came up early in the following year, the grand jury completely ignored the bill for a conspiracy and instead merely found two people guilty of a riot; and since technically two people could not constitute a riot, this amounted to the bill being ignored altogether. It caused exultation among the Orangemen and it was a sign of the times that it also gave considerable pleasure to a number of the Lord Lieutenant's own staff. People like Gregory had always favoured the Orangemen, and when later these were to make a declaration, Gregory had a thousand copies of it printed surreptitiously, while the Chancellor gave the opinion that the ban had been 'unwise, unconstitutional and oppressive'.

Meanwhile, Humanity Dick had not failed to maintain pressure on the Lord Lieutenant for promotion for Richard, and early in 1823 the good news arrived at Clareville that he had been appointed to the living of Dunboyne, a village in the rich county of Meath, about ten miles from Dublin. It was reckoned to be worth between £400 and £500 a year, and the previous incumbent had left a certain amount of furniture which the young Martins were able to purchase at their valuation price. Richard was now twenty-three, and this was the first occasion since he and Emmy had fallen in love that Richard's parents were able to feel at ease about his circumstances.

When, as usual, Humanity Dick was due that spring to return to Westminster after the assizes, the packet *Alert* was lost on the West Mouse rock near Holyhead only eighteen months after the wreck of the *Earl Moira*. There were appalling scenes, with women and children screaming on deck while they waited to be submerged. Two men were saved by clinging to a crate of eggs which was floating about, but a hundred people were lost. A few days later, *The Courier* announced: 'We are sorry to learn that accounts have reached town on Saturday of the death of Richard Martin, Esq., M.P. for Galway.' All the London papers carried similar reports.

As one paper pointed out, Humanity Dick's friends were 'numerous and sincere', and the news must have filled them with dismay. However, after a few days of potential mourning had elapsed, *The Courier* was able to publish another account. This stated there was no truth in the previous report; Humanity had merely been suffering from a violent bilious attack, but had now recovered and would be 'at his post during the motion of Mr. Brownlow, and the more important one of Mr. Plunkett in the ensuing month'.

There was something indestructible about Humanity Dick, a fact to which he did not hesitate to draw attention as opportunity offered. On one occasion in London, having arrived with the journalist, William Jerdan, before the other guests for

215

dinner at the house of an Under Secretary, after some talk of a mutual friend's duels, Humanity solemnly opened his frilled shirt, unbuttoned his vest and insisted on showing the scars of a multitude of pistol shots. It was no doubt things like this and the occasional false reports of his death, as much as his immense vitality, which led his friend, Jonah Barrington, to write somewhat incredulously: 'If *ever* Martin should become defunct. . . . '

The two motions for which Humanity Dick was making a point of getting back to parliament dealt with the Catholic question, and they followed closely upon the formation of a new movement in Ireland, the Catholic Association, founded by Daniel O'Connell. In order to avoid any possibility of being proscribed by law, it was not to be in any sense representative. The Catholic population had risen from three to six million, and O'Connell saw the possibility of a broadly based, popular movement. The parishes were to be the local centres and the priests the recruiting agents. Associate members were to contribute a penny a month to the funds, and full members a guinea a year. The income, nicknamed the 'Catholic Rent', soon rose to £1,000 a year, and was used to pay for publicity, to form public opinion, and to contest in the courts the unlawful proceedings of landlords and Orangemen.

Once again the cabinet was divided on the Catholic question, and Canning and Plunkett, like all advocates of the Catholic cause when they came to power, were accused of soft pedalling. The Opposition insisted that the Catholic question should be brought on by the cabinet, but since its members were not in agreement on the subject, this could not be. Consequently, the Opposition threatened to walk out in protest.

This was the usual Opposition stratagem of trying to monopolize the Catholic cause; Humanity Dick was soon on his feet calling their bluff. Their threat to walk out reminded him, he said, of a man who was challenged to a duel and shot himself in order to avoid being shot by his antagonist. He accused the Opposition of giving up the game before it had started and warned them, as usual, that the Catholics were not prepared for their cause to become a party matter. The question, nevertheless, was lost by 313 votes to 111.

Strangely, Humanity Dick voted against an enquiry into the conduct of the High Sheriff of Dublin on the question of the

216

trial of the Orangemen who attacked Wellesley. Yet when the enquiry was under way, and Bradley King, the former Mayor of Dublin who had called so ill-advisedly for a toast to King William during the King's visit, was brought to the bar of the House to be questioned about the Orangemen's oath, Humanity doggedly insisted that he must be made to reply.

Despite this, and his having, of course, voted for the Catholic question, his behaviour during the Catholic debate had not gone unnoticed by Daniel O'Connell. The latter was described as being 'not a little embarrassed in endeavouring to restrain his indignation within the limits necessary to guard the expression of his feelings' when he accused both Humanity Dick and Valentine Blake of Menlo, one of the members for Galway Town, of being worse enemies to the cause than the Protestants because they were prepared to combine with them. Furthermore, he made his accusations in Galway and called upon its electors to take note. It was a rift which was to take some time to mend.

Meanwhile, Humanity Dick had not forgotten about the 'sanguinary temper' of the criminal code, although he was to reverse his attitude on the Insurrection Bill on the grounds that it was impossible to assemble an impartial jury in Ireland and that, consequently, those brought to justice would have a better chance from an intelligent sergeant than from a jury of their neighbours. He had been working on a bill at the same time as the philosopher, Sir James Mackintosh. Sir James's Criminal Law Bill came up for the third reading on 26 June 1823, and Humanity Dick immediately pointed out that he had himself presented the draft of a bill on the same subject to Sir James who had scarcely looked at it. Yet now he was submitting to the House a bill containing a clause which was copied verbatim from this. He protested that he was being treated indecorously.

Sir James promptly rose to explain, but before he had uttered more than a couple of words, Humanity Dick jumped up and declared, 'I'll go for the bill.' Amidst roars of laughter he walked briskly out of the chamber, and within a few minutes returned bearing the famous bill in his hand. But it made no difference. Mackintosh's bill was dropped until the whole matter was taken up by Peel.

Chapter Twenty

Humanity Dick now had two principal aims: gradually to get his act extended to cover more animals, and to see that it was put into effect in its existing form. The most blatant cruelty to animals was that practised in baiting them and in pitting them against one another in contrived fights. The bull-baiting described by Lawrence and Crowe was popular throughout England, and dog fights were almost as general. Encouraged by the sympathy his description of the Westminster Pit had aroused in the previous session, he applied for leave on 21 May 1823 to bring in a bill to prohibit both animal fights and baiting.

An old argument with which he was to continue contending throughout his career was produced. Brougham accused him of wishing to abolish the sports of the poor whilst overlooking the equally cruel sports of the rich—the hunting, shooting and fishing gentlemen. Humanity Dick replied with an argument he was also to use frequently: if five hundred people were placed on a rock on a desolate island and they could not all be saved, the attempt should be made to save at least one of them.

This left open the question of whether field sports were cruel or not, but that great philanthropist, Florence Nightingale's grandfather, William Smith, took up the challenge. He drew the distinction between baiting to torture and hunting to kill. Any pain animals suffered in the field was 'incidental and unavoidable', whereas in the pastimes to which Humanity Dick referred, the degree of pleasure was proportionate to the suffering inflicted on the animals. The *reductio ad absurdum* followed: Sir W. Ridley, after reiterating the argument that the subject was beneath the dignity of the legislature, feared they would be called upon next to provide suitable punishment for the spinning of cockchafers and the destruction of flies.

The same objections had been raised to Pulteney's and Dent's bills on bull-baiting, and Humanity Dick could foresee how the discussion would develop. Dogs, however, were a different matter from bulls. There could scarcely be a member who did not own one, or at least know one intimately. He decided to ask if leave would be given him to bring in a bill solely to protect dogs. But at this sign of withdrawal there were loud cries of 'No, no!' from his friends, and he persevered, only to be defeated by twenty-nine votes to eighteen.

He now concentrated all his energies on picking out culprits in the streets of London. He must be the only man to have got a bill through parliament and then to have seen personally that its provisions were carried into effect. Whether on foot, in his carriage or in his gig, he gradually became a menace to all who had dealings with animals. There was not a coachman or carter or knacker or dog-owner who was safe from his inquisition. Due to its proximity to both the House of Parliament and Manchester Buildings where he lived, he virtually patrolled the area around Whitehall and Charing Cross, and unsuspecting individuals who had never heard of Martin's Act were apt to find themselves unaccountably confronted by Humanity Dick and his indignation.

Such was the plight of John Wells, the driver of stage-coach No. 4391. He had no reason to suspect that he was being watched with anything but admiration as he raced another coach up Whitehall one May evening. He was flogging one of the leading horses to make her keep up, and when she fell he continued beating her to make her rise. She knocked her head against the pavement and kicked violently. The next thing Wells knew was that he was face to face with a florid, stocky, angry gentleman.

Fortunately for Wells, due to his ignorance of what was afoot, he was polite. When a few days later he found himself in the police court, his behaviour was to stand him in good stead. He admitted flogging the horse, but explained that she was broken-winded and could not be driven fifty yards without falling. The gentleman who had accosted him was sitting on the bench, and now to Wells's astonishment, this previously irate person began to intercede for him with the magistrate. Because Wells had behaved very civilly when confronted, the gentleman asked that the fine should be mitigated to the minimum of ten shillings and costs.

As long as the lesson was driven home, Humanity Dick felt he was achieving something, and he flung himself headlong into his crusade without regard either to his personal safety or to the ridicule he might incur. When he saw a man breaking a sheep's leg in Smithfield market and found there was no officer around to whom he could hand over the offender, he did not hesitate to catch the man by the collar and hold on to him whilst the drovers gathered around and ganged up against him.

He managed to be in so many places apparently at the same time that he was described as an absolute 'meteor of ubiquity', and his activities did not go unnoticed in his home town of Galway. The *Galway Advertiser* published a paragraph about a member of the legislature 'with praiseworthy tenderness for his fellow creatures' who had lost the best part of a night's sleep through the 'unobtrusive caresses of a grateful flea. . . . Unwilling to transgress the enactments of his own bill by effusion of blood, and regardless of the cold and inconvenience, the gallant colonel transported his troublesome friend into the chamber of his cook, and deposited him safe and cosy between the blankets.' It only gave Humanity Dick a foretaste of what he was to expect.

An objection repeatedly raised to his bill had been that the magistrates might have difficulty in interpreting it; it would consequently become a nuisance and waste the bench's time in fruitless litigation. When Erskine had introduced the word 'wanton' into his bill, Windham had questioned how it was to be construed, and now John Stevens, a waggoner in the service of a greengrocer, was to provide a test case.

Humanity arrived one day at Covent Garden in his gig with his groom, Martin Whelan, and came upon Stevens lashing his horse. The animal was standing with his head tied to another waggon, and when Humanity remonstrated with Stevens, he was informed that the animal had a sore on his wither and kept kicking because of the pain caused by the collar chain pressing against the spot. To make matters worse, while Humanity was talking to Stevens, his master, Fitch, came up and announced that he had instructed the man to beat the horse.

When Stevens and Fitch appeared at Bow Street police station before Sir Richard Birnie and Mr. Minshull, Humanity Dick was as usual on the bench. He asked the master what had been his object in ordering the horse to be beaten.

'To make him stand still,' replied Fitch.

'Ah! Ah! That is very good,' said Humanity Dick, 'and reminds me of an anecdote bearing upon this case. A French financier under the ancient regime had among his stud a horse which had a knack of devouring another's corn as well as his own, and in order to put a stop to a practice so injurious to the robber and the robbed, he ordered the execution of death to be put in force upon the offender, and the horse—a beautiful animal, by the by—was shot. But egad! the financier found that his execution had very little effect in the way of example, for other thievishly inclined horses still robbed their neighbours and his friends told him he might shoot his whole stud before he cured the evil; so he ordered no more executions.'

Mr. Fitch insisted that a horse was intelligent enough to know why it was being beaten. 'Nonsense, man!' retorted Humanity Dick. 'As well might you beat a horse today for kicking this day week. I tell you what now you should do to make a horse good and obedient. Just go whisper in his ear, "You are a good horse and I am a bad man," and I engage he will be as quiet as a lamb.'

But Mr. Minshull was having difficulty interpreting the words, 'wantonly *and* cruelly' in the act. A thing might be done cruelly, he held, without being done wantonly.

'If there be no apparent wantoness, I think a man must be permitted to exercise his own judgement as to the chastisement he may inflict upon his horse,' said the magistrate.

Humanity Dick could scarcely contain himself. 'O, by God!' he exclaimed. 'If a man is to be judge in his own case, there's an end of everything.'

Sir Richard Birnie intervened: 'I must fine you five shillings for swearing.'

'I am sworn already,' replied Humanity Dick.

'Yes, but you have just sworn an unnecessary oath,' Mr. Minshull explained.

Humanity Dick took out his purse. 'Well, I'll pay.'

Sir Richard was only joking and let him off, but Minshull continued to maintain that a man must exercise his own judgement. Humanity Dick was at bursting point. Jumping up from his seat on the bench and throwing down a bar which was used to keep off the crowd, he declaimed from *Macbeth*:

'Time has been
That when the brains were out the man would die.'

'My brains may be out now,' Minshull replied, 'and I am still alive. But I shall act upon my own judgement as far as it goes, and I cannot make up my mind to convict in this case.'

'Then I tell you,' replied Humanity Dick, 'that it is time you were relieved from the labours of your office.'

He was moving with great agitation to and fro when Minshull declared: 'That was a very kind and gentlemanly remark, certainly Mr. Martin, but I will keep my temper whatever you do. I dismiss the case.'

Upon that Humanity Dick snatched up his hat and, declaring that he would apply for a pardon for everybody who had ever been convicted under the statute, he hurried away.

He was quick to fly into a temper, but equally quick to forgive and forget, and within two days he was back in court, this time at the Guildhall, his sense of humour fully restored. His case was against Benjamin Squires, a carman employed by a firm of coal merchants called Goudge and Thrupp. Humanity Dick declared that he had seen the man cruelly beating his horse. The man explained that he had to do it because the horse was of a fretful nature. The carman's master gave him a good character, and having apparently achieved his object of teaching the man to behave better in the future, Humanity once again intervened to have the fine kept down to ten shillings.

'Now, to show you that your horse wants no flogging,' he concluded, 'I'll tell you what I'll do for you, if you please. I'll walk for half a day with your waggon and deliver your coals, and I'll engage he shall do all his work without any flogging at all.'

But Messrs. Goudge and Thrupp were so little accustomed

Mr. Martin and the Dromedary: The Hoax . . .

. . . and Humanity's reply

Literary Squibs and Crackers or Dickey's Visit to Bow Street

Daniel O'Connell.
Engraved from a
portrait by
T. Carrick

Humanity Dick in old age,
holding in his hand his bill to
abolish the penalty of death
in cases of forgery

to having their coals delivered by a member of parliament that they declined the offer.

As the days went by he must have realized that his outburst against Minshull was both unjustified and unwise. Now, only a few days after the incident he found himself bringing a case in the Mansion House. He made a habit of saying a few words about cruelty to animals before beginning a case, but on this occasion instead he expressed his acknowledgements to the magistracy for the ready assistance they had never failed to give him. Then he went on to the case in point, that of an itinerant greengrocer, Thomas Worster.

'I shall stand excused for the liberty I am going to take,' he declared, 'in addressing you by way of appeal on behalf of a much injured portion of the brute creation. The species which I now allude to is that of asses, or as they are often called, donkeys; and everyone who hears me will bear me out when I say that every person who has resided in London for ever so limited a time, must have been a witness to the cruel and merciless treatment which those wretched animals too often suffer from their employers. This man now before you, Thomas Worster, is one of that class of drivers who, though human in form, have no other signs or emblems of the human nature in their composition.'

He had come across the man in Fleet Street beating his donkey with a leather strap with a strong iron buckle on the end, and at least ten people had been so incensed at the man's cruelty that they had helped Humanity Dick to stop the cart and take the number.

'Please, your worship,' said Worster in his defence, 'I always uses the animal well. He's as fat as a mole, your worship, and as good a creature as need be; only he's a little obstinate, and shies and flies back at the stages, he's so *timersome.*'

'Why, man,' interrupted Humanity Dick. 'You are justifying your conduct. I thought you said you was very sorry for what you had done.'

'Yes, your honour,' continued Worster, 'I owns I beat him, but I say I always feeds him well. Only go and look at him, your honour; there isn't a hair awry in him. I am very fond of him: he's a countryman, your honour; but he shied, and ran back from one of the stages, and he put me in a passion. I never beat him but when I'm in a passion, and I'm always sorry for it afterwards; and I'm very sorry for it now, and if your honour will look over it, I will never beat him again as long as I live.'

The donkey stood outside the court, but Humanity did not need to examine him. Once again the man's penitence went to his heart, and he begged that the penalty should be kept down to ten shillings. But Worster's wife claimed they were too poor to pay even that and the man himself continued to protest his contrition.

Humanity Dick decided his object would be served if he extracted a promise from the man that in future he would always lead his donkey instead of driving him, and, into the bargain, that he would tell his fellow donkey-drivers to do the same. Worster made the promise and Humanity, offering immediately to go halves on the fine, handed the man a half-sovereign.

So far as Humanity Dick was concerned, it was a good day's work, and the fact that a cartoonist portrayed him leading the ass into court was only grist to the mill; it proclaimed his cause.

Instead of returning home to Connemara as usual when parliament rose, he continued to comb the streets for examples of cruelty. His family scarcely saw him. His tenants had to depend on Thomas and the agents, and his entangled monetary affairs grew more entangled. His energy was boundless. His brisk step resounded through the police courts, and he trudged through the dust and mud of Smithfield market in all weathers. He harangued and cajoled, with a typically Irish capacity for fun, and with every breath he pleaded mercy for those who could not plead for themselves and who would never express their gratitude to their liberator.

Although on the surface, and in the context of the times, his activities seemed like mad antics, there was always method in his conduct. He was not just keeping his act in operation; he was establishing precedents which would govern the whole future of animals' welfare. Sometimes he tested the magistrates successfully, as when he secured a conviction for the overloading of a cart. Sometimes he failed, as when he tried to get some bull-baiters convicted on the grounds that the bull was covered by the words 'other cattle' in his act; but to a man of his tenacity failure only pointed the way to future action.

He employed an inspector, and was not only trying to put a

stop to cruelty through example, but was studying the conditions which encouraged it. Some of the worst abuses were those committed in Smithfield market. He visited it regularly over several months and picked out some of the flaws in the organization.

In the first place, there was a shocking lack of officers, and many of the existing ones were old men. He promptly proposed to the Court of Aldermen that the older officers should be pensioned off, and in their places four energetic young men should be appointed who would be capable of handling the tough frequenters of the market.

Next, he noticed that a great number of the accidents were caused by carts, waggons and even carriages being allowed to pass through on market days. All too often they came into collision with sheep or cattle, and the men in charge of the animals often had to beat them mercilessly in order to make them move fast enough to avoid accidents.

He tried to persuade his good friend, the Lord Mayor, to prohibit all thoroughfare on market days, and when this proved to be outside Heygate's competence, Humanity personally drew up a series of regulations which would diminish the causes of accidents and brutality, and petitioned the Board of Aldermen to allow him to lay his suggestions before them.

At the end of the year he at last returned home to the west of Ireland. When in Galway he always stayed at Black's Hotel in Merrick Square, and there one evening his watch was stolen. A little later in one of the public rooms he encountered a man who was actually wearing the watch on a chain, and, having identified it, Humanity pulled out his sword, and with the tip dexterously lifted up the watch by its ring, to the evident terror of the thief.

But Humanity also had more serious business in Galway. A dinner was given early in the new year in the Assembly Rooms to celebrate the coming of age of the young Earl of Clanricarde, the heir to the de Burgos with whom the Martins had come to Ireland, and the descendant of a family which had played a notable part in the history of Galway.

The city now looked to him to liberate the Corporation from the domination of the Daly family who had usurped its offices and set aside its ancient royal charters. On the evening of the banquet, at the special request of the stewards, it was Humanity Dick who made the final speech conveying to the young noblemen the enthusiastic welcome of the citizens and their conviction that, with his help, Galway would now recapture some of its former prestige.

Chapter Twenty-one

As soon as parliament reassembled in 1824 Humanity Dick prepared to immerse the House in the animal question. He started by bringing in an amendment to his own act so as to extend its protection to 'dogs, cats, monkeys and other animals'. He no doubt threw in 'and other animals' in the same way that he had thrown in the controversial 'and other cattle' in his original bill, hoping that the benefits would spread without the words being too precisely noticed. The Attorney-General took him to task for having tried since Martin's Act was passed to argue in court that the bull was covered by the words 'other cattle', and objected to the bull being insinuated covertly. The honourable member, he claimed, should take the bull by the horns and introduce it openly.

That was precisely what Humanity Dick was planning to do, but first he decided to soften the members' hearts with two examples of mistreatment of dogs. He told of one over whom a kettle of boiling water had been poured before he was turned out into the streets to die, whereas another had been rubbed all over with sulphuric acid and left to perish in the most atrocious agony. Apart from extending the benefits of his act to such creatures, he wanted offences under it to be classed as misdemeanours which would render offenders subject to imprisonment.

Humanity's supporters were soon on their feet. Fowell Buxton, who was married to a sister of the great philanthropist, Mrs. Fry, and had supported the abolition of the death penalty for forgery, asserted that Martin's Act had put an end to half the cruelty that previously existed in the country. Mr. Warre denied a statement that most of the cases brought before the magistrates were so doubtful that there was no conviction. Most of them, he assured the House, were so atrocious that conviction followed regularly, while Alderman Bridges maintained that there never had been such a measure for humanity. He reminded the House, as Romilly had done years before, of Hogarth's series of pictures, 'The Progress of Cruelty', in which a man started by tying a canister to a dog's tail and ended by committing murder.

Huskisson, a former Secretary for War, who was Canning's close friend and was to become famous as an advocate of free trade, was basically sympathetic, but tried to turn Humanity Dick's own benevolence against him. The fact that he so often had to pay the fine himself because the accused was too poor to pay was, it seemed to Huskisson, proof that the punishment under Martin's Act was sufficiently severe. But it was Humanity Dick's persuasions, and not his, which prevailed upon the House. He was given permission to introduce the amendment to his act, and by 5 April it had passed through the House of Commons.

But on the very day on which he had introduced the amendment he had given the Attorney-General the satisfaction of seeing him take the bull by the horns, so to speak. He moved for permission to bring in a bill to abolish all cruel sports, and this included bull- and bear-baiting. The familiar arguments about abolishing the entertainment of the poor while leaving their cruel sports to the rich were produced once again, and Windham, the great exponent of the theme, being dead, Peel now took over where he had left off. Referring to the hunting, shooting and fishing gentlemen of the House, he even rose to a little rhyme, hoping they would not

> 'Compound for "sports" they are inclined to
> By damning those they have no mind to.'

He enlarged upon the enormities of fishing, which he described as a cruel fraud practised on innocent and defenceless animals. As for hunting, he could not see why it should be made an offence to encourage the antagonisms between two animals in bear-baiting, while allowing the same thing in fox-hunting,

228

and although he was an enthusiastic shot himself, he put in a special plea for the abolition of partridge-shooting. He even went so far as to question upon what principle we retained animals in confinement at all.

Humanity Dick replied by using William Smith's argument. There was a world of difference, he declared, between hunting to kill and baiting to torture. There was no inconsistency in not prohibiting field sports while putting down the gross and atrocious cruelties which depraved the morals of the people, and he told the House he had received letters on the subject from all over the country.

He was eventually persuaded to abandon his motion on the grounds that it was already covered by the amendment he had brought in to his own act, but he charged ahead and proposed the establishment of a committee to enquire how far cruel sports, if persevered in, tended to deteriorate and corrupt the morals of the people. He claimed that if the hunting, shooting and fishing gentlemen in the House did not vote for him, they would be proving that they were as cruel as those who wallowed in the appalling spectacles of which he gave two examples relating to the suffering of badgers. One was brought out day after day to be baited until it was torn to pieces by the dogs. The other was baited for two years and then had to be shot because there was nothing left for the dogs to fasten on.

He now showed how well he had been preparing the ground outside parliament. It was part of his system to canvass public support either personally or through his sympathizers; then, when he had it, he would face the House with their obligation to respond to the wishes of their constituents. He had a petition from Manchester, he announced, signed by all the resident physicians and the hospital doctors. There was one coming from Liverpool asking for the abolition of all forms of baiting and signed by seven hundred people, mostly members of the Society of Friends, including seven clergymen, while a petition from St. James's called for the suppression of cruelty to all domestic and other animals.

He now encountered some of the criticisms he had, no doubt, expected, and the fact that they were ridiculous only served to emphasize that he was committed to what seemed absurd. He had already been asked if he intended that rats should be protected along with dogs and cats. Now Sir Robert Heron, the brother of the Chief Secretary for Ireland whose wife had so feared Dublin social life, wanted to know if he was going to outlaw the boiling of lobsters and the eating of oysters alive. Did he intend to ask the King to enter into an agreement with the King of France to forbid the torture of frogs in that country, to say nothing of the agonies inflicted on geese in deliberately swelling their livers in order to make *pâté de foie gras*.

Humanity Dick did not feel that there was any need to reply to these pleasantries. But he did reply to Peel. He reminded the Home Secretary that he was fond of shooting and indulged in it frequently. He could see no reason why he should not now also indulge in a little bear-baiting, and he invited him to visit the Westminster Pit.

He countered the suggestion that he should go further and deal with all kinds of sport with a question he was to repeat often in varying forms. If he could not save seven hundred men on a field of battle, why should he not save 50 per cent or 25 per cent. The more there was to be done, the less repugnance the House should feel against allowing him to do a little. But when he declared that he would not press for a division he was suave, as only he could be; he declared that it was out of a feeling of tenderness for the House. There were gentlemen there who had not uttered a word, but he was certain they would not want to have their names given to the public as forming part of the majority which he felt he would have against him.

With his determination to bombard the House with the predicament of animals, he had meanwhile turned his attention to another aspect. During the parliamentary recess, when he had been inspecting the animal population of the city, he had found that the most dreadful conditions prevailed in knackers' yards where horses were frequently kept for days without food pending slaughter, as Erskine had pointed out to the Lords years before.

In one case in Whitechapel he had found eight to ten horses some with their eyes knocked out, others hopping around on three legs, all maimed and half-starved. He gave the man in charge some money to buy bales of hay, and when they were brought in, the horses fell upon them like hounds and devoured them so rapidly that the man said: 'There now, you'd much better ge'd me the money to buy drink.' Humanity's reply was prompt: 'I would see you d——d first.' The man was so incensed at this that he declared he would trample down the hay so as to make it inedible. In order to pacify him and save the horse's food, Humanity had given him another two shillings. But he did not let the matter rest there. He took his revenge: he sent the man over two hundred letters appointing him to go to various parts of the town to collect dead cows and horses.

As a result of experiences such as this, he introduced the Slaughtering of Horses Bill on 31 May 1824. According to it, every occupier of a licensed slaughter-house would have to enter in a book kept for the purpose details of the food given to the animals in his care. On the first Monday of every month he would have to swear to the truth of his entries before a Justice of the Peace; the book in question would have to be available for inspection at all reasonable times. Furthermore, nobody was to carry a living horse on any waggon or truck, dray or cart, or drag any horse having a disabled limb by attaching him to a vehicle, under penalty of paying £5 or being subjected to three months' hard labour. A clause was later added requiring licences to be renewed annually, to be operative only in the parish where the slaughtering was to take place, and to be suspended in cases of public nuisances. The bill got as far as the report stage on 15 June, but was then defeated.

The following day, and while the fate of the amendment to Martin's Act was still hanging fire in the Lords, a momentous meeting took place at a coffee house in St. Martin's Lane called, ironically, Old Slaughter's, from the name of the proprietor. The gathering arose out of a correspondence started by the Reverend Arthur Broome in the *Monthly Magazine*, and was made up of the Friends of the Bill for the Prevention of Cruelty to Animals, Humanity Dick's bill. Fowell Buxton took the chair, and, of course, Humanity Dick himself was present. When at one juncture of the proceedings grave doubts were expressed of parliament's ever agreeing to their demands, S. C. Hall, *The Times* parliamentary correspondent, who had also come along, heard Humanity Dick deliberately adopting an Irish accent for effect and saying that 'By Jasus, he'd make 'em do it!' From the very look of him, Hall knew that this was no idle boast. He described him as 'a short, thick-set man, with evidence in look and manner, even in step and action, of indomitable resolution'.

The outcome of the meeting was the Society for the Prevention of Cruelty to Animals. It issued a prospectus declaring that its object was 'the mitigation of animal suffering, and the promotion and expansion of the practice of humanity towards the inferior classes of animated beings'. The Reverend Arthur Broome was appointed Honorary Secretary, and two committees were set up. One was to superintend the publication of tracts, sermons, and so forth. The fact that it included both Wilberforce and Sir James Mackintosh shows the prestige the movement had already acquired, principally thanks to Humanity Dick. The other committee was to adopt measures for inspecting the markets and streets of London, slaughter-houses, the conduct of coachmen, in fact, all the things Humanity Dick had already been doing on his own, and, of course, it included him. The foundation of the SPCA may have done something to compensate him for the fact that on that very same day the amendment to Martin's Act was lost in the Lords.

There were other signs that his message was being heard. Nobody who read the newspapers could have failed to realize that something like a revolution had been going on quietly for a couple of years, and now there were occasional instances of members of the public intervening to prevent cruelty to animals. A Mr. Grey prosecuted his own coachman for cruelly beating his own horse. A Mr. Fessenege was almost assaulted by a man whom he had tried to stop beating a restive horse in a cart, and the coachman of Madame Pasta, the opera singer, was smartly taken off the box in Downing Street and charged with cruelty to his horse.

It was now generally known that Humanity Dick was perpetually on the prowl, and one man called him 'the devil to any coachman'. Another said to him: 'I tell you what, Mr. Martin, there's not a hackney coachman will drive you, or if they do, they'll only walk you, for fear you should put them up for using the whip.' Humanity replied coolly: 'That's strange, indeed, for I always pay more than my fare.' The fact was he had been a veritable Society for the Prevention of Cruelty to Animals in person for a number of years.

Then one day in July 1824, he was involved in a case in which he claimed that the accused man's wife had said he was ill-tempered. The owner of the horse, which was the object of the case, intervened in court to say: 'She meant the horse was ill-tempered, not the man.' On this Humanity Dick turned to his friend, Sir Richard Birnie, the magistrate hearing the case, and said: 'Now I will appeal to you, Sir Richard, whether this defendant does not bear the outward and visible signs of a bad temper. Any man who knows anything of physiognomy can see that in a moment.'

The owner of the horse immediately retorted, pointing to Humanity: 'Now I will make an appeal to your worship. Look at this man's physonomy and tell me if it is not worse than the physonomy of any man.'

Sir Richard declined to pronounce on so delicate a matter as Humanity Dick's personal appearance, but he fined the man and then noticed that a well-known actor, Joseph Munden, was standing by and that Humanity Dick, who was a friend of his, had not even noticed him. When he asked Humanity if he did not realize that it was Munden who was standing beside him, Humanity immediately burst forth: 'Oh, by God so it is. My dear fellow, I am very glad to see you.'

'Pray, Mr. Martin,' interposed Sir Richard, 'do you not know that you are subject to a fine for swearing in front of a magistrate?'

'By God, Birnie, you're right,' replied Humanity, promptly taking out his purse and paying five shillings. Then he departed.

> 'O place me where Dick Martin rules
> The houseless wilds of Connemara'

wrote his friend, Tom Moore, parodying a Horatian ode, but it was a long time since Humanity had been home, and economic distress in the west of Ireland continued. There now appeared a letter in *The Times* addressed to him and signed 'A Casuist of Connemara'. This took him to task for failing to be amongst his tenants and constituents, organizing relief, rather than amongst cattle-drovers and magistrates, reserving his humanity for animals. Instead of being at his post in his vast demesne, the writer chided, 'We were . . . surprised to learn that, at the Police Office in Bow Street, you was yesterday fined by the magistrates for wanton and profane swearing. You should be reminded, Mr. Martin, that "charity begins at home".'

It was an impressive and well-reasoned letter, and to one who worshipped every square-inch of Connemara and every man, woman and child in it, the reproach would have been wounding except for one small detail. It appeared in *The Times* on the very morning after the swearing incident in front of Birnie, long before news of this could have reached Connemara and a reply been returned. *The Times* was clever at teasing Richard Martin M.P., but not quite clever enough.

A couple of weeks later *The Times* published another long paragraph on 'Mr. Martin of Galway' saying that they understood he was about to act on the advice given by the correspondent a few weeks earlier and to return to his numerous tenantry in Connemara. There followed a garbled version of the family background in which Robert, Humanity Dick's father, was confused with Nimble Dick, his great-grandfather, and there followed what purported to be a description of life on the Martin estate.

'The kelp, or seaweed,' *The Times* continued, 'is the great support of the family. When groceries, or clothes, or other necessaries are to be paid for, Mr. Martin loads a couple of asses (for there is no horse on the estate) with kelp, and the asses return with the produce. Money is a thing unknown at Connemara; and that which is spent in the services of the public to the terror of the Smithfield drovers, never reaches the country without going through the hands of the soap-boilers of Galway or the surrounding country. When he wishes to dispose of some land, he never says "give me so much an acre for this or that piece of ground"; but he takes the purchaser up a hill, and pointing to a bush (for a bush is a landmark on the estate, there being scarcely a tree to be seen), he says, "I'll let you all that, from that tree across that bog, to the foot of that mountain, with all that coast for so much kelp and so much butter." But although a bailiff would no more live in the air of Connemara than a serpent, the town of Galway is not so destructive of the vermin. When a dissolution of Parliament takes place, Galway, as well as Smithfield, may run riot. The retreat of Connemara then is more honoured than it is at any other period; but the moment the return is made, a flag is hoisted upon the hustings over the Court-house, and then the worthy representative rides off to his constituents and assures them that the question of Catholic emancipation shall receive his strongest support.'

The writer went on to assert that Humanity Dick owed his continued return to parliament to the fact that he had settled Catholic refugees from Northern Ireland on his estates in 1797 and made them freeholders. 'He keeps a storehouse of brogues,' it continued, 'which he opens at the time of election to his constituents, and they sally forth in genteel though exceedingly inconvenient style, to vote for the "veisther" [master].'

With his keen sense of humour, Humanity Dick would have appreciated this typically English skit on Irish life, but the grain of truth in it may have irritated him, for his circumstances were becoming progressively more embarrassed. The kelp to which the newspaper had referred now fetched only a quarter of what it had been worth when things had been going relatively well twenty years previously. The mines had still produced nothing but expense, Thomas was pathologically extravagant, and Humanity's own debts were such that were it not for the immunity he enjoyed as a member of parliament, he would find himself being sued on all sides.

Jonah Barrington claimed to have met one of Humanity Dick's servants from Connemara who gave his occupations as butchering, burning kelp, working at the still, smuggling, tanning the brogues for Humanity's yeomen, acting bailiff-bum and making out election registers. 'And when I've nothing else to do,' he added, 'I keep the squire's accounts, and by my sowl that same is no easy matter, please your honour, till one's used to it. But, God bless him, up and down, wherever he goes here and hereafter, he's nothing else but a good master to us all.' As for the writ-servers who pestered him, they were easily dealt with. They were merely forced to eat their parchment and to wash it down with a few glasses of poteen. 'Only that our own bailiffs and yeomen keep the sheriff's officers out of Connemara,' the man concluded, 'we'd have a rookery of them afore every 'sizes and sessions, when the master's amongst the sassanachs in London city.'

Chapter Twenty-two

CANNING WENT to Dublin in September 1824. His daughter was about to become engaged to Lord Clanricarde, at whose coming-of-age Humanity Dick had made a speech in Galway earlier in the year, and the young man came up to Dublin from the west of Ireland with his guardians to meet his future father-in-law.

But whatever personal aspect this might give to the Foreign Minister's visit, the fact that he was in daily consultation with a Viceroy considered to be, like him, sympathetic to the Catholics, was viewed in London with the deepest suspicion. The King, who only three summers previously had been fêted in Dublin as the religious conciliator, was revealing that his views on the Catholic question were, in fact, the same as his father's. Only a couple of months before, when Peel had turned down the Lord Lieutenant's request for letters of precedence for an Irish Catholic barrister, the King had sent Peel a message saying that even had the cabinet approved, he would not have consented. 'The King,' the message ran, 'desires Mr. Peel to remember this, as it may be a guide for his future conduct relative to the Catholic question.' Peel scarcely needed such guidance, and his views were shared by the Prime Minister, Liverpool, and Wellington, to name but two of his colleagues.

The Catholic Association was made the excuse for a hardening of attitudes. It united the whole of Catholic Ireland, from the aristocracy who dominated the previous Catholic Committee, to the peasantry, and it established O'Connell as a formidable organizer and effective demagogue. To those who were prejudiced against the Catholic claims, it was that most dangerous of all things—a powerful organization which was, nonetheless, law abiding. But O'Connell was a natural rabble rouser, and even when he himself was prepared to compromise, the extremists among those whom he had excited were not. They frequently indulged in the kind of invective which had been totally absent from the earlier Catholic movement, and Humanity Dick was among those who, like the Lord Lieutenant, regretted this.

Humanity dined at Dublin Castle with Canning during his visit, and while the Catholic Association would no doubt have been one of the subjects of conversation, there was a cause of discord brewing which might well also have been mentioned. In the next election it was known that Daly, as usual, would put up a candidate for the town of Galway and himself stand for the county. But now Canning's future son-in-law, to whom Humanity had made such an eloquent appeal earlier in the year to liberate the town from the Dalys' domination, was responding in a strange way. He was putting up a candidate for the county in opposition to both Daly and Humanity Dick.

The news resulted in a good deal of political activity. When Humanity went down to Galway during Canning's visit for the quarter sessions, Daly suggested that he and Humanity should back one another in the county to keep out Clanricarde's candidate. In exchange Daly was prepared to bring in Thomas as his candidate for the town on condition that he undertook to be the guardian of the corporate rights of Daly who would reserve the exclusive patronage of the town. But the Martins had been pledged since time immemorial to the independence of Galway. Thomas could not accept the conditions, and so, after some weeks of uncertainty, the proposed junction between Daly and Humanity Dick was abandoned. Clanricarde had an unencumbered estate worth about £18,000 a year, and, as things now stood, Humanity Dick would have the whole weight of this wealth and influence lined up against him at the next election.

He could have benefited from a prolonged stay among his constituents. Besides, Charles Peshall, who had now come into the title and was British Consul in South Carolina, was at home with Laetitia and young Charles, now aged fifteen; and Richard was on a visit to Ballinahinch. But Humanity was not a man to procrastinate. So long as something remained to be done he could not rest, and, abandoning his estate and his family, he returned to Dublin, and while Canning was still there he proceeded to deal with the Catholic Association as only one with his background and prestige could do. He decided to show them how even a sympathizer could feel about some of their manifestations, and on 25 September he went to the Association's headquarters in Capel Street and addressed a meeting.

He went there, he explained, as the oldest parliamentary advocate of the Catholics in existence. In fact, at seventy he was the sole survivor of those who had voted for Luke Gardiner's Catholic Relief Bill in 1778, which had granted Catholics the right to lease land, thereby starting a new era. He spoke as the close relative of Lords Trimelstown and Gormanston who were now and had been for several generations among the leaders of the Irish Catholics and, going back to his visit to Ballinasloe Fair in 1803 and his consultations then on a county basis with the Catholic gentry, he reminded the meeting that he had been the first man to encourage the Catholics to organize and press their cause during the period of general apathy that followed the disappointments of the Union.

All this established him as a man who had a right to speak frankly, and he proceeded to do so. More and more people now saw the justice of the Catholic cause, he declared, but while prejudice was being conquered in England he urged the Association to conquer among themselves any tendency to intemperance, lest those among them who were intolerant should wrest from the Catholics the fruits of a victory so hardly won.

The English Lord Chancellor, he claimed, had done them a singular service. In declaring that the English Catholics could with safety be granted liberties which could not be allowed to the Irish, he had caused a reaction among all moderate people who were shocked at his illiberality. The Prime Minister himself had opposed the Chancellor's exclusiveness, and the best means of preserving so valuable an ally was a strict adherence by the Catholics to temperance and forbearance.

As to having the honour of becoming a member of the

238

Association, he did not think it would be in keeping, and, into the bargain, as a member he would not be able to serve them as he hoped always to do. The Catholics now had a mighty engine to assist them in the form of the Catholic Rent, he concluded, and the surest way to prevent its failing was 'to bridle their feelings and not let them escape through their mouths with impetuosity or lack of control'.

However surprising his continued expressions of faith in Liverpool, his meaning was clear: he had come as a sympathetic critic. The speech was given full coverage in the press, and the *Dublin Evening Post* went so far as to say they had been informed that it was Humanity Dick who had first recommended the Catholic Rent; but *The Times* gave way to a growing tendency to extend to his politics the sneers that greeted his crusade for animals. Their Dublin correspondent, after referring to Martin's having dined with Canning, wrote, evidently before reading the report of his speech to the Catholic Association: 'You will be amused at hearing that he has been speeching today at the Catholic Association in approbation of the measures of that body. It is true a general election is at hand; but this is almost too shallow even to excite a laugh.'

Even the *Dublin Star* misinterpreted the spirit in which he had gone to address the Association, and treated him as a turncoat. It published a skit which *The Times* reprinted under the title, 'Mr. Martin of Galway, Brahmin', which ran:

'It is a fact more curious than surprising, when it is considered in connexion with Mr. Martin's love of the brute creation, that the honourable gentleman has lately become a steadfast believer in transformation, transmigration, and metempsychosis!!!—hence, we learn, has been produced his philanthropic suit of feelings with regard to the lower order of animals. Mr. Martin never, like vulgar people, speaks of death. He talks only of metamorphosis. Nothing, we are persuaded, would shock the member for Galway more than his merging into a water-rat, a church-mouse, or a watch-dog. Only conceive for a moment, how Mr. Martin would look were he transformed into a huge, surly mastiff, chained to a kennel.'

The ridicule did not dampen Humanity Dick's ardour for either the Catholic cause or that of animals, and instead of returning to Connemara as in former years to await the reassembly of parliament, he hastened to London to get on with the work in hand. He was collecting fresh information on baiting, and had some alarming details on vivisection. Following up his basic plan of putting pressure on parliament through public opinion, he called on aldermen and got in touch with magistrates up and down the country in search of support. Then he began extracting opinions from leading medical men on vivisection.

In the midst of this concentrated activity, he received notice that there was a dromedary at a certain place in Woolwich which was being grossly ill-treated by overloading. His energy was unabated and his spontaneity undiminished. He dropped everything and made off at once to the scene of the crime expecting, no doubt, to find a menagerie. It was early November and, therefore, not the best of weather for a visit to the Thames estuary, but the robust countryman that he still was basically was ready to face anything. On arrival at his destination he found no menagerie and no camel. Instead, anchored in the river, he found one of the outward-bound convict ships which it was customary to overload, and it so happened that she was called the *Dromedary*.

But the practical joker who had originated the story had not only forgotten that his victim was an Irishman noted for his quickness of wit, but a member of parliament who had always shown a particular interest in everything concerned with the penal code. Before long, he was aboard the ship, launched upon a tour of inspection, looking into every detail, and within a few days he had a note inserted in the press which ran:

'On Friday last, Mr. Martin went over the Dromedary, outward-bound convict ship lying off Woolwich, and humanely inspected all the prisoners sentenced for transportation. He expressed satisfaction at the arrangements for their comfort and cleanliness, and their generally healthy appearance. He examined the calendar and made special enquiries about the characters of several of the unfortunate men, who appeared to be sentenced for light offences. The case of R. Mitchell, who was suffering from a severe rupture, and who stated himself to have been convicted for stealing twenty potatoes, appeared to Mr. Martin to merit particularly further enquiry.'

While Humanity Dick pursued his campaign to counter

opposition, serious or ridiculous, and to muster the magistrates of England in his support before parliament should reassemble, the Catholic Association was increasingly occupying the time of Government. Canning called it the most difficult problem a government had ever had to deal with, and the Lord Lieutenant wanted both the Association and the Orange Lodges put down; but Plunkett, the Attorney-General, pointed out that there was no basis for proscribing the Association as it was not representative in character. The only method of intervening was conveyed by Peel to Wellesley on 18 December 1824. 'If a proper opportunity should occur of prosecuting an individual, either for delivering or for publishing a speech, the delivery or publication of which would subject him, under the existing law, to punishment, such an opportunity should not be lost.'

The opportunity had, in fact, already arrived. On 16 December O'Connell had addressed the Association and was reported as saying that if parliament did not meet the claims of the Catholics, he hoped that another Bolivar might arise in Ireland to vindicate the rights of the Irish people. He was arrested for sedition, but after five hours of deliberation, the grand jury ignored the bills against him, much to the satisfaction of the Irish Catholics.

By the time parliament reassembled in February and O'Connell had arrived in London to consult with the English Catholics how best to proceed with promoting their mutual aims, the course events were to take was established. The King's speech declared the Catholic Association 'irreconcilable with the Constitution' and calculated 'to endanger the peace of society and to retard the course of national improvement'. The Government followed by bringing in a bill drafted by Goulburn to declare the Association illegal.

If either *The Times* or the *Dublin Sun* were still in any doubt as to Humanity Dick's attitude to the Association, they could now be set right. He started by saying that he could positively assert that the Association had the support of the great mass of Irish Catholics. They might not all subscribe to everything said in every speech made in the Association, but as far as the acts of that body went, the Catholics were resolved to adopt them. A magistrate of his own county had observed to him that, as the Catholics of Ireland had no hope from justice and the laws, although the equity of their claims was generally admitted, they were compelled to unite to adopt those measures which could oblige the Government to do them justice. He confessed that there was nothing surprising to him in that determination.

He would not, he declared, consent to the bill that was before the House because he could see that it would fail in its operation. At the same time, he did not approve of the conduct of the Catholic Association in many particulars, and he had been to a meeting and taken the liberty of pointing out errors into which they had fallen and those into which he feared they would fall. He was not inclined to think the Association was less dangerous because it had tranquillized Ireland; if they could allay the angry billows, they had the power to raise them again. But he would suggest that they committed an error in entrusting their petition to a member of the Opposition, Sir Francis Burdett. In fact, Humanity had few more staunch supporters in his fight for animals' rights than the energetic Whig baronet whose favourite pastime was fox-hunting, and who became the champion of freedom of speech. He revered Humanity as the precursor of a new world, but the older man, who believed that emancipation could only be achieved through the government in power, resented the fact that Burdett had the previous year walked out of the House rather than discuss the Catholic question with Ministers whose sincerity he claimed he doubted.

The Times, which had been so ready to scoff at Humanity, now took up his main argument, and wrote: 'Of a bill which cannot, in the nature of things, be effectual if brought to maturity, its authors would have surely no reason to lament the strangulation in the hour of giving it birth.'

Meanwhile, Humanity Dick's friend, Canning, who was well acquainted with his future son-in-law's plans, put his own interpretation on Humanity's reactions. Writing to Granville of his daughter's engagement to Clanricarde on the day *The Times* leader appeared, he said: 'Martin is running a race with him for Galway and popularity, and means for that purpose to vote against the Bill, though he wrote to me from Ireland that interference was absolutely necessary.' And a couple of days later he wrote further, referring to those who would oppose the bill: 'among them Martin, who is in alarm lest Lord Clanricarde should set up a candidate for the county; and who, therefore, seeks to fortify himself with the aid of the priests and of O'Connell.'

Canning may not have known that it was rumoured Clanricarde's candidate would be James Lambert, and that he had been the only man in County Galway who had refused to sign the Protestant petition of 1812 in favour of the Catholics. Canning himself voted for the suppression of the Catholic Association, and when a few weeks later Burdett brought up the Catholic question for debate, Canning abstained from voting, thereby seeming to justify Burdett's theory of the insincerity of ministers.

As for Humanity Dick, after forty-three years of fighting for the Catholics' rights, it is questionable if he was in need of renewed support from the priests and O'Connell. Certainly, his speech to the Association and his statement in the House did not suggest that he was courting O'Connell, but, rather, that he was pained by any extremism which might cause a set-back to the Catholic cause. He and O'Connell had much in common. They shared the belief that what was needed was the granting of civil rights to the Catholics within the British Constitution. They both stood by the British connection, and the Catholic Association's emblem was the same as the Volunteers' of the previous century—an Irish harp surmounted by a crown.

It may have been a signal that the rift between the two men was mended that ten days later at a big meeting in London, O'Connell claimed that the Association had preserved tranquillity 'from the north to the south of Ireland—from the Giant's Causeway to Cape Clear—from the East to the West— from the Hill of Howth to Mr. Martin's wide domains'. But neither the advice of *The Times* nor of Humanity was taken.

The bill outlawing the Catholic Association passed by 278 votes to 123, and the Association held its last meeting in Dublin on 31 March 1825. But Humanity Dick's analysis was to prove true. It was no longer possible to quash the great popular movement or to put down O'Connell, but meanwhile the Orange Lodges continued afoot.

Humanity Dick was now to have one of his busiest sessions. Scarcely was the Catholic Association business out of the way than he once again presented a bill for the abolition of bear-baiting, to which he added once again 'and other cruel practices'.

Now, however, he was not just a zealous crusader, but the wily lawyer. A great many of the performances to which he drew attention were outside the jurisdiction of the police because no admittance fee was charged, but he now held in his hand a poster which told a tale. Billy, the phenomenon of the canine race and champion vermin-killer, was to perform in aid of his late owner's widow; a fight between two dogs and two fresh badgers was to follow; and then several dogs were to be tried at a bear. Admittance to each fight was to cost three shillings and this would entitle the police to intervene.

But the punch line was to follow: the entire performance was at the 'express invitation of several noblemen and gentlemen of the first distinction'. He threw this out particularly for the benefit of Peel, who had accused Humanity Dick of meddling only with the sports of the poor, and had gone so far as to say: 'Show me that the nobility take part in these sports and I will join with all my heart in putting them down.' Now Humanity called upon Peel to redeem his pledge and to give the bill his strenuous support.

Next he set about shocking the House. He gave them a detailed description of some of the experiments carried out in one of London's anatomical theatres the previous year by an eminent French surgeon, Majendie, adding that those who witnessed without interfering were in his opinion no better than criminals. Majendie had bought a greyhound for £10, nailed it alive to a table and dissected the nerves of its face— those affecting sight, hearing and taste. He had then turned to the spectators, saying: 'I have now finished operating on one side of the dog's head; as it costs so much money to get an animal of this description, I shall reserve the other side till tomorrow. If the servant takes care of him for the night according to instructions I have given him, I am of the opinion I shall be able to continue tomorrow with quite as much satisfaction to us as I have today; but if not I shall have the opportunity of cutting him up alive and showing you the peristaltic motion of the heart and viscera.'

The House was universally horrified, and while Humanity Dick waved at them written declarations from Abernethy and Home, the Professors of Medicine at Cambridge and Oxford, condemning outright such cruelties, he told his listeners that

Majendie was due to return to England shortly to repeat his experiments. What he hoped was that he could stir up so much antagonism that the Frenchman would have no audience and would be obliged to return home in search of a theatre.

He claimed that the magistrates whom he had canvassed and who had called for a law to put down cruel practices were entitled to some respect, and challenged any man to stand up and say: 'I am such a lover of cruelty that I will not even allow a measure to be discussed which tends to abolish it.' He feared, nevertheless, that he would be defeated, but after the familiar argument about such matters being beneath the dignity of the House had been produced, Fowell Buxton and Alderman Bridges came forward with valuable support, and on the division, there were forty-one for permission to bring in the bill, and twenty-nine against. Writing of the debate to his wife the next day, Fowell Buxton, after remarking that the House had a tendency to laugh at Humanity Dick, concluded: 'We have saved the bill, and all the dogs in England and bears in Christendom ought to howl us a congratulation.'

An account of Humanity Dick's diatribe against Majendie was soon read by Dr. John Shiel, a former President of the Royal Medical Society of Edinburgh, then living in Paris. He lost no time in bringing it to the attention of the French surgeon, who authorized him to write a letter which was reproduced in *The Times*. In it Shiel asserted that the experiments described by Humanity Dick 'never had existence but in that honourable gentleman's fancy', and he resented that the facts had been communicated to parliament by a member 'whose exquisite benevolence might have taught him a little more of candour and respect for the feelings of a stranger who had no immediate opportunity of vindication'. He concluded by pointing out that Majendie was held in veneration by scientific men of every country, that his experiments had conferred considerable benefits on mankind, and that he had been elected a member of the Institut de France at a very early age.

Humanity Dick's utterances in parliament were privileged, but he had no desire to shelter behind this immunity. The very morning after Shiel's letter had appeared in *The Times* he stalked down to St. Bartholomew's Hospital, which had refused Majendie the right to operate there. In order to give the

Frenchman the opportunity of proceeding against him if he wished, he there repeated publicly what he had stated in parliament.

When he went to the House the next evening to move the second reading of his bill on cruel practices, Sir James Mackintosh, who had known Majendie in Paris and thought highly of him, spoke in his favour. But Humanity Dick countered by producing fresh medical testimony, that of the Professor of Anatomy at Oxford who maintained that the country should be informed of what was happening. Then he proceeded to make members' flesh creep once more with a further detail on Majendie's experiments. While operating on a dog in England he had whispered in the dog's ear: 'Restez tranquille'. He had then explained to the audience: 'Il serait plus tranquille s'il entendait français.' Nobody could hear the details without squirming.

One of the criticisms most frequently produced against the kind of legislation for which Humanity Dick was fighting was that the powers would be abused, and Sir Francis Burdett now answered it. Contrary to being abused, he feared that they would fall into disuse entirely unless the member for Galway could find a successor as industrious and persevering as himself. But Fowell Buxton had spoken too soon. Humanity's bill on cruel practices was lost by thirty-two votes to fifty. The time had not yet come for all the bears and dogs to howl a congratulation.

When a few weeks later Humanity Dick moved once again for permission to bring in a bill to prevent cruelty to dogs he withdrew it by calling Peel's bluff. The Home Secretary was fond of complaining of the number of motions the member for Galway introduced for the protection of individual animals; he wished there could be one bill to cover them all. But when Humanity announced that he would withdraw in order to introduce a more comprehensive measure later, Peel hastened to prepare the way for retreat. He approved of the withdrawal, but wished it to be distinctly understood that he did not pledge himself to support any future bill. This could only prove to Humanity that by trying too much he would lose all. Progress must be by degrees and time was needed to allow public opinion to develop.

The signs that this was happening were multiplying, including the fact that the butchers and drovers of Smithfield had sent in a petition in favour of Humanity Dick's latest bill, and, largely due to his exertions, the subject was being kept constantly before the public through the press. Whatever *The Times* leader writers might say, their parliamentary correspondent faithfully reported the debates on cruelty to animals. Mudford, the editor of the *Courier* was on one of the committees of the SPCA and not only reproduced reports, but gave editorial space, and from March 1825, he waged a constant war against the *Morning Chronicle*, which missed no opportunity for jeering. It even accused Humanity Dick of himself writing the editorials in the *Courier* which it referred to as his 'organ'.

There was nothing surprising in Mudford, who was in constant contact with the dynamic member for Galway, writing:

'Mr. Martin is indefatigable. . . . He is the man to carry a good cause through a host of opposing prejudices. He has that quality of steady, unflinching perseverance, which turns neither to the right, nor to the left, but moves, however, slowly, straight onward to his point, satisfied that, so long as he does not stand still, nor retrograde, he must get to the object at last.'

And even if Mudford did write with Humanity Dick looking over his shoulder, that did not render his words less true.

Chapter Twenty-three

THE CATHOLIC ASSOCIATION might appear to be dead, but the Catholic cause seemed to be on the eve of a triumph. The Government which had brought in the bill to suppress the former, immediately prepared to introduce a bill to ensure the success of the latter. O'Connell, who remained in London, was consulted at every stage, and the bill was largely drafted by him.

It was to permit Catholics to sit in parliament and, thereby, it met their principal complaint that they were ruled by laws they had no part in formulating, but, as on all previous occasions, the question of securities for the Protestant establishment arose. O'Connell realized that emancipation would not be obtained without these, and he was, at the same time, sufficiently aware of the agitation he had stirred up at home to want to get it through as speedily as possible.

The securities were contained in two bills which came to be known as the 'wings'. One was to reduce the Catholic electorate by disenfranchising the forty-shilling freeholders. The other provided for state remuneration for the Catholic clergy as a means of rendering them more dependent and, thereby, more loyal. In one of the largest divisions ever known the Commons voted by 292 to 265 in favour of admitting Catholics to parliament. It was thirty-three years since the last Catholic Relief Bill, and the disappointment it had caused by not providing for this basic right had helped to pave the way for the Rebellion. For those old enough to remember, the new turn of events was particularly heartening, if overdue.

Among these people was Humanity Dick, but when it came to the 'wings' he had some observations to make. The Catholic clergy, he pointed out, had not asked for any financial support and would be much happier without it. They received more from their flocks than they would receive from parliament, and in accepting it they would lose a great deal of the sway they held over their parishioners. But he would support it, and one of his reasons for doing so was that it would relieve the Protestants of what he considered a just reproach. At present they assessed the Catholics, without allowing them a vote on the subject, for their church rates, the repair of their churches and other matters. If the bill went through, at least the Protestants, in their turn, would be taxed for the payment of the Catholic clergy. He did not consider state aid necessary in itself, but he would vote for it because he thought it would advance the great question of Catholic emancipation.

As for the forty-shilling freeholders, it was they who put him into parliament. It was not in Humanity Dick's interest to disenfranchise them, although he admitted that they were often subjected to undue pressure. Reluctantly, he was, however, prepared also to vote for this 'wing' and for the same reason— it would advance the Catholic cause. He had persuaded himself that it was proper to do a little wrong, for the sake of obtaining a great right.

The 'wings' also passed the Commons, and brought emancipation nearer than it had ever been. For Humanity Dick it meant that he had little prospect of getting back into parliament again, and must abandon his campaign for the protection of animals; but he would have been jubilant despite this. His cousin, Lord Gormanston's son Edward, was in London with the Irish delegation, and wrote home that he had been seeing Cousin Martin, as he called Humanity, and that he was confident the bill would pass the Lords.

But the shadow of the mad old King still lay across that assembly. His son, the Duke of York, the heir apparent, speaking through tears, reminded the House of George III's qualms about his coronation oath, and declared that he himself had always opposed political power for the Catholics. 'The Roman Catholics,' he ranted, 'will not allow the Crown or the Parliament to interfere with their Church. Are they, nevertheless, to legislate for the Protestant Church of England? . . . I have been brought up in these Protestant principles . . . and in whatever situation I may be placed in life, I shall maintain them, so help me God!' He had many willing followers, and his declaration acted as a fan to the prejudices of others. When the question came to a division, the admission of Catholics to parliament was defeated by 178 votes to 130.

While the Catholic bill was being debated, *Blackwood's Edinburgh Magazine* came to the support of Humanity Dick's bear-baiting bill, and threw ridicule on those who compared baiting with field sports. The quality of every act of violence, the writer maintained, depended largely upon the relative conditions of 'the thing that strikes and the thing that suffers', and he made a precise distinction between those who paid money 'expressly to *purchase* the protracted agony of a helpless and unoffending (note: unoffending) creature' and field sports.

Such support was welcome, and Humanity now had a powerful ally in the SPCA. A couple of weeks before he applied for leave to bring in an amendment to Martin's Act so as to increase the penalties for wounding and maiming horses and cattle, the society circularized all members of parliament who were considered sympathetic, asking them to attend in the House for the second reading, but the bill was defeated, as was the Slaughter of Horses Bill which Humanity had introduced again, although this reached the third reading.

As always, Humanity Dick lived in a frenzy of activity, with time for both man and beast. He was, for instance, a member of the Society for the amelioration and gradual abolition of Slavery throughout the British Dominions which had been formed in 1823, led by Fowell Buxton and Wilberforce, and at the annual general meeting of the society in May 1825, he was on the platform next to Wilberforce. The next day he would be in Smithfield arguing with drovers, or else in the police court battling for horses. Anybody who had praise for him wrote to the *Courier*, such as the man who wrote that he deserved 'the thanks of the whole human race'. Those who had any criticism wrote to the *Morning Chronicle*, as did the man who objected to castration. It was known that Humanity Dick rode regularly in the Park, and the correspondent wanted to know if he always rode entire horses.

A controversy was now to begin in the press which was to involve *Blackwood's Magazine*, the very publication which had given Humanity Dick such valuable support. It was started by the *Morning Chronicle*, which had taken to calling Humanity Dick the Professor of Humanity, and had kept up a sustained campaign against him. It ridiculed him when it could, and when it could not it gave pride of place to his political adversaries. Now it raised the question of an informer being at the same time a witness. It was a travesty of justice, they claimed, for them to be one and the same person, thus striking at the very essence of the legislation for animals, namely, that it was to protect the dumb.

The paper maintained that the difference in people's reactions had to be taken into account. What might not appear cruel at all to one might seem atrocious in the eyes of another person of morbid sensitivity whose heart, as the writer put it, 'was a menagerie of birds and beasts'. Yet here was Mr. Martin stalking about London laying down the law about what was and was not cruel with the authority of a dictator. Inadvertently the paper even paid tribute to his status of a king at home by complaining that he disposed as arbitrarily of His Majesty's subjects 'as of the subjects of his own wilds of Connemara'. It then raised the question of reliability. Could the informant, who in the heat of his zeal had detected what he considered a case of cruelty, be relied upon as a dispassionate witness in court?

An incident now occurred which gave the *Morning Chronicle* ammunition for battle and enabled it to continue its protests for several months. One day when Humanity Dick was walking up Regent Street, he saw a lad of about fifteen beating a donkey so violently that the noise of his blows could have been heard even if he had been out of sight. Furthermore the donkey had a bit on him as sharp as a saw. Humanity immediately intervened. The youth was insolent and replied that he would do as he pleased with his own donkey. He had the tin plate with the number of his cart, and Humanity grabbed at it in order to take the number. Upon this the youth began to hurl abuse at him, and a crowd started to collect. Then, as Humanity still clutched the plate, it became detached from the boy's arm, and a fight started. Humanity's only way of defending himself was to wrest from the lad the cudgel with which he had been beating the donkey, and although he was seventy-one and the boy was in his teens, Humanity succeeded. Feeling then that the crowd was likely to attack him, he made a dash for safety and took refuge in the house of General Ross in Portland Place, where he left the offending stick.

When the case came up at Marlborough Street police court a couple of weeks later, the *Morning Chronicle* published its report under the heading, 'Mr. Martin, M.P. and Another Unfortunate Ass'. Its rival, the *Courier*, took exception to the insinuation, but this was not the crux of the problem. It arose over the evidence. Humanity Dick claimed that the lad had struck the ass with a bludgeon such as the Irish use to fight one another; he realized that the word 'shillelagh' would not be understood. But when the lad claimed that it was not thicker than his finger, Humanity continued: 'It was a little thin switch, which the young wretch used for about 300 yards upon the poor donkey's head and ears; and, besides, he wanted two shoes, which is an offence. You see I have quick eyes.'

One of the *Morning Chronicle*'s grouses against Humanity Dick was that he patrolled the streets, detected what he considered cruel, took up the time of police courts with charges which he invariably prefaced with a speech on the evils of cruelty to animals, and then frequently ended by pleading for leniency for the offender or paying the fine himself. But in this case, after the accused youth had remained impudent to the very end and was then unable to pay the penalty of ten shillings and three shillings and sixpence costs, Humanity told the father who was present that it would do the boy good to have some exercise at the treadmill. From having attacked him for his benevolence, the *Morning Chronicle* now passed over to attacking him for his severity. But it was his qualities as a witness that came in for the paper's sharpest criticism. Having said that the boy had beaten the donkey with a bludgeon, had he not later said it was with a thin switch?

But he was left in peace for a few weeks until the *Morning Chronicle* carried an article under the heading, 'Blackwood and Mr. Martin', which ran: 'It is well for the former that a considerable interval separates him from Mr. Martin. Otherwise we think, his friends might be in some apprehension for him. Our hair absolutely stood on end when we read the following attack in the last number: "That Irish jackass Martin throws an air of ridicule over the whole matter by his insufferable idiotism. I hope to see his skull, thick as it is, cracked one of these days; for that vulgar and angry gabble with which he weekly infests the Police Offices of the Metropolis, is a greater outrage to humanity, than any fifty blows ever inflicted on the snout of a pig or the buttocks of beeve, blows which, in one and the same breath, the blustering and blundering blockhead would fain prosecute, punish and pardon. . . . " '

The article in *Blackwood's* was one of a regular series in the form of a dialogue, and after another paragraph in which the writer defended the Smithfield drovers against Humanity's persecution, the *Morning Chronicle* finished with the comment: 'We dare not quote what follows about *murdering*.'

The *Courier* expressed surprise that *Blackwood's Magazine* should sink to such buffoonery, and Humanity Dick got in touch with his solicitors, Messrs. Madox and Sydney. The words which the *Morning Chronicle* had hesitated to publish in reference to the Smithfield drovers and Humanity, were 'Why don't they murder him?' Following up the *Morning Chronicle*'s habit of calling him the Professor of Humanity, *Blackwood's* went on to say that he was about to be made Chancellor of the University of London, the establishment of which was then under discussion and subject to much ridicule. Meanwhile the *Morning Chronicle*, realizing from Madox and Sydney that something was afoot, took to referring constantly to 'good Mr. Martin'.

On 21 September 1825, Humanity Dick turned up at Bow Street police court accompanied by a young solicitor from Madox and Sydney's. He took his seat on the bench behind the magistrate, Mr. Minshull, with whom he had once had an altercation, bared his head, removed his gloves and proceeded to deliver an oration. His object was to apply for a warrant against Mr. Clement and Mr. Black, respectively the proprietor and editor of the *Morning Chronicle*. He drew attention to the paper's having kept up a continual campaign against him and maintained that the obnoxious paragraph now in dispute was addressed to a mob, the Smithfield drovers, and was obviously an incitation to assassination.

The *Morning Chronicle* laughed its way through the affair.

Far from approving of calling Mr. Martin a jackass, it could think of no animal he resembled less. 'What! The fiery, mettlesome Member for Galway, whose very enemies cannot accuse him of patience or long suffering, like that poor drudge, an ass!' As for wanting to get rid of him, Mr. Martin was being far too modest in not recognizing his value to a newspaper whose readers should be grateful for accounts of so diverting and original a performer. It was obviously in the paper's interest that Mr. Martin should live a thousand years, whereas he insisted it would be the death of him. 'Lord love the good gentleman! Since the man killed the goose that laid the golden eggs, so foolish a deed was never dreamt of.'

The following day, however, Humanity Dick reappeared at Bow Street to say that he did not consider the *Morning Chronicle*'s statement that it should preserve his life so that it could have a little more fun with him was a rational answer to his charges. He enlarged upon his claim that the paper's campaign was of long duration, and in particular set out to answer its criticisms of him as a witness, since the truth of his testimony would be relevant to the present case. He explained that it was 'the little ruffian' who had claimed that he had been beating the ass with a switch and not a bludgeon; and anybody who wished to see the object could do so at General Ross's house. In fact, he had probably originally used the words 'little thin switch' rhetorically.

Minshull ordered Clement, the proprietor of the *Morning Chronicle*, to attend next day. In the meantime Humanity Dick did a foolish thing. He did not want his enemies to get away with the idea that they were adding insult to injury by making a laughing stock of him. His case had turned into a *cause célèbre* and he wanted to humble the *Morning Chronicle*. On the evening before Clement was due to appear in court, Humanity visited the paper's offices to tell them of the benefits in publicity he was deriving from their attacks. These, he declared, were just nuts for him to crack. The paper had made him the most popular man in the world.

And, sure enough, next morning the court was thronged. But Clement failed to turn up, due to an injury to his foot, and while the court awaited the arrival of his counsel, a Mr. Adolphus, Humanity Dick said: 'In the *manetime* I have a few observations to make.' This Irish habit of deliberately lapsing into a brogue for humorous effect was completely ignored by the *Morning Chronicle* which reported his words as though the member for Galway knew no other method of speaking. He then informed the bench that he had now discovered that the offending paragraph from *Blackwood's* had first been copied by the *Morning Herald* and that he intended also to proceed against them.

When Adolphus appeared, Humanity Dick's affidavit, in which he claimed that his life was in danger, was read, and then Adolphus proceeded to demolish it by repeating, by and large, the attacks the *Morning Chronicle* had been making for some time. When he came to the point about Humanity Dick having been called a jackass, Adolphus let himself go on a positive eulogy of the animal which, he pointed out, was incidentally called 'Dickey-ass' in Essex. The ass he claimed, was a most respectable member of the brute creation. There had been one that spoke, yet never told a lie. One had made a philosopher laugh by the way it had eaten a basket of figs. In the ancient Greek 'feast of the asses', the highest honours were paid them; they were preceded in procession by bands and girls singing, '*Io asine, Io asine.*'* Were such honours ever shown to the honourable member for Galway in celebrating his election? Had not Lucian, the greatest of wits, considered the ass worthy of his pen. If Mr. Martin could prove that he had ever received any of the honours enumerated there might be some grounds for complaint, but in the meantime, on the score of comparison, Adolphus declared that he felt it was to the ass that an injury had been done.

Throughout this discourse Humanity Dick kept gesticulating to the magistrate to let Adolphus have his say, and even the bench joined in the general laughter. But a serious point was to follow. Here was a man, declared Adolphus, who was complaining that his life was endangered by a paragraph in a paper. Yet, only the night before he had gone to that paper's office to say he was delighted with the whole business. It was necessary to enquire if Mr. Martin really considered his life in danger.

Humanity Dick had patiently listened to all the ridicule, knowing that in due course his turn would come to reply, but

* 'Up asses, Up asses.'

what had now been said was a different matter; it cast a doubt upon his word. He leant across the table to Adolphus, and in the kind of voice he used in the theatre he boomed: 'How *daer* you, you scoundrel, doubt my affidavit!' This time the *Morning Chronicle* accurately reported the rolling Irish 'r'.

The magistrates were startled, but Humanity repeated that Adolphus was a scoundrel. Words began to fly between the two men, and Humanity was called to order. Then he came forward to address the bench, but Minshull intervened. He could see that an altercation was about to take place, and decided to cut it short. He concluded the case by ordering that Clement should give bail since he saw sufficient ground for it. But this did not satisfy Humanity. He wanted to reply to Adolphus's accusations. But every time he tried to give his explanation, Minshull interrupted, until at last, consumed with anger, he thundered: 'I – do – on – my – oath – really and truly believe – that the *Morning Chronicle* – had in view – the destruction of me – and I positively – swear – that I think – my – life – is – in – danger.'

The following day the *Morning Chronicle* published an epitaph under a quotation from the *Bucolics*, 'Happy for him if Herds had never been'.

> 'Alas, and well-a-day, he's dead—
> The *Coster's* fear, the Drover's dread
>   Is all *a-mort* and gone!
> How shall we write the Epitaph
> Of him, kill'd by a *paragraph*
>   As dead as any stone?
>
> A paper bullet hit his head,
> *Which* quickly turn'd it into *lead*,
>   And brutes lost all their joys—
> For Howard, the philanthropist,
> Compared with him was little miss'd;
>   *He* made not half the noise!
>
> His cup of charity was full
> For ass, horse, sheep, and bear and bull—
>   But as I hear from some,
> His gallantry was not so great,
> Hence *Ladies* grieve not at his fate,
>   Who only loved the *dumb*!

Neigh, bleat—bray, roar, straight-hair'd and curl'd—
"The admiration of the World"
  Is gone!—thus all things pass;
But not so bad the donkey's lot,
For e'en in death he's not forgot,
  If true—all flesh is *grass!'*

Humanity Dick also intended to proceed against *Blackwood's*, but Bailie Blackwood sent a couple of letters of the deepest apology, explaining that the scurrilous article had got into the magazine without his knowledge. The October number made full amends by carrying a long text praising Humanity and all his works, and comparing him in all seriousness with Howard.

Both the *Courier* and the *Morning Chronicle* reproduced the text in full, the latter with a comment. As with the pieces in the *Courier*, the paper believed it could detect the pen of the Professor of Humanity in the article which should be 'framed and glazed, and hung up on one of the walls of his palace in Connemara'. As usual, the writer could not resist the temptation to put a bit of a brogue into Humanity's mouth, and described him as one who would exclaim at somebody 'for *bating* a poor *baste* for standing still under his load when he could not walk *aisy* under it'. But they were sailing rather close to the wind when they remarked that *Blackwood's* called Mr. Martin a gentleman of ample fortune, large estate and splendid connections, and commented: 'Mr. Martin himself is, of course, best acquainted with his own affairs, and no one else would have been justified in hazarding a statement of this kind.' No doubt it was common knowledge that Humanity Dick's financial situation was by now extremely precarious.

He did not proceed against *Blackwood's* or the *Herald*, and the affair with the *Morning Chronicle* appears to have been amicably settled, but his crusade for animals' rights for which the *Morning Chronicle* now named him 'Don Quixote', had received more publicity than at any time previously.

Chapter Twenty-four

AT THE height of the controversy with the *Morning Chronicle*
Humanity Dick had said that some people laughed at him, but
there were more who laughed with him. A barrister friend
writing of his effect on his contemporaries in the House bore
this out. 'He holds them,' he wrote, 'by the very test and
characteristic of the human race, laughter; and while their sides
shake, their opposition is shaken and falls down at the same
instant. There is a beautiful symmetry, a perfect keeping, as it
were, in the whole man of Richard Martin, Esq. Every limb of
his body and every feature of his face is round and solid. He
lets drive at the House like a bullet and the flag of truce is
instantly hung out upon both sides.'

And Humanity knew full well how to take advantage in the
House of his reputation for eccentricity. On one occasion when
he was pleading the cause of animals he heard a mock Irish
brogue from the Opposition benches. The words used were
'Hare, hare.' He finished what he had to say and then very
deliberately stepped across the floor, asking the speaker to
reveal himself. The culprit, however, knew better than to own
up; but somebody pointed out one of the city fathers, who were
known to be Martin's supporters. 'Oh,' exclaimed Humanity,
turning and walking quietly back to his place, 'it was only an
alderman.'

His increasing years did nothing to diminish his activities in
London's streets. He continued to patrol them, his originality
unaffected by any stir he might cause, his wit always fresh. One

day when walking through St. James's, keeping to the side of the pavement nearest the wall to avoid being spattered with mud, he came face to face with somebody who had some grudge against him, and who growled: 'I never give the wall to a blackguard!' Stepping politely aside to make way for the other man, Humanity replied: 'I always do.' The next minute he might be seen calmly sitting up on the box of a cab driving the horse himself to prove that it did not need beating. Then, his mission completed, he would step down, pay his fare, and promptly summon the driver for ill-treating his animal.

He neglected his private affairs more and more, and it was typical of his benevolence that people frequently took advantage of him. Very shortly after the *Morning Chronicle* episode he had found himself once again in court, this time over a Galwayman named de Courcy Ireland who had been involved in a series of frauds after Humanity Dick had allowed him, like many others, to use his address for correspondence and his name as a reference. When it turned out in court that Humanity had mistaken the man for his brother, the *Morning Chronicle* resumed its teasing. 'We confess,' they wrote, 'from all we have ever heard of the Honourable Member for Galway we think it much more likely that he should be a dupe himself than that he should attempt to make dupes of others. Many a man has confounded one brother with another, who would not mistake a bludgeon for a switch, or a switch for a blundgeon.'

However, the crusade which the *Morning Chronicle* had held up to scorn was advancing. The Society for the Prevention of Cruelty to Animals had gone through some difficult times. At one stage it was bankrupt and the Reverend Arthur Broome, as President, was imprisoned for the society's debts; but Humanity Dick and the very active Secretary, Gompertz, had succeeded in extricating the society from its financial difficulties. For some years Humanity Dick had himself paid for an inspector to keep track of what happened in the street, but now the society had a team of its own and support for it was growing steadily. Guy's Hospital had followed Bart's and St. George's in forbidding experiments on live animals, and the SPCA published a pamphlet containing a collection of medical opinions protesting against vivisection. Jeremy Bentham had come forward to condemn not only this, but baiting and fox-hunting as well, while even in France there was a reaction against Majendie and the College of Surgeons had asked him to relinquish his experiments.

The SPCA had grown from a group of Friends of Martin's Act, but it is doubtful if it could have advanced as it did had it not been for the energy and dedication of the man who fathered this first piece of legislation for dumb beasts. His name became synonymous with animals' rights, and even in Germany Heine claimed that he read the papers in order to find out 'whether Richard Martin had not again presented a petition to Parliament for the better treatment of poor horses, dogs and donkeys'.

While Humanity Dick was hurrying about London, saving the destitute with money he himself did not possess, something had nevertheless been happening in his remote 'kingdom' of Connemara to brighten his financial horizon. It was already known that the area was rich in marble, but a couple of years before a series of green serpentine, which was considered every bit as good as the best verd-antique, had been discovered on the estates. The part which for so many years Humanity had been waiting for his mines to play, had been transferred to the quarries which he was now working in partnership with Thomas.

It was an expensive business, involving costly tools and machinery for extracting the marble and even the construction of roads on which to transport it, but he had at least the satisfaction of knowing that he was giving much needed employment. He was paying for his share of the undertaking out of the rents from the lands he had retained for himself, and the money was handed over directly by his agent for the works in hand. But trying to keep in touch from London with the enterprise created inevitable problems, and there was constant friction between himself and Thomas.

In the early part of 1826 he tried again unsuccessfully to get through parliament a bill to prevent bear-baiting, and to have his own act extended to cover bull-baiting. As always on such occasions, he had a tale with which he hoped to capture members' sympathy. On this occasion he described a bull-baiting at Oxford in which the animal's tongue had been wrenched out and handed around on a plate for a collection. When he went on to introduce once again a bill for the prevention of cruelty to dogs, he told the story of some ruffians who had skinned a dog alive and then flung him into the river.

One of his principal opponents on everything concerning animals was the Scottish member, Hume, who was notorious for the dreariness of his speeches which almost always dealt with accounts. He now tried to ridicule the proposed bill by asking if Humanity intended to include in his legislation cats which were so often teased by dogs. Humanity reminded Hume that outside the House he had promised him his support, but he knew that the reason why he now withheld it was that he, Humanity Dick, had refused to vote against flogging in the army. As he spoke there were loud cries of 'Order, Order,' which according to *The Times*, must have been caused 'by certain gesticulations used by the Honourable Member for Galway and directed towards the Honourable Gentleman for Montrose.'

About the same period, Lamb, a member of the Opposition, brought in a bill to allow counsel to felons. Humanity Dick supported it with the observation that he had himself brought in such a bill three times and had scarcely been able to get twenty people to attend a division. If the measure were now successful he would be persuaded to transfer to the members of the opposite bench all those measures which had failed when he had introduced them himself. He also gave notice that he would bring in again a bill to reduce the punishment for forgery, but was prepared to withhold it temporarily, in the hope that it might prove unnecessary. In fact, shortly afterwards Peel brought in a Criminal Justice Bill which covered Humanity Dick's proposals.

With a dissolution imminent, all the implications of the electoral contest which lay ahead were becoming clear, and Humanity Dick, speaking against a proposal for parliamentary reform, conveyed some of his apprehensions to the House. He declared that a corrupt opposition had been set up against him. Yet, he added, whether he was again returned to sit in parliament or was deprived of that honour, he would never attribute his defeat to parliamentary corruption.

It was from Clanricarde's money and influence that he had most to fear. Canning had looked after his son-in-law well. He had pressed for him to be made a representative peer of Ireland, but Peel had raised the objection that the young man had contributed to the Catholic Rent. He had, however, been given a marquisate and took his seat as an English peer. Into the bargain, Clanricarde had been made Under-Secretary to Canning at the Foreign Office.

By the time Humanity Dick was ready to return to Ireland for the elections, the truth of his forecast about the Catholic Association had already been proved. The act suppressing it specifically did not apply to any organization set up for charitable purposes, and O'Connell had been quick to seize upon this opening. He had launched the New Catholic Association with the perfectly legal object of 'public or private charity'. At the same time the Catholic Rent continued to be collected 'for the relief of distressed Catholics'. In order to avoid any suggestion that the Association was representative, they held what they termed Aggregate Meetings—gatherings of associates—and a number of these had taken place in preparation for the election.

The forty-shilling freeholders, who had so nearly been disenfranchised, were now selected to play an important role, and it was no doubt in this knowledge that Humanity Dick had endeavoured to get a measure through parliament which would protect them. He proposed that by showing a receipt for all rent up to the election, they would become free to vote as they pleased, or the landlord, if he wished them to do so any way, could give a receipt for the arrears if there were any. In this way the freeholders would be protected against the recriminations of their masters. The measure was not adopted, but the Catholic Association was now mobilizing the freeholders to take the unprecedented step of voting for the Association's candidate rather than their landlord's.

The situation in the different constituencies was reviewed by the Association, and that in Galway was found to be highly unsatisfactory. An analysis revealed that Clanricarde, apart from putting up Lambert, who had refused to sign the Protestant petition in favour of the Catholics, as his candidate in the county, was prepared to back Daly in the county in exchange for Daly's candidate giving way to his candidate, Bourke, in the town. It was suspected that Daly, who wished to save himself the expense of a double contest, had made the same kind of bargain regarding the seat in the town as he had proposed to Thomas some time previously, and that Clanricarde would guarantee his continued domination of the Corporation. This presented a formidable threat to Humanity Dick whose unswerving devotion to the cause of unqualified and unconditional emancipation was praised at a meeting of the Association of which he was now a member. On his way back from Westminster to Galway for the elections, he dropped in at one of these meetings and all present cheered loudly and waved their hats.

A year previously Humanity Dick had written to Canning about his son-in-law's activities, and had received the reply: 'If ever I shall have any influence on Lord Clanricarde it shall be exerted to procure an easy time for *you* at the election.' But when Humanity Dick heard that Clanricarde was determined to oppose him and asked Canning to arrange a meeting for him with the young lord in his presence, Canning had merely replied: 'I hate all local politics and if I could would draw Lord Clanricarde out of such pursuits, and not drag myself in. I do for you all that I can, and more than I would for any other, and I send your letter to Lord Clanricarde just as I receive it.' When in fact the two men met, Clanricarde merely reiterated that he intended to oppose Humanity.

Clanricarde arrived in Galway before even the Sheriff received the writ for the election, and rumours began to reach Humanity Dick of his activities. Valentine Blake of Menlo, it was said, had been promised the post of minister of a legation for his support, and John D'Arcy of Clifden was supposed to have been promised a living in the Church for one son, and some official appointment for the other, besides £3 a head for one thousand freeholders, £300 of which had been paid in advance. The Honourable Martin Ffrench was to be made a Distributor of Stamps for Limerick in exchange for obtaining his grandfather's support for Mr. Lambert, and Clanricarde had even written to the Chief Secretary, Goulburn, but had received no encouragement. All of this Humanity Dick outlined in correspondence to Canning, urging him to recall his son-in-law from County Galway to attend to his official duties. The reply he received ran:

'My dear Sir,

I hardly can think for two reasons that Lord Clanricarde made the promises you refer to. First, I never gave him any authority of the kind and secondly Lord Clanricarde assures me he never made any such.'

At this point Humanity Dick seriously considered asking the cabinet to intervene, but decided not to do so, as he later explained to Peel, 'from motives of great delicacy for Mr. Canning'.

Intrigue and counter-intrigue were characteristic of every election, but the 1826 Galway election surpassed all its predecessors in this respect. The press was deeply involved, and Humanity Dick was fortunate in having the support of the *Dublin Evening Post* whose editor, Conway, was a former tutor of young Richard's. Thomas made a last-minute, but unsuccessful, attempt to have himself adopted as a candidate for the town. All three of those aspiring to the candidature of the county, including Lambert, announced that they stood for Catholic rights. Commenting on Lambert's declaration, Humanity remarked in an address: 'Granting his conversion to be as perfect as it was sudden, his *promise* is too recent to outweigh with the Catholic body the zealous and undeviating services of my whole life.'

At the county meeting for the selection of candidates, Humanity spoke, as always, with much humour. He warned the meeting against believing that his own best friend, Canning, was a party to the bartering which was going on, and harried Lambert once again about the Protestant petition. As for having all his election expenses paid by Clanricarde, Lambert if he were returned to parliament would be so subservient to the young Lord's wishes that he would scarcely know how to vote if Clanricarde happened to be out of town.

Lambert produced an explanation of how he came to give the only negative to the Protestant petition of 1812. Humanity Dick, he said, who had originated the petition, had declared that he would hold up to public execration anybody who refused to sign, a threat to which he, Lambert, had not been prepared to submit. Humanity Dick had another version of the incident. According to him, Lambert had declared: 'I object to that petition.' Now Lambert claimed that Clanricarde's support was completely constitutional, and that if he entered parliament he would be under no obligation to any man as to how he should vote. As to his election expenses, he got in a wounding dig at Humanity Dick: if they could not be covered without robbing a just creditor of his rights, he would never solicit from the assembled company the honour of representing them. At the conclusion of the meeting, Daly, Lambert and Humanity Dick were all selected as candidates for the two seats in County Galway.

Humanity Dick's daughter, Hatty, was to convey admirably the atmosphere of a Galway election in her long story, *Canvassing*, many years after the momentous events which were about to take place.

'The eventful morning came,' she wrote, 'and the whole town was alive at the dawn of day; crowds of partizans of all ages and ranks gathering around the Committee rooms of the opposing candidates; electioneering agents, oratorizing, explaining, or mystifying, as suited their purpose; looking over certificates, and "making Pat Conny sinsible he was only to be Pat Conny the first time he voted, but Dennis Sleevan the second time, in regard of poor Dennis not being convenient just then, because he was burried last week." And reminding Martin Donovan, he mustn't forget to slip a flea inside his lase, that he might swear with a safe conscience, that the life in it was still in existence, and other trifling, though necessary, arrangements for the proper carrying on of their employer's interests. And voters were eating, drinking, shouting, and whirling their ferrals to give "the raal fighting touch".'

The 1826 Galway election was to be characterized by all these acts of personation and great violence besides. Skirmishes between the tenantry of contesting parties were a commonplace on such occasions, but on this there were confrontations like pitched battles.

It was claimed that the tenants of Humanity Dick's cousin, John D'Arcy of Clifden, who was supporting Lambert, were beaten back by Martin supporters who held all the roads and passes into Connemara and prevented most of them from reaching Galway to vote. Kirwan's tenantry in east Galway, who were going to vote for Martin, were attacked by those of Bingham, who was supporting Lambert, and the police had to intervene. Lambert's and Martin's supporters clashed, and Lambert's brother shot dead a man called O'Sullivan and was lodged in prison. The tenants of Blake of Menlo broke down Anthony Martin's gates at Dangan, and when Anthony met Valentine Blake he horsewhipped him. A thatched warehouse in which tenants were lodged waiting to vote was burned to the ground and a yacht that was to fetch others suffered a similar fate. Humanity Dick's tenants were described as landing on the quays and patrolling the streets to 'the spirit-stirring drum and ear-piercing fife', while somebody opened up the whiskey supplies, the crowd rioted and the military were so slow in acting that there were several deaths.

The mob was for Humanity Dick, but as always, due to the great distance his tenants had to come to vote, he got off to a bad start in the poll. But as the days went by he began to catch up, and finally, on the fifteenth day, he was declared to have a majority of eighty-four over Lambert, and he and James Daly were duly elected. Some of the feuds engendered by the election survived, and as a result of an argument with John D'Arcy of Clifden, Humanity Dick found himself being bound over.

In an address to his electors, he declared that their cause was that of civil and religious liberty, adding that the time was at hand 'when all the subjects of His Majesty shall be placed upon equality of civil rights'. A decisive step in that direction had, in fact, been taken during the election. In Waterford, the Beresford tenantry had ignored their landlord's orders and, by voting for the Catholic Association's nominee, Villiers Stuart, had ousted Beresford and seated a liberal Protestant. In Louth, Monaghan and Westmeath the tenantry had behaved with equal independence. It was the beginning of a new era, and a New Catholic Rent, to which Humanity Dick contributed, was collected to compensate Catholic tenants who were being penalized for their stand by their landlords either by eviction or pressure for arrears of rent.

When Humanity Dick set off for Westminster in the autumn of 1826 he knew that Lambert intended to petition against his return, but such petitions were usual after almost every election. He felt safe once again from his creditors, protected as he had been for years by parliamentary immunity, but he now had greater hopes than ever of being able to pay off his crippling debts. 'Browne,' he wrote to Richard, 'who has been two years in Italy purchasing marble says that our coloured marble and the best verd-antique very far exceeds any marble to be found in Italy, and he adds that our marble must command in every part of Europe a superior price. This all we can desire. I see, short as I may live, that I may have plenty of money, but peace with such tempers as Thomas's and Julia's is not to be expected.'

Before the end of the year he presented several petitions in favour of the Catholics to parliament. In one case the petition was inscribed on several sheets of parchment, and as he carried it up to the table he unfolded it and, showing it to the House, declared: 'There sir, there. The manner in which this petition is signed will prove that Irish people are not so ignorant as they are said to be.'

But Lambert's petition was now laid before the House and was sufficient to cause Humanity considerable anxiety. He was accused in general of having fomented rioting, and his cousin, James Martin, the High Sheriff, was accused of having failed to use his authority to stop it. The petition further stated that he was not qualified to sit for the County Galway, 'either as the eldest son or heir apparent of any person so qualified, and had not any sufficient estate in lands, tenements, or hereditaments, freehold or copyhold'. The irony of the 'King of Connemara' being possibly unseated because he had not enough land would not have been lost on the House, but it would have been typical of him to have overlooked this detail in dividing up the estates with Thomas.

He now proceeded to fight back on other grounds. In a lengthy address to his electors he admitted that *great indignation was felt*, and violently demonstrated' every day during the election, and that it was 'loud and deep—unappeased and unappeasable. There was no need of incitement, and restraint was hardly practicable.' All of this, he claimed, could be attributed to the unprecedented behaviour of Clanricarde who had ostentatiously exercised his unconstitutional influence. With some justification he asserted that it was only in Ireland that such operations could be undisguisedly carried on. If a member of the Foreign Office were boastingly to control and corrupt the right of free election in England, the Government would intervene.

In the House he had to take back what he had said there about corruption before the elections. He openly accused an Under-Secretary of State of having opened a bank to defray the expenses of his nominee, whom he called his 'man'. The same

Under-Secretary had promised a peerage to somebody in exchange for supporting his candidate, and had applied before the election for offices for those from whom he expected support.

Humanity was an old man of seventy-three making an appeal for what he considered justice, but the greater part of what he said was inaudible due to the laughter and general disturbance that went on throughout his speech. He concluded by stating that Lord Clanricarde was the Under-Secretary to whom he referred, whom he then, in that House, denounced, and against whom within twenty days he would appeal for a special report.

While this matter was agitating Humanity Dick, Sir Francis Burdett once again brought forward a motion in favour of the Catholics. Much familiar ground was gone over, but this time the question was brought up of Catholic freeholders in Ireland having been forced by their priests to vote for certain candidates in the recent election, and reference was made to the reprisals now resorted to by some of the landlords.

Humanity Dick denied that the priests exercised any spiritual coercion, and deplored the attitude of those landlords who were persecuting their tenants, but the remedy, he claimed, was in the hands of the House. 'We must interfere,' he said, 'and that interference must be to grant to one party "that withholding which, not enriching us, makes them poor indeed".' This was greeted with general cheering. As to the landlords, he pointed out that if the House had adopted the measures for protecting the tenants which he had proposed in the previous session, what was happening would have been impossible.

He went on to say that he considered the Treaty of Limerick violated as long as the Catholics were excluded, but another treaty of more recent date was also being broken, namely the Union. He had supported it because Cornwallis had given him an assurance that emancipation would follow, and, armed with that authority he had persuaded the inhabitants of County Galway. 'Sorry I am,' he declared, 'to have deceived them, but I was disappointed myself, and deceived *others* in consequence. The Union I consider a benefit to England and Ireland and that benefit we owe *to the Catholics*. And if that be the case, is it just that they should be the sufferers by what has benefitted the Empire in general?' As for the Irish clergy, he maintained that their influence was great, adding 'and will every hour become more dominant if we persevere in withholding from six millions of men their rights'. Once again there was an exceptionally large division, and once again the motion was defeated, this time by the narrow margin of 276 votes to 272.

Humanity Dick had heard in the meantime that Canning took exception to the motion he intended to make on Clanricarde, and he wrote to Peel mentioning this and telling him the whole story. He further pointed out that in his address to his electors he had not mentioned that Clanricarde had actually sent out a circular letter asking for contributions towards the costs of the petition against him. He felt that if the charges he made were untrue, Canning should, in the interests of Clanricarde's character, proceed with the enquiry, and if they were well-founded, only the young lord himself could be held answerable. He enclosed a résumé of his correspondence with Canning and said that after being disappointed in Canning and having relinquished any idea of asking the cabinet to intervene, he now appealed to the Foreign Secretary through Peel to decide how the matter could best be settled. 'All I want,' he concluded, 'is fair investigation and by that I will stand or fall.'

Peel's reply solved nothing, but left the door open. He had not heard, he said, that Canning had taken any offence at Humanity's proposed motion and assured him that Canning 'was not cognisant of, much less a party to, any undue interference with regard to the Galway election'. He informed Humanity that he expected Canning would 'leave the House of Commons to dispose of your motion as if it were a motion in which he had no personal or private concern'.

Humanity Dick then went ahead, but when he announced that he would bring forward a motion concerning Clanricarde's behaviour, several members asked him to postpone it until the Select Committee, which was then taking evidence on the Galway election, had reported. The Speaker went further; he pointed out that if the motion contained anything which could afterwards be enquired into by the Committee, it could not be heard by the House. Humanity declared that the matter could not be examined by the Committee, and expressed his determination to proceed with the motion, but later changed his mind and decided to refer it to the Select Committee.

Witnesses for both sides had been brought over from Ireland

to be heard by the Committee, and there was at least one clash in the lobby of the House. Humanity Dick's counsel asked for a Commission to be granted and sent into Ireland to examine 320 people, some of them members of the most respectable families, but counsel for the petitioners objected.

At one juncture the Committee asked the Speaker to send to the House of Lords for the Marquis of Clanricarde and his brother-in-law, the Marquis of Sligo, to appear before them to give evidence on behalf of Humanity Dick. The Lord Chancellor informed the messenger from the Commons that the Lords would send back an answer by their own messenger, but the Chancellor forgot. As a result of this omission, Humanity Dick had to close his case without the benefit of evidence which could have been decisive.

The Committee started sitting on 22 March, and soon they were striking off Humanity Dick's votes by the dozen, tenants having voted twice, even three and four times. On 6 April Humanity proposed that Lambert be considered as having the majority of legal voices, but that an adjournment take place in order to allow him to produce evidence showing such corrupt practises as would disqualify Lambert for a seat in the House; but this was not allowed.

By 11 April, the Committee had finished its deliberations and Lord Forbes, the Chairman, informed the House of the result. In the opinion of the Committee an organized system of rioting had prevailed during the election. Furthermore, the local authorities had failed to make use of the ample forces at their disposal to preserve the peace, and the Committee recommended that an enquiry should be held in order to ensure free election in Galway. Meanwhile, they had decided that Mr. Richard Martin was not duly elected, and that Mr. J. C. Lambert should have been returned as the member for County Galway. The clerk of the crown was ordered to attend in order to amend the return.

At a crucial moment in politics, Humanity Dick no longer had a seat in parliament. Liverpool had been struck down by paralysis and the very day before the Select Committee had given their verdict, Canning had replaced him. Never since the Union had the Catholics' hopes been greater. They were on the threshold of success, and Humanity Dick would not be in his place to share in their triumph. Further, James Daly had realized his ambition of escaping from 'the rascality of elections and electioneering' and been raised to the peerage, so that in their hour of victory the Catholics of the most Catholic county in Ireland were to be represented in parliament by a man who had refused to sign a petition claiming their rights.

Very fittingly, Humanity Dick's last speech in parliament had been in favour of the Catholics, just as his first vote had been for them. But, as Sir Francis Burdett had asked years before, who was to carry on his work for animals? He had supporters, but who among them would persevere as he had done in the House and risk ridicule to keep the message alive outside it?

These disappointments would have been bitter enough, but his being unseated had another and more alarming implication. He no longer enjoyed parliamentary immunity and was liable for all the debts which the mines and the quarries had not yet succeeded in eliminating. He determined to make one more attempt to obtain justice, and on 13 June presented a petition to the House of Commons. He asked to be heard at the bar of the House concerning the undue influence which had been exercised by the Marquises of Clanricarde and Sligo during the Galway election. Ironically, it was to one of his most consistent adversaries, Hume, the very member whom he had so recently addressed with comic gestures, that it fell to reply. Hume stated that the House could not now interfere, the time allowed for producing evidence having passed. The matter ought, he declared to have been brought forward in the Committee. Consequently, he confined himself to moving that the petition should be brought up, and it was then laid upon the table. There it remained and was not heard of again.

As things turned out, the Catholics' hopes had been premature. They did not know that Canning had given the King an undertaking not to raise the Catholic question. Yet when Canning himself died in August, only a few months after taking office as Prime Minister, the Catholics lost one of their most powerful advocates.

Meanwhile, Humanity Dick had urgent decisions to take. His creditors would be pressing him any minute and he would end in gaol for debt. His only hope of avoiding such a fate was to do as many others had done before him—flee. Boulogne, a pleasant little town on the Normandy coast with a flourishing English colony, was a haven for those whose debts were beyond redemption. Humanity hoped that before too long the marble quarries would redeem his, but in the meantime Boulogne was not too far distant. And it was to Boulogne he decided to move with his wife and his three daughters.

It meant a rift with the whole of his past—his place in parliament and in the social life of the period, his unfinished fights for the Catholics and animals, and, worst of all, his life in Connemara which always remained what was nearest to his heart. But by the autumn he was installed with his family in Boulogne, and the *Dublin Evening Post*, which had pointed out a number of fashionable people in the place, was able to write that the ex-member for Galway was among them. 'He is like a fish out of water,' the paper commented; ' "Othello's occupation gone." One may see a Frenchman flog an unfortunate Rosinante to death—but there is no Sir Richard—no Bow Street.'

Epilogue

BOULOGNE AT the time the Martins came to settle there was
a thriving port and watering-place. The old town was built on a
hill and surrounded by ramparts with a tree-lined walk from
which, in fine weather, there was a good view of the English
coast. A new suburb, called the Low Town, had emerged at the
foot of the hill, and there the Martins installed themselves in the
rue de l'Ecu. The area between the High and Low Towns was
still open country composed of steeply sloping fields where two
of the six windmills which had been there in Napoleon's time
remained. The Low Town stretched down to the fine strand
with its pavilion and bathing boxes.

Boulogne had become a popular English resort at the time of
Waterloo, when it had been an English base. Not so far distant
from Brighton, it had much of that town's attraction for the
English visitor, and there was a constant coming and going of
celebrities. In the Martins' time there was a rapidly expanding
English colony which numbered about 1,200 out of a total
population of 20,000 when they arrived and doubled during
their years of residence. Most of its members were people who
found they could live more cheaply in France than in England;
there was a fair sprinkling of chronic defaulters—people like
Humanity Dick who were evading their creditors; the prison
was nicknamed 'l'Hôtel d'Angleterre' because of the number of
English imprisoned there for debt; and the town was a favourite
rendezvous for those escaping from the laws in England against
duelling. All told, the English colony lived well. The rolling

green country around Boulogne, with its hedged laneways reminiscent of England, was studded with charming châteaux and manor houses, most of which were let to English residents who found they could entertain there on a grander scale than their means would allow at home.

Humanity Dick had the cheerful disposition which enabled him to adjust himself to circumstances, but it is hard to imagine that he could have been more than resigned to his new surroundings. A countryman at heart, he loved best of all things the wild majesty of Connemara to which, pretty as it was, the Boulogne area was such a total contrast. He would have missed, too, the mild climate of Connaught, with roses blooming at Christmas and spring flowers beginning to appear in January, whereas in Boulogne spring did not come until late April. When not in the west of Ireland, he had been accustomed to the sophistication of a capital city and to the challenge of the work he had set himself to accomplish. The small-town life of an English colony could not have failed to seem strangely restricted; yet he was to be compelled to live it for seven years.

He no doubt continued to hope that the marble quarries would settle his debts for him and that he would be enabled to return home, and there may be more than a hint of nostalgia in the fact that shortly after his arrival he presented the local museum with a sample of Connemara marble. There were, also, other reminders of home. Among the English residents there was Lady Morgan, the daughter of Owenson who had managed the little theatre in Kirwan's Lane in which his beautiful Elizabeth had made such a name, and one of the leading bookshops was stocking Lady Morgan's book *The O'Briens and the O'Flahertys*, set on the old O'Flaherty estates the Martins now owned. Wolfe Tone's memoirs had, also, been published when Humanity first arrived in the French town. They would have stirred up old memories of life at Dangan, but, fortunately, they would not have given him the shock they might have done. Tone's son, in preparing them for publication, had carefully removed all reference to his father's passion for Humanity Dick's wife. With it went Tone's statement that she had returned his affection without 'in a single instance overstepping the bounds of virtue'—a claim which might have allayed any doubts still lurking in Humanity's mind.

There was a repertory theatre which gave performances alternately in French and English, concerts and balls were given at regular intervals, an English reading-room stocked books and papers from across the water, and there were four posts a week from England. In the beginning there was still the odd request for Humanity to intervene in somebody's interest, particularly as Lord Goderick, the Prime Minister, was married to a first cousin of Thomas's wife, Julia, but it is probable that as the old man's influence waned, such requests became infrequent.

There were, of course, over-driven horses and tortured donkeys in Boulogne as well as in London, and Humanity Dick automatically became their protector. He could be seen walking in the streets with an observant eye, and strolling along the beach at low tide picking up the immature fish the fishermen had cast out of their nets and putting them back into the water. Once in a while some incident would occur to remind him of his old crusading days, such as the occasion on which he came across a young Englishman mercilessly whipping and spurring his horse upon the sands. Humanity Dick remonstrated with him and said that he pitied the horse for having such a bad rider. The young man demanded an immediate apology and presented his card. But when he discovered that the old man facing him was Richard Martin, his ardour cooled and he withdrew. In those days great duelling reputations died hard.

Humanity was still on the Committee of the SPCA, and through Gompertz, the Secretary, to whom he was deeply attached, he kept in close touch with all they were doing. Occasionally he offered sound advice based on long experience, as when Mackinnon was preparing to take up again in the House the question of bull-baiting. Humanity wrote at length to Gompertz, asking him to put his views to the rest of the Committee. He examined with great clarity the law as it then stood under his own act, and stressed several times that it would be 'most imprudent to present any bill that has not passed through the hands of some parliamentary counsel used to drafting Acts of Parliament.' He concluded: 'As to the dissection of living animals, it is in my mind too revolting to be palliated by any excuse that science may be enlarged or improved by so detestable a means.'

He personified the theory he preached—that humanity is all

embracing and must be shown equally to all God's creatures, and it was typical of him that he took no credit for all that had already been achieved. Lever, it is said, was to immortalize him as the benevolent and lovable member for Galway, Uncle Godfrey, in *Charles O'Malley*, but he was also due to be much misunderstood, like all those who are before their time. Dickens wrote of him: 'It was a pity that he could not exchange a little of his excessive tenderness for animals for some common sense and consideration for human beings.' When he had already been dead ten years, a Doctor James Johnston published an account of a tour in Connemara and claimed that the great animal lover was at that moment guilty of committing repeated murders at Ballinahinch. *The Times* many years later was to write: 'The time has passed away when a Martin, unquestioned, could nail a red-hot shoe upon a cruel farrier who had shod a horse with iron glowing from the forge', as though such a thing would ever have been possible. It was a long time before the idea died that one who was humane to animals must be cruel to humans.

Humanity Dick himself had no doubt that his good work would be carried on. When his daughter, Hatty, once remarked to him on the discouragement he had met with, both from people's ingratitude and from the fruitlessness of some of his efforts, he remarked with the kind of philosophical turn of phrase he had so often used in the House: 'Have you ever watched a mason dashing a wall? A great deal falls to the ground, but some will stick.' It was a modest appraisal of the movement he had launched.

Of all the news that reached him in Boulogne probably none caused him to rejoice as much as that which arrived a couple of years after his retirement from politics. O'Connell had pulled off one of the most extraordinary political feats. Although he could not sit in parliament, he had stood for a by-election in County Clare and been elected. The floodgates which George Ogle had declared were being opened when Luke Gardiner had presented his Catholic Relief Bill in 1778 were now burst open with a vengeance, and the peaceful, disciplined method made it the more alarming. It became plain in England that the Irish Catholics now held parliament in a vice; a dissolution would result in their being elected all over Ireland. The

Orangemen reacted by founding a new anti-Catholic movement throughout the country in the Brunswick Clubs, and it would have taken little to spark off a civil war.

Wellington, who was Prime Minister, and Peel, once again Home Secretary, read the writing on the wall. They set about convincing parliament that the situation was so critical, nothing short of emancipation could save it; and they succeeded. But the King, with no alternative to assenting, threatened to emigrate to Hanover. What Humanity Dick called 'the great measure' was at last granted, but not without conditions. Several offices were still closed to Catholics, and the forty-shilling freeholders, who had been principally responsible for the victory, were disenfranchised in order to limit the power of the Catholic peasantry.

The triumph was confined to the Catholic gentry, a fact which may have influenced the course of Irish history in creating a social fissure. It is one of many anomalies that they who had been the object of the Catholic struggle for so long were to disappear more completely from the Irish scene within a century than the Anglo-Irish Protestants who had deprived them of their rights. As for the old warrior sitting in Boulogne, he may have experienced a moment's regret at not being present to share in the success, but it is probable the sense of satisfaction that emancipation had been achieved in his lifetime would have outweighed all else. He may even have still felt that it could not have been brought about without the initial sacrifice made in accepting the Union.

Despite all his and Harriet's party-going, none of his three daughters had married. Hatty, the eldest, gives what seems like a hint of one of the reasons in her story, *Canvassing*, which was appended to *The Mayor of Wind Gap* by the Irish writer, Michael Banim, whom she had got to know in Paris. If Maria Edgeworth could ridicule the Irish, Hatty was no less accomplished at making fun of the English. In the story, which gives an admirable picture of life at Ballinahinch, she says, referring to one of the young characters, Maria, in the presence of Englishmen:

'Unfortunately for her, she possessed much of the humour of her country; and had more than once, not only actually laughed herself, but had caused others to perpetuate a similar enormity.

She was, in consequence, set down as "sadly Irish". . . . Maria was aware that although an Englishman, of a certain *caste*, may perchance be induced to enjoy a jest, he never fails to pretend to undervalue the jester . . . that, conscious how much trouble a witty saying would cost himself, he imagines the gaiety of his lively neighbours to be as great an effort to them as to him; and that, therefore, when they laugh, or are brilliant, in his presence, all *that* is done by self-admitted inferiors to please a superior.'

Further on she makes Maria, in speaking to an English aristocrat at her uncle's house in Ireland, say:

'So you imagine that we laugh to divert you; and that, therefore, you must be gods to us? You are mistaken, my good Lord, we do not laugh to amuse you, but to amuse ourselves; we laugh because we like it; because we can't help it in fact. What would the philosopher of old, who defined man to be a laughing animal, say to you English?'

As for the English hero of the tale, when he arrives at what is plainly Ballinahinch, she comments: 'There is something in the very air of Ireland which acts on the most pertinaciously rigid muscles, and makes those laugh who never laughed before, and who never may again.'

With such views, Hatty at least was unlikely to find an English husband, and the story suggests that her sisters shared her outlook. And the numbers of Irishmen of that, or any period, prepared to marry a woman with such a sharp wit was limited. The young women were known, like their father, for their general benevolence and their love of animals, and they busied themselves among other things with good works.

Richard was an equally unconventional character. He was still rector of Dunboyne, but it is doubtful, given the manner in which he had come to take holy orders, if he was ever more than a reluctant parson. At all events he seems not to have been over-conscientious about prayers, since his wife had to remonstrate with him about never saying grace before meals; but he was not prepared to give in. The most he would concede was to say grace once a year in the cellar where the food and drink were stored, and that, he declared, must serve for the whole year. His sermons may have been inspiring, but one at least was accompanied by an unusual expression for a clergyman. A dog had entered the church while he was speaking, and he had promptly stopped and ordered somebody to 'take that damn bitch out!' He and Emily had five sons and due to Thomas only having a daughter, Richard was the heir to Ballinahinch and the whole Martin estate.

Relations between Humanity Dick and Thomas continued, as always, strained. Thomas resented the demands the old man made upon the estate for himself and his family, and Humanity did not feel that his son always treated him justly. Nonetheless, it must have been with something like the same anguish he had felt when Thomas set off to the Peninsular War that, after a prolonged silence, he received a letter from him saying: 'This letter may be the last that you may ever receive from me. I am to meet Mr. Wm. Macdermot to-morrow at 2 o'clock. I have been compelled to call upon him to apologize for offensive expressions in a letter published in the *Connaught Journal*.' In preparing to take what was possibly his final leave of his father before his duel, he swore that he had never been actuated by anything except a desire to serve him, and recommended to his care his only beloved daughter. 'Unless some effectual steps are taken,' he wrote, 'the property after your death must be sold for the payment of the debts. On my word I believe that the poor desolate creature will not have her mother's fortune out of the wreck.'

But Thomas survived to continue his life and to worry about his daughter's future at Ballinahinch. His collateral, Violet Martin, the 'Martin Ross' of the Somerville and Ross partnership, once asked her mother what Thomas was like. 'I never saw anyone who realized my idea of a chieftain so completely as he did,' her mother replied; 'an absolute ruler, but the protector of his people.'

Maria Edgeworth was impressed by the massiveness of his tall frame, his Connaught brogue, and his overwhelming, though shyly dispensed, kindness, even to the servants of the Culling Smiths, the intimate friends of the late Duke of York, with whom she was on a visit to Ballinahinch. She noticed that Thomas personally brought them each cider or a glass of port every day. Miss Edgeworth found the food and drink at Ballinahinch worthy of the greatest *gourmet*, but the house was in a sad state of dilapidation, with patches of damp on the ceilings and missing window panes replaced by boards, and the battlements and pepper-pot towers which had been added did nothing to raise it to the status of a castle in her eyes.

Apart from that on Catholic emancipation, of the news Humanity Dick received in Boulogne, nothing would have pleased him more than that Thomas had been elected for County Galway in 1831. He was an active member of the SPCA, but he did not attempt to take up where his father had left off in his fight for animals' rights, and the Catholic question, despite certain restrictions retained under the emancipation act, was more or less solved. But as a large landlord, he had plenty to occupy his time in the House, and, in particular, he continued his father's fight to have the electoral laws revised.

Thomas idolized his only child, Mary, and she him. Maria Edgeworth first met her at Ballinahinch when she was seventeen, and with her very fair hair and complexion, and a head particularly well placed on her shoulders, she reminded Miss Edgeworth of a Leonardo da Vinci painting. She spoke fluent French, which she had learned from a French officer, but had what Miss Edgeworth called a barrack-room accent. She had read prodigiously, understood Latin, Greek and Hebrew, and had studied engineering under Nimmo, the Scotsman who had built the road from Galway through Oughterard and Ballinahinch to the coast at Clifden. Miss Edgeworth found her both excessively proud and shy, and rather humourless, but she had grown up with all the Martin concern for the tenants. She did not want ever to live anywhere but at Ballinahinch, and she was something of a paragon, being beautiful, elegant, intelligent and benevolent.

Thomas's adoration of his daughter was to have fatal results for the Martins. An act of 1833 greatly simplified the breaking of the entail, and enabled him to make a will in favour of Mary. And the entail being broken made it easier to raise money which he now did with the object of paying off all the family debts going back as far as the time of his grandfather, Robert. Whether he did this out of a sense of honour or because he hoped ultimately to leave Mary an unencumbered estate, it was too late for it to have any effect on Humanity Dick's life, while he strongly opposed the breaking of the entail. It was unjust to Richard and left the whole future of the estate in jeopardy.

Mary would, doubtless, marry, and the property would pass out of the Martin family. After years of difficult relations with Thomas, all this was now to cause much ill-feeling.

As for Richard, seeing himself dispossessed, he planned to emigrate. He had friends who had gone to Canada, so he now brought valuers into the glebe house, sold his living and set off with his whole family to Canada. There, on the Grand River, he built a house which he named after the beloved Derryclare Lake in Connemara, and Humanity Dick was left to lament the departure of a much loved son.

That year Humanity became involved in what was a typical situation for him. A youth had been found on the ramparts of the High Town in Boulogne, apparently dying, with a bottle of laudanum beside him. He was taken to hospital, where Humanity Dick was among those who called. When the young man, barely eighteen, had recovered, Humanity announced to the family: 'That unfortunate young fellow, I have asked him to dinner today. Perhaps we ought to tell him we shall expect him whenever he has no other engagement, otherwise he may make *surer* work of it next time. I must see what can be done for him.'

From then onwards, the young man more or less lived at the Martins' house. He explained that he had been involved in fighting for some lost cause, and when all was over, finding himself without money or friends, had attempted suicide. He also declared that he was related to an aristocratic English family. In his usual fatherly manner, Humanity Dick wrote to the people in question, only to receive the reply that the young man must prove the relationship. As they had not denied the connection, Humanity Dick felt that there must be some truth in the young man's story, but before he could do anything further, he himself was taken seriously ill.

Fearing that in their anxiety about him the family might forget the young man, he never failed to ask each day if he had come to the house, requesting that he should be sent up to him. On one occasion, thinking that he was going to recover, he asked the family to remind him that the first thing he must do when he got up was to write again to the English family to whom the young man had claimed to be related.

Meanwhile, his grand-daughter Mary was just turning eighteen, and she was to come out three months later at the

London Season. As the sole heiress to the Martin estates, she had now acquired the title of the 'Princess of Connemara', and the old man, now in his eightieth year, was looking forward to hearing how she would fare. He would have expected the best of everything for her, but could not know that Prince Moskowa, Marshall Ney's son, would court her, or that Count Werdinski would follow her back to Ballinahinch in order to propose. Werdinski was the classic Polish count, with forfeited estates, an unverifiable title and a tendency, it was rumoured, to cuddle the maids. To complete the picture he made an unsuccessful attempt in his bedroom at Ballinahinch to commit suicide when the young lady refused him.

But Humanity Dick was never to hear of any of these things. He died at four o'clock in the afternoon on 6 January 1834 at 6 rue de l'Ecu. In his last days he had realized that he was about to pass away, and had concerned himself with his family's welfare, and worried about his favourite dog for whom he would be irreplaceable. A year after his death, Martin's Act was extended to embrace all cruelty to all domestic animals, and the work which had absorbed so much of his heart and mind was completed. It was a contemporary on the bench, describing him at the height of his fame, who wrote the most fitting epitaph: 'In life he never was equalled, and when he dies by whom shall he be replaced?'

Only twelve years later Ireland was struck by the great famine. Thomas spent a fortune in assisting his tenants, only to be carried off himself by famine fever after visiting some of them in the workhouse. He died uttering the characteristically Martin words, 'My God, what will become of my people!' His tenants were ravaged, and died or emigrated in thousands, no rents were coming in, the estate became bankrupt, and the mortgagees foreclosed on his daughter.

Soon no Martin was left in the little kingdom Nimble Dick had founded and King William had honoured with his patent. But the vision Humanity Dick had seen there did not fade; he had started a movement that continued to gather force with the years. One country after another followed the example set by the British parliament, until civilized men everywhere came to admit that animals have rights on the earth which was theirs before it was man's.

Those to whom he had given so much of his heart could not express their gratitude to their liberator, and millions of men were to cherish his ideals without ever hearing of the reckless, eccentric, generous member for Galway. But every beast that breathes freely from the Arctic to the jungle creates hourly a living memorial to the man who held one of the noblest titles in the world.

References

Manuscript Sources

National Library of Ireland
Bellew Papers
D'Arcy Papers
Gormanston Papers
French Papers
Heron Papers
Lords Lieutenants' Union Correspondence
Teeling Papers
Teresa O'Neill's thesis *The Sixth Parliament of George III, 1798-1800*

British Museum
Cornwallis Papers
Hardwicke Papers
Law Hedges' Journal
Peel Papers
Letter Book of the first Marquis of Buckingham
Liverpool Papers
Wickham Papers

Public Record Office (Ireland)
Ballyglunnin Papers
Maggs Mss.

Public Record Office (England—Crown Copyright)
Home Office files, series 100/ and 101/

Irish State Papers Office
Westmoreland Papers.

Library of Congress
Verbatim reports of the debates in the Irish House of Commons, 1776–89, 37 vols.

MSS in Private Hands
Erskine Papers
Kilmaine Papers
London Corporation Repertories
Martin Papers
RSPCA Papers

Selected Reading

A LATE PROFESSIONAL GENTLEMAN. *Recollections of Ireland.* Collected from fifty years practice and residence in the country. Printed for the author, 1865.

ALKEN, HENRY. *National Sports of Great Britain . . . with descriptions in English and French.* London, 1821.

ARCHDEACON, MATTHEW. *Legends of Connacht, Irish Stories, etc.* Dublin, 1839.

BABEAU, ALBERT. *Les Hôtels et les Salons de Paris en 1789,* in *Le Correspondent.* Paris, 10 May 1889.

BANIM, J. *The Mayor of Windgap—Canvassing.* Dublin and London, 1865.

BAINVILLE, JACQUES. *Histoire de France.* Paris, 1924.

BARKER, EDMUND HENRY. *Parriana.* London, 1828.

BARRINGTON, SIR JONAH. *Historic Memoirs of Ireland, etc.* London, 1833.

BARRINGTON, SIR JONAH. *Personal Sketches of his Own Times.* London, 1827.

BOLTON, G. C. *The Passing of the Irish Act of Union; a study in parliamentary politics.* Oxford, 1966.

BOWDEN, C. T. *A Tour through Ireland in 1790.* Dublin, 1791.

BURKE, OLIVER J. *Anecdotes of the Connaught Circuit.* Dublin, 1885.

BUXTON, CHARLES. *Memoirs of Sir T. Fowell Buxton.* London, 1848.

BURKE, SIR JOHN BERNARD. *Vicissitudes of Irish Families.* London, 1859.

CALLWELL, J. M. *Old Irish Life.* Edinburgh and London, 1912.

CANNING, GEORGE. *Some Official Correspondence of George Canning. Edited with Notes by Edward J. Stapleton, in two volumes.* London, 1887.

CAMPBELL, JOHN, LORD. *The Lives of the Lord Chancellors and Keepers of the Great Seal of England from the earliest times.* London, 1847.

CARR, SIR JOHN. *The Stranger in Ireland.* 2 vols. London, 1806.

CLARKE, WILLIAM SMITH. *The Irish Stage in the County Towns, 1720–1900.* Oxford, 1965.

CONNELL, K. H. *The Population of Ireland, 1750–1845.* Oxford. 1950.

COOTE, CHARLES. *History of the Union.* Printed for the author 1802.

CROLY, GEORGE. *Life and Times of His late Majesty George IV.* New York, 1845.

CROWE, REV. HENRY. *Animadversions on Cruelty to the Brute Creation, addressed chiefly to the lower classes.* Bath, 1825.

CROWE, REV. HENRY. *Zoophilus, or Considerations on the Moral Treatment of Inferior Animals.* Buckingham, 1819.

CURTIS, EDMUND. *A History of Ireland.* London, 1950.

DE LATOCNAYE. *A Frenchman's Walk Through Ireland,* translated by John Stevenson. Dublin and Belfast, 1917.

DESBRIÈRE, EDOUARD. *Projets et Tentatives de Débarquement aux Iles Britanniques.* 2 vols. Paris, 1900.

DE QUINCY, THOMAS. *Autobiographic Sketches.* Edinburgh, 1862–1863.

DOYLE, JAMES WARREN. (Bishop of Kildare and Loughlin). *Letters on the State of Ireland; addressed by J. K. L. to a friend in England.* Dublin, 1825.

EDGEWORTH, MARIA. *Tour in Connemara and the Martins of Ballinahinch.* London, 1950.

EDGEWORTH, MARIA. *Castle Rackrent and The Absentee.* London, 1910.

ELLIOTT, GRACE DALRYMPLE. *Journal of my Life during the French Revolution.* London, 1859.

ERSKINE, THOMAS, BARON. *The Farmer's Vision.* London, 1819.

ERSKINE, THOMAS, BARON. *A Letter to the Proprietors and Occupiers of Land, on the causes of, and the remedies for, the declension of agricultural prosperity.* London, 1823.

FIELD, WILLIAM. *Memoirs of the life, writings and opinions of the Rev. S. Parr.* 2 vols. London, 1828.

FITZGERALD, GEORGE ROBERT. *Memoirs of G.R.F.* London, 1786.

FLOOD, WARDEN. *Memoirs of the life and Correspondence of the Right Hon. Henry Flood.* Dublin, 1838.

FREEMAN, T. W. *Pre-Famine Ireland.* Manchester, 1957.

FROUDE, J. A. *The English in Ireland in the Eighteenth Century.* 3 vols. London, 1881.

GRATTAN, ENSIGN. *In Colburn's United Service Magazine, vols. IV to XVII.* London, 1829–41.

GRATTAN, HENRY. *Memoirs of the Life and Times of the Right Hon. Henry Grattan, by his son.* London, 1839–46.

GUNNING, JOHN P. *The Volunteers and the Irish Parliament.* Limerick, 1903.

GWYNN, DENIS. *The Struggle for Catholic Emancipation.* London, 1928.

HALL, S. C. *Retrospect of a Long Life.* London, 1883.

HARDIMAN, JAMES. *The History of the Town and County of the town of Galway, from the earliest period to the present time, 1820.* Galway, 1958.

HARDY, F. *Memoirs of the Life of James Caulfield, Earl of Charlemont.* 2 vols. London, 1812.

HAYES, RICHARD. *The Last Invasion of Ireland: when Connacht rose.* Dublin, 1937.

DUTTON, HELY. *A Statistical and Agricultural Survey of the County of Galway, with observations on the means of improvement; drawn up by the direction of the Royal Dublin Society.* Dublin, 1824.

JERDAN, WILLIAM. *Men I have Known.* London, 1866.

JOHNSTONE, JOHN. *The Works of Samuel Parr. . . . With memoirs of his life and writings.* London, 1828.

JOURDAIN, LIEUT. COL. H. F. N. and EDWARD FRASER. *The Connaught Rangers, 1st Battalion, formerly 88th Foot.* London, 1924.

LAWRENCE, JOHN. *The Sportsman's Repository.* London, 1820.

LAWRENCE, JOHN. *The Rights of an Animal.* With a reprint of part of J. Lawrence's chapters 'On the Right of Beasts', 'On the Philosophy of Sports' etc. 1879.

LAWRENCE, JOHN. *A philosophical and practical Treatise on Horses and on the moral duties of man towards the brute creation.* London, 1796–98.

LECOUR, LOUIS. *Grande Monde et Salons Politiques de Paris.* Paris, 1860.

LECKY, W. E. H. *History of Ireland in the Eighteenth Century.* London, 1902–3.

LECKY, W. E. H. *The Leaders of Public Opinion in Ireland.* London, 1861.

LELAND, THOMAS. *The History of Ireland from the Invasion of Henry II, with a preliminary discourse on the ancient state of that kingdom.* Dublin, 1773.

The Life of George Robert Fitzgerald. . . . To which is added a number of facts, relative to his trial and execution. Anonymous. London, 1786.

MACCARTHY, MARY. *Fighting Fitzgerald and Other Essays.* London, 1930.

MACDERMOT, FRANK. *Theobald Wolfe Tone.* Tralee, 1968.

MCDOWELL, R. B. *Irish Public Opinion, 1750–1800.* London, 1944.

MᴄDᴏᴡᴇʟʟ, R. B. *Public Opinion and Government Policy in Ireland, 1801–1846*. London, 1952.

MᴄNᴇᴠɪɴ, Tʜᴏᴍᴀs. *The History of the Volunteers of 1782*. Dublin, 1845.

Mᴀʀᴛɪɴ, Aʀᴄʜᴇʀ E. S. *Genealogy of the Family of Martin of Ballinahinch Castle in the County of Galway, Ireland*. Winnipeg, 1890.

Mᴀᴜʀᴏɪs, Aɴᴅʀé. *Histoire de la France*. Paris, 1947.

Mᴀxᴡᴇʟʟ, Cᴏɴsᴛᴀɴᴛɪᴀ. *Dublin Under the Georges*. Dublin and London, 1946.

Mᴀxᴡᴇʟʟ, Cᴏɴsᴛᴀɴᴛɪᴀ. *Town and Country in Ireland Under the Georges*. Dundalk, 1949.

Mᴀxᴡᴇʟʟ, W. H. *Wild Sports of the West with Legendary Tales and Local Sketches*. London, 1838.

Mᴏʀɢᴀɴ, Lᴀᴅʏ (Sʏᴅɴᴇʏ Oᴡᴇɴsᴏɴ). *Memoirs: Autobiography, Diaries and Correspondence*. London, 1862.

Mᴏss, A. W. *Valiant Crusade*. London, 1961.

O'Bʀɪᴇɴ, Gᴇᴏʀɢᴇ. *Economic History of Ireland in the Eighteenth Century*. Dublin and London, 1918.

O'Bʀɪᴇɴ, Gᴇᴏʀɢᴇ. *The Economic History of Ireland from the Union to the Famine*. London, 1921.

O'Fᴀᴏʟᴀɪɴ, Sᴇᴀɴ. *The Autobiography of Theobald Wolfe Tone*. London, 1937.

O'Fʟᴀʜᴇʀᴛʏ, Rᴏᴅᴇʀɪᴄᴋ. *Chorographical description of West of H-iar Connaught, written A.D. 1684. Ed., from a Ms. in the Library of Trinity College, Dublin, with notes and illustrations*, by James Hardiman. Dublin, 1846.

O'Gᴏʀᴍᴀɴ, F. *The Whig Party and the French Revolution*. London, 1967.

O'Sᴜʟʟɪᴠᴀɴ, M. D. *Old Galway, the History of a Norman Colony in Ireland*. Cambridge, 1942.

Pᴀʀʀ, Sᴀᴍᴜᴇʟ. *Aphorisms, Opinions and Reflections*. London, 1826.

Pᴀʀʀ, Sᴀᴍᴜᴇʟ. *A Discourse (on Prov. xxii 6) on Education and on the Plans pursued in Charity Schools*. London, 1786.

Pᴀɪɴ, W. and E. Fᴀɪʀʜᴏʟᴍᴇ. *A Century of Work for Animals. The history of the R.S.P.C.A. 1824–1924*. London, 1924.

Pᴀɪɴ, W. and E. Fᴀɪʀʜᴏʟᴍᴇ. *Richard Martin (1754–1834)*. Boston, 1925.

Pᴀᴋᴇɴʜᴀᴍ, Tʜᴏᴍᴀs. *The Year of Liberty*. London, 1969.

Pᴇʀᴄɪᴠᴀʟ, Tʜᴏᴍᴀs, ᴍ.ᴅ., ꜰ.ʀ.s., s.ᴀ. *A Father's Instructions consisting of moral tales, fables and reflections*. London, 1781.

Pʟᴏᴡᴅᴇɴ, Fʀᴀɴᴄɪs P. *History of Ireland from its Invasion under Henry II to its union with Great Britain*. 2 vols. London, 1809.

Pʟᴏᴡᴅᴇɴ, Fʀᴀɴᴄɪs P. *History of Ireland from its Union with*

Great Britain, in January 1801, to October 1801. 2 vols. Dublin 1811.

PLUMB, J. H. *England in the Eighteenth Century 1714–1815.* London, 1950.

PRIMATT, Dr. *The Duty of Mercy and Sin of Cruelty to Brute Animals demonstrated from reason and revelation. . . . To which are added a few notes . . . by a Clergyman of the Church of England* (A. Broome). London, 1822.

Projets de Descentes, Angleterre. Ministère des Affaires Étrangères, Paris.

REID, THOMAS. *Travels in Ireland, in the year 1822, exhibiting brief sketches of the moral, physical and political state of the country.* London, 1823.

ROGERS, REV. PATRICK. *The Irish Volunteers and Catholic Emancipation, 1778–1793.* London, 1934.

ROSS, CHARLES. *Cornwallis (Charles Cornwallis, 1st Marquis): Correspondence,* ed. by Charles Ross. 3 vols. London, 1859.

SIGERSON, GEORGE. *The Last Independent Parliament of Ireland.* Dublin, 1918.

SIMMINGTON, ROBERT C. *The Transplantation of Connaught.* Irish Manuscripts Commission, 1970.

SIMMS, J. G. *Jacobite Ireland.* London, 1969.

SIMMS, J. G. *The Williamite Confiscation in Ireland.* London, 1956.

STAPLETON, A. G. *George Canning and his Times.* London, 1859.

SUMNER, MARY. *Quelques Salons de Paris au XVIII Siècle.* Paris.

TEELING, CHARLES H. *Personal Narrative of the Irish Rebellion of 1798.* Glasgow 1828.

TEELING, CHARLES H. *Sequel to Personal Narrative of the Irish Rebellion of 1798.* Belfast, 1832.

Ten Thousand Pounds. Trial between Richard Martin and John Petrie for criminal conversation with the plaintiff's wife. Taken in shorthand by a student at the Temple. Dublin, 1792.

The Trials of George Robert Fitzgerald Esq., Timothy Brecknock, James Fulton, and others . . . for the murder of Randall McDonnell and Charles Hipson. Dublin, 1786.

THOMSON, DAVID. *England in the Nineteenth Century.* London, 1950.

WAKEFIELD, EDWARD. *An Account of Ireland, statistical and political.* London, 1812.

WALL, MAUREEN. *The Penal Laws.* Dundalk, 1967.

WALSH, E. W. *Ireland Ninety Years Ago.* Dublin, 1876.

WATSON, STEVEN. *The Reign of George III.* Oxford, 1960.

WYSE, SIR THOMAS. *Historical Sketch of the late Catholic Association of Ireland.* 2 vols. London, 1871.

YOUNG, ARTHUR. *A Tour in Ireland; with general observations on the present state of that kingdom; made in 1776, 1777 and 1778, and brought down to the end of 1779.* London, 1780.

YOUNG, THOMAS. *An Essay on Humanity to Animals.* London, 1798.

Journals

Analecta Hibernica
Animal World
Blackwood's Edinburgh Magazine
Dublin University Magazine
Galway Reader
Irish Sword
Journal of the Galway Archaeological and Historical Society
Monthly Magazine
Notes and Queries
Royal Irish Academy, Transactions
Royal Irish Academy, Proceedings
Walker's Hibernian Magazine

Newspapers

Anti-Union
Connaught Journal
Courier
Dublin Correspondent
Dublin Chronicle
Dublin Evening Post
Faulkner's Journal
Freeman's Journal
Galway Advertiser
Morning Chronicle
Saunders Newsletter
Times
Volunteer Gazette

Works of General Reference

Journals of the Irish and English Houses of Lords and Commons.
The Parliamentary Register of debates in the Irish House of Commons.
Cobbett's and Hansard's debates in the English Houses of Parliament.
Reports of the Historic Manuscripts Commission.
Calendar of State Papers, Domestic Series.
Reports of Public Records in England and Ireland.
The Dictionary of National Biography (1908).
Burke's Peerage (105th edition, 1970).
Complete Peerage, ed. by Vicary Gibbs (1910).

Index

Criminal Law Act (1823), 217
Cromie, Sir Michael, 13, 83
Crowe, Rev. Henry, 205–6, 208, 218
cruelty to animals, prevention of: Erskine's bill, 152–5, 157, 220; Martin's bills, 196, 198–9, 205–8, 220, 227–32, 243–6, 250
Curly, Patrick, 90

Dalgin Castle, 172, 174, 175
Daly, Bowes, 122, 143, 147, 149, 176, 237; and 1812 Galway election, 172, 173, 174; and 1818 election, 181–2; and 1826 election, 262, 265–6
Daly, Denis, 13, 50, 51, 76
Daly, James, 172, 174, 181, 271
Daly, St George, 103
Dangan (Martin family seat), xv, xvii, 1, 2–3, 13, 46–7, 60, 61, 65, 90, 91, 99, 147, 265
D'Arcy, Count Hyacinth, 74
D'Arcy, James, 141
D'Arcy, John, 263, 265, 266
D'Arcy, Patrick, 140
Darley, Alderman, 203
De Latocnaye, M., 102
De Quincey, Thomas, 128
Declaratory Act (1719), 17; repeal of, 38, 40, 44
Devereux, John, 185–6
Dickens, Charles, 276
Douglas (Home), 48, 50, 66, 67
Downshire, Lord, 204, 205, 207
Dromedary (convict ship), 240
Duane, Mr, 146
Dublin, 3, 4, 48–9, 65; social life in, 14–16; Volunteers' National Convention (1783), 51–5; anti-Union feeling, 125–6; Emmet rebellion (1803), 140–1; George IV's visit (1821), 200–203; Orangemen demonstrations, 213–15, 216–17
Dublin Chronicle, 67, 81
Dublin Evening Post, 239, 264, 272
Dublin Patriot, 203
Dublin Star, 239
Dunboyne, Richard Martin jun. as rector, 215, 278–9
Dungannon, 37, 38, 39, 51
Dunlo, Lord (formerly Richard le Poer Trench and later Lord Clancarty, qq.v.), 140, 141
Duty of Mercy and Sin of Cruelty to Brute Animals, The (Primatt), 208

Earl Moira (steam packet), 202
Eden, William, 36
Edgeworth, Maria, 89, 132, 279, 280
Elliott, Grace Dalrymple, 72
Emmet, Robert, 140–1
Emmet, Thomas Addis, 107
Erskine, Thomas, first Baron, 81, 83, 127, 194, 196, 198, 206, 230; bill for prevention of cruelty to animals, 151–5, 157, 207, 208, 220
Espinasse, Marie de l' (Mrs Anthony Martin), 140, 147
Eyre, Giles, 147, 148, 172, 173

Fair Penitent, The (Rowe), 65
Fisheries, Martin a Commissioner of, 188
Fitzgerald, Lord Edward, 107, 108
Fitzgerald, George Robert, 45, 52; grotesque behaviour, 32–6; Martin's challenge and duel over shooting of wolf-hound, 33–6, 48–9, 57–61; trial and execution for murder, 63–4
Fitzgerald, James, 121
Fitzgerald, Pamela, 73, 107
Fitzgerald, Lord Robert, 71
Fitzgibbon, John (later Lord Clare, q.v.), 37, 41, 64, 85, 96, 97, 98
Fitzpatrick, Richard, 42, 43
Fitzwilliam, William Wentworth, second Earl, 96, 97–8
Flood, Henry, 26, 38, 56, 57, 59–60, 83; opposes Grattan, 44–5; Martin's support for, 45, 51; at National Convention, 51, 52–3, 54–5
Foreign Enlistment Act (1819), 185–6, 211
Forgery Punishment Mitigation Bill (1821), 193
Foster, John, 123, 132, 149
Fox, Charles James, 131, 142, 146–7
Franklin, Benjamin, 9, 117
Freeman's Journal, 46n, 50, 56, 60, 65, 67, 84–5, 150, 157–8, 160, 165, 182
French, Martin, 188, 263
French, Robert, 112, 114
French Revolution, 71–77, 81, 86–7
Friedland, battle of (1807), 149
Friends of South American Independence, 211
Friends of Independence, 182
Friends of Toleration, 159

Martin, Richard ('Humanity Dick')—
cont.
93–4; right to hold court, 94; punishment of tenants' cruelty to animals, 94–5; 'King of Connemara', 95; marries Harriet Hesketh, 99; aids Catholic refugees, 100, 104, 235; as member for Lanesborough, 105; urges amnesty for rebels, 110–11, 116; supports Union, 118–26, 134, 136; attacked by mob, 125–6; member for County Galway, 129, 136, 138–9; Commissioner for Stamps, 129, 133; residence in London, 132, 135; seeks other political office, 136–7, 139, 140, 141; death of youngest son, 139; family affairs and finances, 139–40, 147; shows displeasure with Government, 141–2; Commissioner for Hearth Money Collection, 145; returned again for County Galway, 147–8; attacks Canning, 150–1; makes over most of estate to son Thomas, 158; friction with Thomas, 160, 260, 279; 'Pledge' on Catholic emancipation, 160, 188; attachment to Prince Regent, 158, 166; social activity, 167–8; general benevolence, 170–1; nicknamed 'Humanity', 171; forced to relinquish candidature in 1812 election, 171–4; retirement from politics, 173–4, 176, 178–9; legal business, 176; determined to fight for legislation against cruelty to animals, 177, 179; return to Parliament, 180–4, 186; and agrarian unrest, 186–7; supports Queen Caroline, 190–1, 192; rift with George IV, 192; urges reform of criminal code, 192–3, 217, 261; and cruelty to animals, 193–6, 197–9, 205–8, 218–25, 227–33, 240, 243–7, 250–7, 259–61, 275–6; reconciliation with George IV, 202; family and estate matters, 203–4, 215; 'Martin's Act' becomes law, 207–8, 210; displeasure over press reporting, 210–211; false report of death, 215; rift with O'Connell, 217; attempt to free Galway from Daly domination, 225–226, 237; and SPCA, 231–2, 259, 275; reproached for neglecting tenantry, 233–5; *Morning Chronicle* ridicule of,

251–7; reputation for eccentricity, 258–9; improved finances, 260; and electoral intrigue, 261–71; unseated, 270–1; retirement to Boulogne, 271–6; misunderstanding of, 276; death, 282

Martin, Richard (Nimble Dick) (great-grandfather), xi–xiv, xv, 3, 89

Martin, Richard (uncle), xvi, xvii

Martin, Richard (son), 101, 150, 168, 173, 175, 178, 238, 281; in Dragoon Guards, 180; decides to enter Church, 188; father's settlement on, 203–4; marriage, 204; rector of Dunboyne, 215, 278

Martin, Mrs Richard (Emily Kirwan), 188, 279

Martin, Robert (father), xv–xvii, 2–6, 7, 13, 89, 93

Martin, Robert (half-brother), 8, 46, 82, 147

Martin, Mrs Robert (Mary O'Flaherty), 147

Martin, St George (son), 70, 132; death, 139

Martin, Thomas (son), 65, 132, 139, 150, 159, 168–9, 173, 174, 178, 187, 203, 237, 264, 267; and Ballinahinch estate, 158, 212, 260, 279–81; friction with father, 160, 260, 279; at Badajoz, 160–3; marriage, 175–6; death, 282

Martin, Mrs Thomas (Julia Kirwan), 175–6

Martin, Violet, 279

Massereene, Clotworthy Skeffington, second Earl of, 72

Melville, Henry Dundas, first Viscount, 142

Merlin, Dr, 57, 59

Minshull, Mr (magistrate), 221–2, 253, 254, 256

Monthly Magazine, 195, 231

Moore, John, 113

Moore, Thomas, 233

Morgan, Lady, 274

Morning Chronicle, 211, 250, 259; campaign against Martin, 247, 251–7

Morning Herald, 255, 257

Morning Post, 211

Morris, Gouverneur, 74

Moskowa, Prince, 282

Mountgarret, Margaret, Lady, xvii, 4

Mudford, William, 247